ADVANCE PRAISE FOR *THE EBAY ENTREPRENEUR*

I've watched Christopher succeed where so many others have failed—because his eBay Trading Assistant business has truly flourished. No magic beans to success here—just solid information honed and perfected through his years of experience selling on eBay. Anyone considering starting a Trading Assistant business will do themselves a tremendous favor by reading this book.

MARSHA COLLIER
BESTSELLING AUTHOR OF *EBAY FOR DUMMIES* AND *STARTING AN EBAY BUSINESS FOR DUMMIES*

The eBay Entrepreneur *has eye-opening ideas for achieving success. The time and money you spend on this book are an exciting investment. I learned so much! Christopher Matthew Spencer shares successful methods for utilizing eBay to build your own business. Wise people constantly discover what they believe and you'll believe in Christopher after you discover this book.*

KATHY IRELAND
CHIEF DESIGNER AND CEO *KATHY IRELAND WORLDWIDE*

Christopher Spencer has done an amazing job of explaining the nuts and bolts of running an eBay consignment business. Whether you are a one-person operation or a well-staffed business, you'll benefit from Christopher's advice.

IRA STEINER
EDITOR OF *AUCTIONBYTES.COM*

eBay is not only a phenomenal success, it has spun off a vast new economy of entrepreneurs who make their dreams come true on this remarkable platform. Nobody—except maybe Meg Whitman—knows more about selling on eBay than Christopher Spencer, who has already taught thousands of people how to profit on eBay. This book will bring his message to the larger audience he deserves.

CHRIS TUCKER
AMERICAN WAY MAGAZINE

THE eBay ENTREPRENEUR

THE DEFINITIVE GUIDE TO STARTING YOUR OWN EBAY TRADING ASSISTANT BUSINESS

CHRISTOPHER MATTHEW SPENCER

 KAPLAN PUBLISHING

This publication is designed to provide accurate and authoritative information in regard to the subject matter covered. It is sold with the understanding that the publisher is not engaged in rendering legal, accounting, or other professional service. If legal advice or other expert assistance is required, the services of a competent professional should be sought.

President, Kaplan Publishing: Roy Lipner
Vice President and Publisher: Maureen McMahon
Acquisitions Editor: Michael Cunningham
Development Editor: Trey Thoelcke
Production Editor: Karen Goodfriend
Typesetter: Ellen Gurak
Cover Designer: Matthew Eberhart, Evil Eye Design, Inc.

Published by Kaplan Publishing,
a division of Kaplan, Inc.

Printed in the United States of America

06 07 08 10 9 8 7 6 5 4 3 2 1

Library of Congress Cataloging-in-Publication Data

The eBay entrepreneur / Christopher Matthew Spencer.
p. cm.
Includes bibliographical references and index.
ISBN-13: 978-1-4195-8328-5
ISBN-10: 1-4195-8328-X
1. Internet auctions. 2. eBay (Firm) I. Title.
HF5478.S64 2006
658.8'7–dc22
2006015752

Kaplan Publishing books are available at special quantity discounts to use for sales promotions, employee premiums, or educational purposes. Please call our Special Sales Department to order or for more information at 800-621-9621, ext. 4444; e-mail *kaplanpubsales@kaplan.com*
ing, 30 South Wacker Drive, Suite 2500, Chicago, IL 60606-7481.

CONTENTS

ACKNOWLEDGMENTS

IT TAKES AN ENTIRE VILLAGE TO RAISE A CHILD

Writing this book has been a wonderful experience—no, *journey*—for me. But no part of it has given me more pleasure than this page, because so many friends and colleagues generously joined me on this journey. I'd like to thank:

My mother, Dr. Carol Anne Rizvi, whose sacrifices raising me, and whose unconditional love and support throughout my life, have always inspired me and made me the happy, successful person I am.

Jeff Chase, the general contractor for eBay tradeshows and show director of all past eBay Live! user conferences, my close friend and a true mentor. Jeff single-handedly changed my world and moved me into a bigger and better direction with my life. He has been cajoling me to write this book for the past four years.

Mike Richards, my best friend in the world, who gave me the first six items I ever listed on eBay for someone else.

Matt Wagner, literary agent extraordinaire, who made this book a published reality.

Stephen P. Olejniczak, the author of *Telecom for Dummies*, who generously put me in touch with Matt Wagner, his agent as well.

All the Trading Assistants across the country who generously shared their stories—you'll see them at the top of each chapter.

Special thanks to Sally Milo for reaching out to many of those Trading Assistants cited above and getting their wonderful stories.

Donita Woodruff, my research assistant and a published author in her own right, for her intelligence, hard work, and terrific way with people.

John Lovell, my friend and the senior creative director of my company. John, also a published author and former copy editor for *Variety*, provided substantial and invaluable input and editing skills for this book.

All the eBay executive staff, directors, category managers, and product managers who asked me to act as eBay's official spokesperson at over a hundred conferences and tradeshows. And to Joseph E. Sullivan, legal counsel for eBay, Inc., for providing the content for the Appendix.

Special thanks to Jenny Henriques and Monique Svazlian of eBay's tradeshow department, who have kept me so actively involved in public speaking for the past five years. Their endorsement of my speaking abilities has secured my position among the leading speakers for eBay.

Michael Cunningham, senior acquisitions editor at Kaplan Publishing, whose vision put this book in your hands.

My friends and colleagues who graciously agreed to read and critique sections of this book as I wrote them: John Anderson, Zach Cochran, Jason Hand, Jean Heggestad, John Krawiec, Joshua Lewis, David McKenzie (CEO/founder, Dream World Consulting Group), Rae Osenbaugh, Diana Petersen, Taiza Pickering, Adam Smit, Sally J. Suddock, Lance Thomas, Troy Thoreson, and Gary Zaydman.

A very appreciative thanks to every one of my students and eBay community members who educated and inspired me with their personal successes.

And thanks to Meg Whitman, CEO of eBay and one of my first customers, for buying my Army Corps of Engineers compass on eBay.

INTRODUCTION

THE $74,330.60 GARAGE . . .

Photo © 2005 by John Lovell of The Spencer Company

"I wanted to throw it out—it was so ugly. And, of course, I thought it was worthless," she said.

"And I," drawled her husband, "almost dropped it—right out there." He nodded towards the Burbank, California sidewalk in front of my store. "But I talked her out of trashing it."

The young couple and I peered down at what they had just brought to my eBay Trading Assistant store. There, on my counter, was a porcelain figurine of a whimsical nude woman sitting on a pear. The item, standing about ten inches high, was in mint condition and well marked with "Lenci" the date 1930, and the artist's name. Didn't look like much.

The three of us gazed at it with a mixture of skepticism and wild hope—it was an odd piece.

"I figured maybe $100," the young man said, referring to what we might be able to get for it on eBay on their behalf.

The young man's father had recently passed on, leaving a Burbank garage crammed with the fruits of 40 years of collecting with a very interesting eye. The couple was moving to Oregon and wanted to give us the entire contents of the garage to list for them on eBay.

We listed the Lenci figurine on eBay with a starting bid of $9.99. On July 7, 2005, it brought $17,100 and went back to a collector in Italy, where it was made.

The contents of the garage brought $74,330.60.

I'm not going to say, "Just another day in the life of a Trading Assistant" That garage was an extraordinary treasure. But if you decide to become a Trading Assistant, I guarantee that every day there's surprise, gratification, and good old-fashioned creative work.

And my simple eBay Trading Assistant business has made me a millionaire.

THE STREETS ARE PAVED WITH GOLD

First of all, I would like to thank you for taking the time to read my book. I am delighted that you have made the commitment to explore the world of eBay Trading Assistants. Not only have I created a successful business for myself on eBay and made lots of money in the process, but I have also taught thousands of people all over the country how to make money easily on eBay. And with this book, I will help you learn this new kind of entrepreneurialism. This can lead you on the path to financial freedom and a better life filled with interesting, fun (and profitable!) surprises.

Trading Assistants use eBay to help other people sell their items online. Being your own boss is fun. Your clients need you, and you are their hero—creating cash from something they don't need. If you have a computer, an Internet connection, and a basic digital camera, you can easily set up shop as a Trading Assistant. And you won't need to spend another dollar to get started, because you'll be able to sell your clients' items before eBay charges you a single cent.

THE POKEMON INCIDENT

I started selling on eBay in the summer of 1998. While I was visiting my brother Buck and his family one evening, my nephew Matt proudly showed me his Pokemon trading card collection. Pokemon was quite popular at the time, and Matt had acquired these fun collectibles on a new Web site called eBay. His father was helping him learn the art of using this innovative new online service, and Matt was simply thrilled by the whole experience—the eBay experience.

This little random event actually changed my life forever—it gave me an idea for a new and exciting business venture.

Starting as a teenager, I had held various sales jobs and worked in public relations and special events production, and by 1998 I had become a very successful personal manager of actors. The money was fantastic, and I was good at making it. But I am a person in constant need of mental stimulation, and being a personal manager had become routine. Though I worked in the heart of the entertainment industry and was in constant contact with celebrities, I was in a rut. And I wanted to be the master of my own destiny—not a well-paid slave to the whims and demands of my clients.

The little Pokemon incident at my brother's house started the wheels turning in my head. My best friend in the world, Mike Richards, is a Beverly Hills antiques dealer. One of my very first jobs as a teenager was working as an intern for his company, writing letters, running errands, and handling his book work. By 1998, I knew that his business, the antiques business, was on the verge of dramatic changes.

THE EXPENSIVE DOORSTOP

For many years I had tried and failed to get Mike interested in using a computer for his company. I actually forced him to buy a personal computer in the early 1990s, but this state-of-the-art device quickly turned into an expensive doorstop. But now the Internet had really taken off—its growth could only be described as explosive.

Shortly after learning about eBay from my nephew, I suggested to Mike that we try selling a few of his antiques on the eBay Web site. He agreed to loan me six nondescript war medals, in rather poor condition, to photograph and list on eBay. They were just a few bones that Mike threw me as a completely risk-free test case.

At the time, I owned a cool Sony Mavica digital camera. Though very expensive then, with a resolution of 800,000 pixels, my camera was a mere toy by today's standards. I took several pictures of each medal and listed them on eBay. A week later, I returned to Mike with my findings. I had sold all the medals for between $60 and $80 each.

Mike was stunned.

And now Mike was a believer. He promptly prepared another 60 items for me to photograph and list on eBay. Between actor/client phone calls and my regular business meetings, I handled the 60 eBay auctions: answering e-mail questions from prospective buyers, collecting payments, and shipping orders. Quickly this hobby turned into a real enterprise, and Mike, my only client, was bringing me between 100 and 400 items to list on eBay each week.

By 1999, I was shipping well over $30,000 a month in merchandise that I had sold on eBay. This was getting serious! I was now selling a wide variety of items for many new clients besides Mike, and I was getting paid on commission. Most of these clients came to me by word of mouth. eBay hadn't yet coined the term *Trading Assistant*, but I was already doing everything that would eventually define a Trading Assistant.

NO JOKE

One day, while I was busily handling my eBay hobby (that was still the way I thought of it, though it was certainly becoming a lucrative one), I got an e-mail from one of my eBay buyers who said that a relative of hers was a writer for *Time* magazine. *Time* was preparing an Internet-themed edition with some stories about selling online, my buyer told me, and the writer wanted to interview me in this connection. Frankly, I thought this e-mail was a joke, but I played along. The next thing I knew, my entire office was taken over by a *Time* photographer who set up lights and tons of equipment to photograph me for this story. The writer, Sally B. Donnelly, conducted a very pleasant interview, and a few months later the phone was ringing off the hook.

People I hadn't spoken to since grade school were calling to congratulate me on being in *Time*. At that moment I realized I had really started something precious, wonderful, and amazing.

SUBSTITUTE TEACHER

The phone rang, and it was a man named John Slocum. John had written a computer program called Auction Assistant Pro—a listing management tool for eBay that automated and facilitated multiple auction listings, now known as Blackthorne Pro. John knew that I had been using his program, which now belonged to eBay, for my eBay business. He told me that someone from eBay would be calling me shortly, because they were looking for a substitute instructor for a class on Auction Assistant Pro at an event called eBay University. One of their instructors had fallen ill, and they knew that I was an avid and successful user of eBay and their listing tool. Suddenly, I found myself speaking in front of hundreds of eager students who wanted to learn how to use eBay and the listing tool.

I believe this convergence of events happened for a reason. Fate (or something) was making a major change in the course of my life. I quit my job as an actors' manager and started selling on eBay full-time with a new, second job teaching regular seminars for eBay University. Today, I have successfully listed more than 160,000 items on eBay, and I have spoken in front of tens of thousands of students at eBay University events. I have authored so many eBay-related educational presentations and technical manuals, and even produced instructional videos, that I have lost count. As I write this, eBay is currently growing at the rate of well over 80,000 new members each day. I now have a trusted staff that helps me run my Trading Assistant business, and they are my invaluable allies.

My eBay Trading Assistant business started with zero personal investment. I did not have to quit my then full-time job, although I wanted to and finally did. The money I have earned from my eBay sales has enabled me to purchase investment properties such as apartment buildings, houses, condos, and a motel. My eBay business has created great wealth for me and given me the freedom to do whatever I want whenever I want.

NOT AN EASY DECISION

And now I have to speak frankly about my decision to write this book—it did not come easily. I have had no problem sharing my eBay success tips with students these many years, and I believe that there is so much business online that there is enough to go around. I do not feel you are going to somehow jeopardize my business by becoming a success story like me.

There are many how-to eBay books on the market, and much of the material needed to start a successful business is already in print. My dear friend and colleague, Marsha Collier, has written arguably the most successful how-to books on eBay with her *Dummies* series, and I would strongly urge you to buy her *Starting an eBay Business for Dummies* (Wiley Publishing) as a companion to this book.

However, I saw a void in the marketplace on the subject of Trading Assistants. Nobody had really captured the true nuts-and-bolts essence of starting a "hired-gun" Trading Assistant business from scratch. But the reality that most books simply don't get published, even with a great agent, was daunting.

A SCRAP OF PAPER

But I am the most fortunate person on the planet. As fate would have it once again, about a year ago, a couple stopped by my eBay drop-off store in Burbank, California. We had a nice chat about eBay, but for the life of me I could not remember either of their names. In passing, this gentleman mentioned that he had recently landed a book deal through a superb, very talented literary agent. Something inside me yearned to write this book, and meekly, I asked him if he would give me his agent's name and contact information. To my surprise he did! He jotted the information on a scrap of paper, and we said our goodbyes.

Nearly a year passed with that scrap of paper lying dormant on my desk, as I tried to muster the courage to call the literary agent, Matt Wagner at Fresh Books. When I finally did, amazingly, Matt told me that he had just been thinking about eBay and wanted to come up with a book project. The timing for this was unreal, and less than 30 days after Matt helped me get my book proposal together, he landed a generous deal with Kaplan Publishing for me to bring this valuable education to you.

MODEL T TIME

If you are wondering whether you are starting too late and if eBay has already matured—nothing could be further from the truth! This book could be your passport to financial freedom. Online retailing is still in its infancy, and actually you are seizing this opportunity at the perfect time. If you compare the World Wide Web to the auto industry, we are still in the Model T years. There will be plenty of business out there for you. With some determination and patience, you will reap the rewards of trading for others on eBay, and you can be as successful as I have been. You will reach any level of success that you choose, because now you have the tools to achieve it. eBay offers a plethora of free tools to help assure your success as a Trading Assistant as well.

NUTS AND BOLTS

I'm a nuts-and-bolts kind of guy. I wrote this book for *anyone* interested in becoming an eBay Trading Assistant. Maybe you're a mom thinking of starting a Trading Assistant business on your kitchen table. And maybe flipping through this book, you saw a chapter heading about buying a commercial building and thought, "This book's not for me—I'll never buy a building!" Or, "Employees! You have to be kidding." Well, Mom, this book *is* for you. In fact, I wrote it just for you. And everyone else interested in the Trading Assistant business.

This book doesn't have chapters on photography or how to write great eBay listings—plenty of other books out there cover topics like these, and eBay's own help boards and free tutorials are a great resource for these subjects and a lot more.

This book is nuts-and-bolts—a nitty-gritty blueprint for running a Trading Assistant business. It takes you step by step through the entire process of setting up the business and making it a terrific success. If you think you'll never buy a commercial building or have even a single, part-time employee, feel free to skip those chapters. But Mom, you and everyone else who wants to be a Trading Assistant will need to know about contracts, about how to find (and keep) great clients with great (and profitable) merchandise to list on eBay, about how to set your fees, about wonderful software specifically designed for Trading Assistants . . . it's all here—the nuts and bolts of starting and running a successful eBay Trading Assistant business. So have a seat, whether at your kitchen table or the desk in your 4,000-square-foot warehouse, and read on.

In this book, you will find:

- Proven, step-by-step techniques for planning, starting, and executing a successful, profitable eBay Trading Assistant business
- Great ideas for finding the best clients who have valuable items they don't want or need
- Low-cost marketing programs to help even the most cash-strapped entrepreneur get immediate and highly profitable results
- The secrets of unlimited free publicity
- Tips for avoiding technology pitfalls
- Routines for streamlining day-to-day operations, including packing and shipping secrets, inventory handling techniques, accounting procedures, and much more
- Indispensable guidance on client and employee relations
- Profiles and case studies of the most profitable eBay Trading Assistant successes, both home-based and brick-and-mortar

MY BUMPER-TO-BUMPER GUARANTEE

I am so confident about this mission, so convinced of your ability to become a successful eBay entrepreneur, that I will personally guarantee your satisfaction with this book. If, after applying the techniques and tips I have provided, you are not completely satisfied with my book, I will personally refund 100 percent of your purchase price. Simply send proof of purchase and the book to:

Christopher Matthew Spencer
PO Box 1862
Beverly Hills, California 90213-1862

I also welcome you into my sphere of friends. Feel free to write me with your very own tips, ideas, and personal success stories.

You have begun a unique and fascinating journey, and I'm honored to be your guide through this priceless education. We'll have plenty of fun working together as I show you the ropes. With your enthusiasm and a bit of patience and determination, you, too, will be trading online for friends, coworkers, and clients with your very own eBay Trading Assistant enterprise. You will become your own boss. It is time to claim your piece of this growing opportunity.

1

THE TRADING ASSISTANT BUSINESS

A woman brought me a Walt Disney Mickey Mouse light bulb that was made in the 1930s. She had purchased it at a garage sale for $0.50. I sold it for $463.88! My husband started on eBay with baseball cards, and he enjoyed it so much he suggested I talk to businesses around town to help them sell as well. I used to clean offices for a living, and now I own my own business that takes great care of my family. I have five kids and really enjoy the success we have with selling for other people on eBay. I started working from home and eventually opened my own eBay drop-off store.

Amy Reedy, Lowell, Michigan;
eBay user ID "globalduk"; trading on eBay since December 19, 1997

THE NAME OF THE GAME

In October 1999, just when *Time* magazine was talking about eBay success stories, including mine, a man named Walt Duflock started working for eBay. For the previous seven years, Walt had worked for LexisNexis as a program manager and presales consultant. He came to eBay with an extensive background in business and a law degree from Santa Clara University School of Law.

While my business as an eBay seller did not officially have its own name yet, I had started doing something—selling for others—of growing interest to Walt and others at eBay.

eBay University had been formed shortly after Walt came to work for the company, and by the fall of 2001, I had started working regularly as a guest speaker at eBay University classes held at hotels across the country. eBay University was created to educate buyers and sellers about using eBay effectively. eBay had seen my article in *Time* and asked me to join the ranks of their instructors. Students eager to learn how to sell on eBay flooded these classes by the thousands. Many of my students were curious about my particular eBay business—selling for others—and asked for tips on how they could start their very own eBay listing services similar to my own.

At the same time, Walt and his colleagues at eBay noticed that a lot of people seemed to have merchandise they wanted to sell on eBay but, for a variety of reasons, couldn't or wouldn't sell it themselves. Walt also noticed that many of eBay's top sellers, also known as PowerSellers, were doing a good percentage of their business by selling items for others.

And so in 2002, eBay, under Walt's direction, decided to create the official Trading Assistant Program.

Walt's idea was that eBay could leverage the talents of both its top sellers and new, would-be entrepreneurs by creating a special directory on the eBay site where people could locate Trading Assistants—qualified individuals and companies who would sell others' merchandise for a fee. Because Trading Assistants are independent sellers, not employees or agents of eBay, it was important that eBay remain neutral while still assuring prospective Trading Assistant clients that these sellers would perform their services faithfully and successfully.

The Trading Assistant Directory on eBay can be found at *www.ebay.com/ta*, where it provides detailed FAQs, resources, and instructions for setting up your own profile.

THE QUALIFYING ROUND

Walt, who is now the senior manager of the Trading Assistant Program, implemented minimum qualifications for Trading Assistants for them to be included in this special directory.

Currently, to become (and remain) a Trading Assistant, you need to meet the following requirements:

- You've sold at least 10 items in the last 90 days.
- You have a feedback score of 100 or higher.
- Ninety-seven percent or more of your feedback is positive.
- Your eBay account is in good standing.

Once you meet these minimum requirements, you can go to the Trading Assistant Directory and set up one or more directory listings for your Trading Assistant business. This listing will be one of the most successful lead-generating resources for your business, so it is important to qualify for and add yourself to the directory. Many individuals who want to sell on eBay but simply do not have the time or desire to learn how to do so themselves will go to this directory and search by entering their own address. They will then be directed to qualified Trading Assistants in their local area.

Meeting the minimum requirements can be accomplished fairly quickly and easily.

Getting to 10

Selling at least ten items in three months should come easily to you. No doubt each of us has at least ten unwanted items lying around our home or office. I certainly do (still), even though I am an active seller on eBay. If you can't find ten items of your own right away, then start by asking family members, friends, and coworkers. After all, this will be one of the primary ways you will get business for your new Trading Assistant enterprise—by asking people!

This book is not an eBay selling book, it is a Trading Assistant book, so you will find few eBay 101 tips here. However, the basics of selling on eBay are *free* and readily available on the eBay Education Portal. You can find these selling (and buying) resources at *www.ebay.com/education*. eBay makes selling easy—that's why millions of people are doing it. Just take the eBay tutorials and you'll be up and running in no time. You will need digital pictures of your items in most cases, and you can borrow a digital camera if you do not have one. Remember, the goal here will be to get your first ten sales. Don't obsess or get bogged down because of analysis paralysis. You are fully capable and ready to start selling. You will learn with practice and a bit of trial and error.

Getting to 100

Feedback is the heart of the eBay system. Each eBay member can leave another member a feedback comment in connection with an actual transaction between them on eBay. So you must be either the buyer or seller to leave a feedback comment.

Feedback on eBay is straightforward and easy to understand:

- +1 point to your feedback score for each positive comment and rating left for you
- 0 points to your feedback score for each neutral comment and rating left for you
- -1 point to your feedback score for each negative comment and rating left for you

You can reach a feedback score of 100 not only by selling items but also by buying. Because not all eBay community members automatically give feedback comments following a transaction, it is important to communicate with the other member after a successful transaction and ask for feedback if they have not left any for you already. Clearly, maintaining a good relationship with your trading partner is important as a seller (and buyer) during the transaction, so feedback is the natural result of a successful trade. (I will go into much more detail about customer service in later chapters.)

Also, note that the feedback score is actually the net sum of all the positive comments you receive from *unique* eBay members, less the sum of all the negative comments you receive from unique eBay members. In other words, you cannot get a score of 100 if all your feedback comments are from the same member. Each member can only affect your score by one point, so while building your initial feedback rating, you'll want to trade with at least 100 different eBay members.

Remember, also, that you need to maintain at least a 97 percent positive feedback status at all times to qualify for and remain on the Trading Assistant Directory. If you are an honest person with good manners and you treat your trading partners on eBay well, you will never even have to think about this requirement. When you trade often enough on eBay, the possibility always exists that another member may give you negative feedback. You can't make everyone happy all of the time. The key here is that at least 97 times out of 100, you have to make sure your trading partners are happy with you.

> eBay's top sellers, PowerSellers, must maintain an overall positive feedback score of 98 percent or greater to maintain their PowerSeller status.

EBAY RULES

Staying on eBay's good side is also a requirement for being an eBay Trading Assistant. Being on the Trading Assistant directory is very similar to having a driver's license. The privilege can be taken away from you if you don't navigate eBay's roads lawfully. If you break any major rules, you can not only lose your Trading Assistant status, but you can also find your account temporarily or permanently suspended. When eBay suspends a user, eBay is suspending the individual, not just a specific account, so you cannot simply walk away from a suspended account and start a new one.

Keeping an account in good standing is easy, if you take the time to understand the basics. Of course you should sell only legal items, and be sure that none of your items are prohibited on the eBay site. There are a lot of rules, but most of them were created by eBay to protect consumers and prevent bad experiences and, therefore, require only common sense to follow. For example, you may not list items that promote or glorify hatred, violence, or racial or religious intolerance, or items that promote organizations with such views. For example, KKK items are prohibited on eBay and would result in your listing being removed.

Linking from your eBay listing to another Web site is generally prohibited as is selling controlled items such as tobacco, alcohol, or drugs. There are other types of restrictions as well. If you use the words *gold*, *silver*, or *diamond*, or other words that describe precious metals or gems, for instance, you have to make certain you are accurately describing the materials that exist in your item. And you can't sell a fake Rolex or a counterfeit Louis Vuitton handbag—or anything counterfeit for that matter. Using your noggin will help here, because you already know these items are illegal and eBay does not allow the sale of illegal or questionable items.

This can all sound rather daunting at first, but in the most basic terms, be honest in your listings and take some time to read eBay's policy about a particular item before making your listings. That way, you'll be in fine shape and out of harm's way. The link to eBay's Rules and Policies can be found at *http://pages.ebay.com/help/policies/index.html*.

With a little care and armed with the right information, you will be able to remain a qualified Trading Assistant and keep your eBay Trading Assistant Directory profile active.

BEFORE GOING "PRO"

Okay, now for a reality check—you really do not need to be a Trading Assistant to sell items on behalf of others on the eBay Web site. Clearly, having Trading Assistant status would be ideal, but if you are new to eBay, you may need to build your sales and feedback before qualifying, and you are probably eager to start selling immediately.

When I first started, I had only one client, my best friend Mike. As my business grew, however, I found that having more clients kept a steady stream of merchandise coming in, and my sales grew along with the acquisition of new clients. There are lots of ways to acquire new clients. The Trading Assistant Directory, to name just one source, brings in qualified clients quite rapidly—after all, if someone is searching the directory, they are clearly looking for a Trading Assistant. I'll address this topic in depth in Chapter 14. For now, rest assured that starting to sell for other people, before you meet the Trading Assistant qualifications, is perfectly okay.

CAT GOT YOUR MING?

If you don't plan to open a brick-and-mortar store, you will most likely conduct your new Trading Assistant business from home. If you live with others, it is important to share the details of your new business with your housemates or family.

You will want dedicated space to handle storage of items for sale, and keeping fragile items out of harm's way will be crucial. The last thing you want is to find that a very expensive painting has a big yellow stain from your faithful dog, or to come home and discover that a pricey vase has been knocked over by your feline pal. It is important to think ahead and avoid these unfortunate possibilities. Maybe you have a spare room, a spot in your basement, a corner in the garage, or some other suitable place to use for your clients' items.

Be sure your family or housemates understand and approve of your use of the living quarters for this new enterprise and don't find your new activity intrusive. You will want everyone's blessing. Keep in mind that in-demand and good quality items will sell quickly and be out of the house pretty fast. (On the other hand, shabby, useless items could be around for a while!)

You will also have to convince some clients that you can be trusted with their valuable items, and in many cases, the most skeptical of clients will have the best items for sale. You don't want to sell junk (I will drive this point home quite a few times in this book), and a clean, well-organized work space will allow you the possibility of having clients over. Looking professional and on top of things is very important, even when working from home. It's not mandatory that your clients meet you at your residence, but being well organized will help with your sanity and make the business more enjoyable and efficient for you in the long run.

But maybe you already have a business of your own, or perhaps you have a really cool boss who will let you set up your shop part-time at your job (perhaps in exchange for occasionally selling the boss's items for a reduced fee). If so, the same organizational concept will not only still apply but will be even more critical, because as a businessperson, you probably have many other tasks to handle in the course of a day, and you won't want to lose track of things or fall behind in any way. If you have customers or clients coming to your own place of business on a daily basis, their visits will be golden opportunities for you to sell your new eBay Trading Assistant services to them. After all, they already know and respect you.

★TIP

I strongly suggest you maintain physical possession (and therefore control) of the items you are selling on your eBay account for others.

YOUR TOOLBOX

If you have already been selling on eBay, you probably have most or all of the basic equipment you need to start your Trading Assistant business, such as:

- Modern computer system (with an Internet connection)
- Printer
- Copier
- Scanner
- Digital camera
- Tripod (optional)
- Backdrop or background for photography
- Photo lighting equipment

Each of these (and a lot more) is discussed in depth in Chapter 13.

DON'T DOUBT YOURSELF

American households have approximately $2,200 worth of unused items lying around (A.C. Nielsen, "Survey of Unused Household Items," October 2004).

Okay, I really think the time to ask this question is *now* and not later: Are you really sure you want to do this? I personally feel that my Trading Assistant business was the single best thing that ever happened in my professional life, but you may be thinking this is some get-rich-quick scheme, or that I will somehow wave a magic wand over you and turn you into a millionaire.

The reality is that this business, like *any* business, is going to involve some study and work. Are you up to the challenge? I am totally confident that I am taking you down the path of assured success, if you follow my techniques and tips, but your success is measured by you, not by me or anyone else. Your idea of success is all that matters. Perhaps you want to sell a few items here and there for your friends in your spare time and keep a tidy flow of extra money coming in on the side. Maybe you love your job and have no interest in quitting. If you need a hobby, this is a great way to try something fun, interesting, and new.

Perhaps you already run a business and want your customers to keep coming to you to buy new "stuff"; and you want to help them get rid of their old items to keep the upgrade cycle going. After all, you sold them what they have now and want to keep on selling to them.

Maybe you want to set up a dedicated eBay drop-off store and sell items full-time as a brick-and-mortar business. This is a very big undertaking, but if you have the budget and working capital, it is a lucrative and relatively low-cost proposition when compared to many other business opportunities out there.

Whether you are a businessperson, lumberjack, lawyer, accountant, homemaker, sanitation worker, teacher, cab driver—it really doesn't matter—you have made a decision to do something new in your life, whether full- or part-time. Remember, however, that you will be handling other people's items, and even though you will be charging them a fee, at the end of the day, you will have to give them the lion's share of the proceeds from the sale of their items. This means handling money. You are their trusted eBay listing professional, and you have to earn that trust by delivering consistent and quality work.

If you have absolutely no work ethic, it is time to start playing the lotto or asking mom and dad for some dollars. If you have a reasonable amount of determination, a great attitude, and the necessary time, however, you will be well on your way to helping other people relieve themselves of clutter, while pocketing a tidy profit at the same time.

Are you ready to keep going? I thought so! Put aside any fears you may have right now, because I'm going to empower you with the tools, tips, and tricks to make this a great experience!

2

WRITING YOUR
INITIAL BUSINESS PLAN

I sold $21,500 worth of IT equipment, servers, computer monitors, and other items for a New York corporation. I earned $4,300 from the project, which represented my 20 percent commission. The client was in a skyscraper with limited space, and they really appreciated my pickup service. We were both very happy from the sales.

Jack Cheung, New York City;

eBay user ID "ebargainnow"; trading on eBay since December 18, 1998

HOLD THE MAYO . . . WHERE'S THE PLAN?

Before you run out of the room screaming in terror over the idea of writing a business plan, it's time to relax and take a deep breath—it's really not hard or complicated to plan your successful future as a Trading Assistant. If you are a seasoned businessperson, this chapter can serve as a review; or if you are already familiar with the writing of business plans, you can certainly meander on to the next chapter. You may also be asking yourself: Why in the world do I need a business plan, if all I want to do is sell a couple of items a week for close friends and family?

If your new Trading Assistant business will serve simply as a fun new adventure and handling and making a lot of money is not part of your future ambitions, then a professional and formally written business plan won't be terribly important. But even when you make the decision to buy a computer, invest in a camera, purchase supplies for your new business—or basically make any decision about money—you have made a *plan*. A business plan can be a simple set of notes or guidelines you use in your everyday activities or it can be a comprehensive written guide created for securing outside financing to start a brick-and-mortar eBay drop-off store. Establishing fees for your work and budgeting expenses will be part of some form of real, practical business plan to keep the operation running smoothly and profitably. Whatever your goals, however large or small, you'll need a plan to be successful.

The nuts and bolts of a professional business plan will accurately establish your business model, set goals, and create a "resume" for your business. Using a business plan for your operations will help you to allocate resources (money, employees, time, etc.)—incalculably important decisions when the unexpected inevitably happens. And a great business plan will be critical if you seek financing from someone else, unless you have a rich uncle who loves to write you checks.

ROLL UP YOUR SLEEVES

I have already discussed the eBay Trading Assistant Directory (*www.ebay.com/ta*), where you can find a list of Trading Assistants simply by entering any street address or zip code. This will provide you with a quick and easy way of determining your competition in your immediate community. Each Trading Assistant has set up a profile (as will you) that explains their hours and days of operation, areas of specialty, languages spoken, services, fees, and terms and conditions.

As part of your research, it would be a good idea to start a three-ring binder with a set of tab separators to help you stay organized. Some logical tabs to create for this binder might be:

- Company information
- The competition and fee-pricing ideas
- Management/Employment
- Marketing
- Operations
- Financials

These tabs are suggestions, of course, which you can change or add to as your needs dictate.

Company information. In this section, you will want to add information regarding your planned business structure (we'll chat about this in Chapter 3 and Chapter 6), possible licensing requirements, registered business/trade name paperwork (your d/b/a or doing-business-as name), and anything else that might relate to your new company's formation.

The competition and fee-pricing ideas. Here you can keep notes on your Trading Assistant competition's fees and how they charge. You might consider that your competition also includes other types of businesses, such as consignment shops, consignment malls, co-ops, auctioneers, etc. You can regularly update this information as you survey the competition quarterly, biannually, or however often you feel is helpful. This might well be one of your most important tabs, because you will be keeping "tabs" on the competition.

Management/Employment. Here you will be adding any documents relating to people you hire, if and when you decide to hire employees. You can also add information on any outside experts who might join your team part-time to help list specialized items for you. My company often uses such experts, and we keep a list of them. These resources can come in very handy. You can also add the contact information for any accountants, attorneys, or other professionals who will eventually make up the management team of your business.

Marketing. This can be your ideas tab, where you keep marketing ideas, plans, and programs. If you decide that you want to cast a net larger than just the Trading Assistant Directory, you will want to fill this section of your binder with as many good free and paid marketing concepts and ideas as you can.

Operations. You'll often need supplies, and lists of vendors, price lists, and other details can be retained in this section. I find it very helpful to keep a master list of my suppliers. I spend a great deal of time finding the best prices for the everyday things I need; and with a busy company to manage, I like to keep good records so that I can quickly determine where I obtained the best price on photography backgrounds or bulbs or just plain old staples, printer paper, and the like. Ordering online is quite a time saver, so I keep Web site addresses as well as vendor names and phone numbers.

★TIP

Research eBay for packing and office supplies. Use eBay's distance-based search to help find local sellers and cut down on shipping costs—you can even pick up your purchases if the seller offers this convenience.

Financials. Eventually, you will set up a separate bank account for your business, and you may also want to retain monthly financials to help you track your income and plan taxes. Remember that you are now your own boss, and any money you make is income upon which you most likely will have to pay taxes to Uncle Sam. Keep receipts in envelopes and put them in this section. An easy way to do this is simply to punch holes in the envelopes and secure them in your binder with the receipts inside.

KNOW YOUR NEIGHBORS

Print a copy of the profile for each Trading Assistant within 10 to 20 miles of your home, office, or the location where you plan to start offering your services. Carefully study the scope of services offered by each Trading Assistant from the profiles you printed and determine how you might be able to set yourself apart from them. Here are some questions you might want to ask yourself:

- How much experience do they have?

- How long have they been in business?
- Can you offer better hours?
- Would you be willing to pick up items from your clients? Does your competition?
- How do they structure their commissions and fees?
- Are their fees easy to understand, or are they too complex for an average person to grasp?
- Do they charge an up-front listing fee for accepting an item and listing it in addition to a success fee for completing the sale?
- Do they charge eBay, PayPal, or other expenses in addition to their commission, or do they include all fees in their total compensation?
- Are their fees graduated (i.e., do they vary depending upon the final sale price of the item)?
- Do they have restrictions on the value, size, or type of item they will accept?
- Do they specialize or generalize?
- Do they have a drop-off location (physical store), or do they work from home?
- What is the quality of their photography and listing descriptions?

Take the time to thoroughly understand your competition's operations and try to think of ways you might be able to compete with them. If you are not a competitive person by nature, you will eventually develop a sense for these details; but in the meantime, seek out other business owners in your sphere and ask their opinions. But don't forget that simply offering great service itself goes a long way: Referrals from happy clients are the lifeblood of a Trading Assistant and can put (and keep) you ahead of your competitors.

YOUR RECONNAISSANCE MISSION

You have uncovered a great number of secrets about other Trading Assistants simply by browsing their profiles on eBay. Remember that, although Trading Assistants are not your only competition, they will be the primary competitors for your clients' attention and dollars. Let's try something possibly a little unorthodox and even a bit scary—let's pay them all a visit! Commit yourself to an entire day to visit and evaluate every Trading Assistant you've found nearby.

I have dropped into the physical stores of many eBay drop-off businesses and learned a great deal in the process. One of the great confidence-building elements of this concept is that most Trading Assistants are real people, not big corporations with fancy equipment and elaborate marketing campaigns.

Take your binder with you and drop into each of your competitor's stores. Be sure to review the prior checklist of questions before arriving and have a positive and open-minded attitude. As you walk in the door, prepare to mentally answer all of the questions we posed earlier. You may want to write each question down on an index card so that you can have them handy, in case you want to peek at them during your visit. Before you jump into a conversation with your competitor and get butterflies and knots in your stomach, be sure to see if they have brochures on display and, if so, immediately ask if you can have one.

Scan the operation and see how it is run. If you are planning to open a brick-and-mortar store, analyze the store layout, the equipment in view, and the supplies being used.

Introduce yourself and explain that you are looking into starting your own eBay Trading Assistant business. Gauge the reaction and determine if you are being perceived as friend or foe. You might be delighted to find that most businesspeople are very friendly and also willing to help someone new to any business venture. The average businessperson has worked hard to start their business and, in actuality, they respect anyone willing to try to make a go of it in the business world. But if you sense that you are not welcome, thank them for the brochure, mentally scoop up all your observations, and make a courteous exit. Then immediately write down everything you observed and discovered while visiting.

If you are met with a smile and a friendly attitude, it would be great to chat a bit and gather some tips and ideas from your fellow Trading Assistant. Many of the Trading Assistants, as well as local businesses near me, provide client referrals. Amazingly, a good deal of my referrals

> **★TIP**
>
> If you are not met with a friendly face when you visit your competition, perhaps you can recruit a friend or family member to act as your very own "secret shopper." Your secret shopper can then go to the competitor with an actual item in hand and go through the entire selling process with the competing Trading Assistant.

come from other Trading Assistants who feel I am more knowledgeable or better qualified than they, or who simply have too much business and cannot handle all of it. Smart businesspeople always view a competitor as a potential ally before proven wrong. A nice person attracts other nice people, and in business you will need friends. Be sure to make written notes on the Trading Assistant profiles so that you will be able to recall quickly which Trading Assistants were friendly and which were not.

Spend as much time as you can talking with your new friend and let them do as much of the talking as possible. Pay close attention to any mention of challenges that come up in their day-to-day operations and, again, when you leave their store, immediately write down everything you have learned for later reference. You may find that many of these observations fit into your Competition tab, but some of the informational jewels you carry out might become ideas for your Marketing tab.

Some additional questions you will ask the very friendly operators:

- How seasonal is your business?
- Do you get a lot of referrals?
- What are some of the ways you attract new clients?
- Do you get a lot of repeat business from existing clients, or are most one-shot deals?
- Have you run into any pitfalls? What were they?
- How much could a person expect to make in the industry working full-time?

The last question might be getting a bit personal, but with the right amount of diplomacy, you can often get a straight answer about how much the Trading Assistant is netting from their operation. Any such information must be kept in perspective, however, as sometimes people boast, or they may be overly conservative.

After you have spent the day visiting with each of the Trading Assistants in your local area, review your notes and transfer the best ideas onto index cards. You will appreciate having taken the time to do this when you write your final business plan.

WHO ELSE IS ON YOUR HEELS?

As mentioned earlier, other Trading Assistants are not your only competition.

One possible source of competition will be trade-in programs at your local stores. Many retailers offer to take used merchandise as a trade-in towards the purchase of something new. In most cases, your would-be clients would not get nearly as much in value for their trade-in as they will receive when you sell it—even after your commission is deducted.

Charities in your local area pose an interesting situation, as they are both competitors and prospective clients. Often, items donated to local charities are then sold at costly and time-consuming fundraising events. Many items are even disposed of, because the organization has no suitable way to convert them into cash. You can actually form a symbiotic relationship here. You can help the charities by having them direct their patron saints to you and then sell their donations for them on eBay. In this way, the charities will ultimately receive more in real dollars.

Also, some individuals want to make charitable donations, but the charities cannot accept the types of items they have to offer. As in the above situation, you can help the philanthropist give cash to the charity instead.

In such cases, you may be left out of the loop simply because people aren't aware of you and your services. One very prominent charity here in Burbank actually used the services of an out-of-town Trading Assistant, because they didn't know we existed. A top priority goal for growing your business is maximizing awareness that you exist.

Auctioneers and consignment shops, ostensibly competitors, may also turn into valuable clients. Friendly auctioneers and consignment shops can be great sources for merchandise. Auctioneers often have unsold items, and in your professional hands, this dead stock can turn into cash. Many consignment shops also run into this situation, and a heavy mink coat hanging in a consignment shop in Southern California might do better on eBay. There aren't many cold days here!

You may also educate customers by exposing or creating a need where there was none. Many of us don't think of the money sitting idly in our garage or attic.

KEEPING IT REAL

Let's bring all of this into focus and have a reality check. An eBay Trading Assistant business, like any other business, requires patience and time to develop. Don't quit your day job until you have explored a bit more and have tested the waters. If you are still reading this section, you obviously consider a business plan an important part of your future. But if you are becoming a bit overwhelmed at this point, don't worry—that's natural and okay. You should bookmark this section and come back after a day to digest everything you'll do to collect the data, ideas, thoughts, and notes on the business plan.

If you are seeking financial assistance to start this business, especially with a brick-and-mortar drop-off store, you will be pitching your idea to family members with money, investors, or banks. It is imperative that you express, in fair and real terms, the risks inherent in this industry. You will have acquired quite a bit of knowledge at this point, and you will be able to articulate these risks in realistic terms. Remember that anyone investing in you will not believe that this or any other business is a "sure thing." A solid business plan will include an explanation not only of the competition but of any other potential risks, such as seasonality factors. Giving due consideration to the downside will display your forethought and risk-planning ability. Your business plan must also foresee all working capital requirements and a contingency allowance to cover any margin of error. If this is your first business, it is very easy to underestimate the total costs involved. Be conservative until you have a handle on both the income and expenses associated with this endeavor.

WALKING IN THE SHOES OF THOSE BEFORE YOU

Unlike a lot of what you were taught while growing up and in school, it is perfectly okay to copy another business plan closely (but not to steal one!). If you know of anyone who has successfully obtained financing through investors or a bank, ask if you can borrow their business plan and rework it and model it for your own use. Many business plans are simply repurposed from other plans, and there is no point in completely reinventing the wheel. I seriously doubt you will get much resistance from most businesspeople when asking for this permission, because their mission is accomplished. They won't need that plan again, and they will very likely be willing to help out a new fellow entrepreneur.

Copying the plan verbatim is not a great idea. You will want to start taking out those index cards, comparing your notes with the sections in the plan you are using as your model. It is never okay simply to take someone else's document from the Internet (or anywhere else) without permission. Ask for permission, however, and you will probably get it.

Some superior ideas on how to write a good business plan come from the United States government. The Small Business Administration (SBA) has great tips on writing your plan, which you can find at *www.sba.gov/starting_business/planning/basic.html*.

If you hate typing long Web addresses as much as I do, you can simply type the phrase *business plan* into Google and find the same page in seconds. Take the time to review the SBA's best practices for business plans, just to start generally absorbing the concepts. There is a large amount of information on this Web site, and it can become a time bandit if you are not careful. Don't obsess too much about it; simply review some sample business plans. There is also a commercial Web site that provides dozens of free sample plans called Bplans.com, found at *www.bplans.com*.

No doubt you are noticing that I am referring you to a lot of Web sites. It is important to realize that there are literally *millions* of Web sites that provide resource materials for virtually any topic on small businesses. I provide my recommended sites here, but if you know of any better resource for a particular subject, by all means please use it.

"Hey, wait a minute!" you exclaim to yourself. "Wasn't this chapter about writing a business plan?" But we have not shown you an actual *written* business plan for an eBay Trading Assistant business. Why not?

The business plan is like a raw, untouched piece of marble—you get out your tools and start chipping slowly away until eventually a fabulous statue appears—and this is how you will develop your plan. Don't rush it, and it isn't necessary to hold up your new enterprise while you formulate this plan. You can go ahead and test the Trading Assistant water before you have your business plan. In fact, starting to sell items for other people right away will clarify the needs of this business and the possibilities for future growth, and it will help you to create that beautiful piece of artwork on paper that will help to sell your business idea to an investor or a bank.

But if you don't intend to seek financing for this new business enterprise, you have already created a basic business plan! Remember that a professional business plan is typically used when you are seeking financing for your business. A much simpler business plan is all that's needed to help you plan your daily operations, and you will be able to add more valuable information to your binder about financial projections, company legal structure, insurance, and many other details as we progress through our journey.

What goes in a formal business plan to seek financing? Much of what you have already garnered from your research will become the puzzle pieces that make up your plan. You will need to cover:

- Description of the business
- Marketing
- Finances
- Management

You can and should add your resume and a concise autobiography to the plan, as well as any documents to support your theories and projections. The plan should be neatly typed with proper spelling and grammar (thank you, Spellchecker!). There is no right or wrong way to write your professional business plan, as long as it contains the basic elements—who, what, where, when, why, and how—of what you will be doing and why you need money to get started. When you sit down and start typing this all up, you will want to speak in your own voice, without fancy language or complicated terminology. Remember that your target audience (e.g., a bank) will not be an expert in your field. You are the expert, and you should write with confidence and in an informational and educational voice.

Detailing Your Plan

The core elements of a business plan are summarized in this outline. Each section is already supported by much of the factual research you conducted earlier. After you have drafted your first plan, you will want to share it with "safe" individuals, such as other businesspeople, family, and friends, and get their feedback.

Be sure to include:

- A cover sheet with the proposed company name and
  - your complete legal name;
  - address;
  - telephone number;
  - fax number (optional); and
  - e-mail address (optional).
- A mission statement, explaining why you are venturing into this business
- A complete description of the business operation, including a clear definition of the Trading Assistant's job and the benefits to your clients
- A section on your marketing plans and how you intend to keep customers coming. If you have prospective clients already lined up, it is helpful to mention it here and give a complete list of

everyone from whom you have a client commitment. If you have a list of existing clients, ask for permission from them to give out their contact information as references

- A list of your competitors and why you feel you will be able to do better, and/or how you may be able to work with the competition
- A detailed technical explanation of your operation—how you plan to handle photography, listing, storage, shipping, etc.
- A list of the employees you intend to hire and their job descriptions (nothing fancy, just what they will do for you)
- A list of insurance companies who are willing to provide liability and hazard insurance (and, if you hire employees, worker's compensation insurance)
- A list of all the equipment purchases you will need to make, as well as estimates of the costs of improvements on your business location
- Your personal financial statement (the standard form from the SBA can be found at *www.sba.gov/sbaforms/sba413.pdf*)
- A spreadsheet that shows the break-even analysis of your business (the amount you will have to sell to cover all your expenses)
- Income projections to show the future potential of your business operation as your sales grow
- Your personal tax returns for the past three years
- Your business tax returns for the past three years if you presently operate another business or businesses
- Copies of your proposed lease agreement with a landlord or purchase contract for your building
- Copies of any business licenses that you presently hold
- A copy of your resume and bio

If you are not familiar with making spreadsheets and financial projections, it's okay! These projections do not have to be fancy or complex, and in general your services are rather simple and easy to understand. You sell an item and deduct your commission. You know your expenses, such as your rent or mortgage, utilities, miscellaneous office supplies, etc. You can easily put together some basic assumptions and then share them with your peers for evaluation.

SCORE It

America is a great country. The benefits of living here include all of the wonderful organizations set up to help small businesses, of which the SBA is just one. Another tremendously valuable resource is the Service Corps of Retired Executives (SCORE), comprised of successful business owners and executives who provide free and confidential counseling face-to-face and via e-mail. This priceless resource is available to anyone who asks (within a few simple guidelines—see below), whether starting or already in business.

SCORE volunteers will not write your business plan, fill out your tax returns, or run your business for you. Their entire mission is to provide consulting and education to you as a small business owner. You can visit their Web site at *www.score.org* and locate a local SCORE office that services your area, or you can request a consultation by e-mail. Because the SCORE Web site (like the SBA's) provides a plethora of resources, as before, I caution you to avoid the time bandits and stay focused. A volunteer from this fine organization can review your business plan and give you their comments, a valuable step before you present the plan to others.

On the SCORE home page you can enter keywords and locate volunteers who have experience in the specific kind of business you are starting. When I searched the word *eBay*, I found no fewer than seven counselors who provide advice about the eBay site. I found a total of 509 counselors who provide advice about business plans. You have discovered gold, my friend! Imagine getting free help from the retired CEO of a major company in reviewing and critiquing your business plan.

To use SCORE's services, you must be at least 13 years of age (yes, they teach them young!) as well as a U.S. citizen or holder of a Resident Worker visa (green card). Also, as a condition of your free consulting with the SCORE volunteer, you will be required to review and accept their terms and conditions:

- That you will cooperate if selected to participate in surveys designed to evaluate the SBA's small business assistance programs (SCORE is a Resource Partner with the Small Business Administration.)

- That the counselor will ask relevant information from you about the business operations and will agree to keep this information in the strictest of confidence
- That the counselor will not recommend any resource, vendor, or other service in which they have a vested financial or other interest (to avoid conflict of interest)
- That the counselor may not accept fees or commissions in exchange for providing you with their time
- That you will waive any right to bring a claim against SCORE or their related organizations in connection with the advice that they have given you (e.g., if they tell you to jump off a bridge, you can't sue them for the medical bills, pain and suffering, etc.)

Scan the Plan

I have found that scanning documents and converting them into Adobe Acrobat PDF (Portable Document File) format make life much easier, and when distributing your business plan, it will speed things up quite dramatically. Acrobat is a software program that converts documents from a scanner and a myriad of other document file formats (including Word, Excel, PowerPoint, etc.) into the PDF format, which can be viewed on virtually any computer. With the current version of this program costing $299, you will probably not want to make the investment in owning your own copy just for this one project. I suggest collecting any notes, ideas, and comments you garnered that may help to sell your business plan. Take them down to your local copy shop, Internet café, or other computer business and see if you can rent time with a scanner and do the conversion yourself, without the cost of buying the program.

Some free programs are available that will convert documents into PDF format. Although they are less robust in their capabilities than Acrobat, you can certainly get your business plan into electronic form by going for the freebies. For Apple computer users, iFILLE is available from Apple's Web site (*www.apple.com/downloads/macosx/*

system_disk_utilities/ifille.html). PC users can try OpenOffice (*www.open office.org*), which is a free, robust office suite and a very good substitute for Microsoft Office. I'll talk more about this program later in the book.

If you intend to e-mail your plan, the scans will be invaluable—you can always make hard copies if you are mailing or hand-delivering your plan. And remember, you will come across as a complete pro when you include the printed profiles of your competition. This shows that you did the work to investigate your business thoroughly and will help to seal the deal with prospective investors.

Get Two Cents from Others

I'll admit it: The business plan chapter is rather dull and dreary for someone who hates homework (and that's just about everybody), but we already agreed that if you got this far into this section of the book, it's because you wanted to use someone else's money to start your business, and reading this section was a necessary evil. Don't worry—if you feel as though you're in a dentist's chair, the ordeal is just about over.

After you have created an initial business plan and had it reviewed by a SCORE counselor, it's time to distribute copies to your family, friends, and business peers. One purpose this serves is earning their support for your new business venture. Emotional support is important when starting a new business. Additionally, your peers in business for themselves can comment on the plan and give you feedback. Keep those index cards handy for all the comments, and you will start to see what may need to be changed.

Your business plan will develop gradually, and you will add to it both as your understanding of the Trading Assistant world grows, and as you read through the rest of this book and learn the other details that will make it complete.

If your friends and peers have given you the green light and you feel you are ready to go, be sure to check grammar and spelling, then get it all into one PDF document or make a master copy that you can use for photocopying. Avoid putting this into your binder, because the three binder holes you would make will show up on the copies. Keep your master plan clipped with a large binder clip or paper clip and protect it in a large manila envelope or folder. If you have absolute confidence that you are ready, it is now okay to send out copies to your prospective investors and/or banks. But if you plan to start a brick-and-mortar store, you may want to hold off just a bit and discover the rest of what I have to say on the requirements of opening a physical drop-off store.

3

CONSIDERING YOUR LEGAL STRUCTURE

I have been a live auctioneer for 15 years. I opened up my own auction gallery and was struggling with regulatory problems. My 18-year-old assistant showed me that items we were selling were doing better on eBay. He taught me how to use eBay, and my first auction, of tools and equipment, ended up selling on eBay for over $40,000. We now use eBay to auction off virtually all of the items we sell. Where I would hire seven to nine people to run a live auction, I am able to hire just two and put more money in my clients' pockets.

Michael Odell, Edmonds, Washington;

eBay user ID "tradermicksgallery"; trading on eBay since March 10, 2004

I have been doing my duty to keep you motivated by constantly reminding you that nothing about starting a business should really scare you. That being said, if you are a business newbie, you should consider all the angles and make sure that you do things right the first time. Your legal structure (i.e., the way you manage your business and the legal entity you use for that business) is an important decision. When working as a house dad or soccer mom, you will be keeping things simple and doing business as a *sole proprietor*, which means no fancy paperwork and nothing revolutionary at tax time. If you decide to own a brick-and-mortar business or if your work-at-home Trading Assistant job becomes massive, however, you will want to consider a legal structure to protect yourself, your family, and your personal assets from possible legal liability in the event something unforeseen happens. And, of course, it's very important for potential investors to be aware of the legal structure you have chosen for your business.

Since the day I started on eBay, no buyer has ever sued me for an unhappy transaction, and no client has ever taken legal action because they were disappointed. In all probability, this will never be a concern for you either, but it would be unfair to you if I failed to mention all the possibilities. If you take on a partner or decide to take plunge into the physical store concept, you will want to do some soul searching on whether to form an entity such as a limited liability company, a corporation, or the alternative S corporation. I can't stress too much the importance of getting good accounting and legal counsel, as personal liability can be a risk, depending on how deals and contracts are structured.

PICKING YOUR HOUSE OF CARDS

In the business world, there are quite a few common legal structures with which you can operate a company. Some (but not all) of the types of entities are:

- Sole proprietorship
- General partnership
- Limited partnership
- Limited liability partnership
- Corporation (including the S corporation)
- Professional association
- Limited liability company
- Business trust
- Professional corporation

For our purposes, it's not necessary to define each of these entities, and personally, I find a lot of talk about legal structures dull and dreary. We're here to have fun, while of course making certain that you are operating with the correct type of business structure to meet your goals. So let's keep it lean while still covering what you need to know. The following issues primarily determine the type of organization you'll form:

- Taxation

- Liability
- Risk and control
- Continuity of existence
- Transferability
- Expense and formality

I'll focus on the four most popular ways to do business: sole proprietorship, limited liability company, corporation, and S corporation (the *S* is from the Internal Revenue Service code). The rest of the above ways of forming a company are not really applicable to you, but if you feel we don't adequately cover *your* situation within these four areas, it is time to call in a CPA, and possibly an attorney, for some further advice.

SOLE PROPRIETORSHIP

The simplest and easiest way to start your new business will be as a sole proprietor. My accountant informed me early in my business life that anyone grossing less than $175,000 from all business activities should operate under this type of business entity. Much of the consideration here is the inherent additional expense of operating a separate legal entity. In addition to the costs of forming the organization and filing additional tax returns, accounting may also cost you more, especially if you hire a bookkeeper to help.

As a sole proprietor, you can simply start doing business—and you are immediately a company. You may need to contact your state and local city licensing agency regarding appropriate licenses or permits (even when working from home), and you may wish to file or register a business name (also known as a d/b/a or doing-business-as name). Many local newspapers run the mandatory printed publication notices required when filing a d/b/a, and they may also keep copies of all the paperwork required to file. My local paper not only had the forms, they even filed them with the appropriate government agency, published the required notices, and returned my conformed and certified copies back to me. Your local chamber of commerce can also help, even if you are not yet a member. I strongly suggest that you open a distinctly separate bank account to keep your business separate from the rest of your life.

> Not all areas have mandatory d/b/a notices. With the advent of the Internet, it is very likely that most cities/states will soon fulfill any publishing requirements via the Internet on a searchable database (as Alaska does).

As a sole proprietor, you have total control—and total responsibility. You get all the profits from the business, you can hire any number of employees, and, as the owner, you are fully responsible for all taxes, claims, and debts of the business. You will need to claim the revenue from your business on your tax return. Your accountant (or you) will simply add the additional revenues to a schedule on your normal tax return called a Schedule C (Profit or Loss from Business).

With the sole proprietorship, all your business expenses will be in your name, with vendors and banks requiring a personal guarantee on any credit extended to the business. You will also need to pay estimated income tax to the government quarterly, and you may be required to pay your own Social Security, Medicare, and federal unemployment taxes for the additional income. Because you are the employer of yourself, you are required to handle the employer's portion of the taxes on your net income. The business *is* you. And you will be responsible for all debts, even if you decide to discontinue the business.

If you don't want or need to create your own company name, a d/b/a is not a mandatory part of the process; you can simply start your Trading Assistant business and bank your profits. If you start making some good money, you will want to speak to an accountant about handling the taxes. There are some great software programs out there to help you with the process of estimating and filing taxes, but use caution—if you are not comfortable using such programs, seek professional help.

If you hire employees, you will also need to apply for a Federal Employer Identification Number (FEIN), a number given to you by the IRS to identify your business that can be thought of as analogous to your Social Security number. The IRS uses this number to track various activities of your business, including your collection and payment of payroll taxes. In most states, you will need to apply for a state identification number for handling employees' tax withholdings as well. Don't worry: it's not as complicated as it may sound, as you will see in Chapter 21 about employees.

For now, if you think all of the above sounds like you, you are probably going to start off small and keep it simple—be a sole proprietor. To review:

- *Taxation.* You will be taxed once. You will simply add Schedule C to your normal federal return, while state returns and rules may vary by state.
- *Liability.* You are personally liable for all debts and legal actions against you.
- *Risk and control.* If you are a very small business, the risks are minimal, and you have a tremendous amount of control.
- *Continuity of existence.* This type of entity is *you*, so it cannot survive your death or be passed on to heirs.
- *Transferability.* Selling the business to someone else is not as easy as other business structures.
- *Expense and formality.* The least expensive way to operate your business, with the least formality.
- *Financial management.* You can use your existing bank account, but a separate account is recommended

As a sole proprietor, you will have more difficulty raising capital and seeking investors, because many will consider you "small potatoes." But if you want to be small, this structure is ideal.

LIMITED LIABILITY COMPANY

This type of entity is a rather popular way for individuals or partners to start and maintain a business. The limited liability company is commonly referred to as the LLC. This type of organization is relatively easy and inexpensive to form and operate and has many of the benefits of a corporation, such as limited liability (as the name suggests) and the flexibility of a partnership (which we do not discuss at length here). This is a very common way for sole proprietors to protect personal assets and secure loans. It is not as economical as the sole proprietorship, because you may have to pay someone to form the organization and there will be additional tax returns. This business structure can be formed in any state. You can allocate the profits and losses of the LLC in flexible ways in different percentages to and from the ownership of the organization.

There is no double taxation issue, because the LLC is not treated as a separate taxable entity, and you do not need to be a U.S. citizen to own or invest in this type of organization. The LLC can also be owned by a combination of individuals or business entities. This might prove handy if one of your investors wants a piece of your business, perhaps taking part ownership through one of their own companies.

An LLC can be formed in one step, while an S corporation, though similar in its benefits, requires first the formation of your corporation and then election to the S corporation status. If you are not a U.S. citizen, an LLC will be your ideal structure as well, as only citizens and resident aliens may own an S corporation. With the universal adoption of the LLC by every state, it has become extremely popular.

If more than one person will own your company, the LLC can form an operating agreement that sets forth how the business will be managed. The members (owners) of the LLC typically contribute capital to the enterprise, and the profits are distributed at your discretion. Unlike corporations, no stock is issued when the LLC is formed, and no minutes of the board are required.

To review:

- *Taxation.* The corporation will be taxed separately, and you can pay yourself as an employee of the corporation. Dividends to stockholders are taxed separately as well. Profits flow directly to the members of the LLC in proportions designated by you with maximum flexibility. Each member is then responsible for paying taxes on their share of the profits

- *Liability.* The LLC offers substantial protection from legal liabilities
- *Risk and control.* LLCs hold moderate risk and offer excellent control over your taxes, ownership, and finances. Due to the higher administrative burden and higher cost of doing business, it is a higher-risk entity. However, for a large company, the corporation structure provides a great deal of control (financial and ownership), and stock can be easily transferred to others
- *Continuity of existence.* The LLC can have an unlimited number of stockholders (in essence, owners), and it can add members with no limit.
- *Transferability.* Due to the flexible nature of the LLC, it can be transferred quite easily via stock sales
- *Expense and formality.* The LLC will require additional tax returns, and the formality is moderate, but it is a good trade-off if you want to protect assets and assure a fair and level playing field when doing business with multiple owners or a fairly good-sized company. It may be appropriate to create an LLC when you have grown your business somewhat. This is the highest-cost structure due to the administrative burdens, additional tax returns, and legal and professional fees for management of the company
- *Financial management.* A separate bank account is required

---

★TIP

Because of the highly flexible nature of the LLC, you can raise capital more easily, give investors a piece of the pie, and retain control via the operating agreement documents you create when forming the LLC.

C CORPORATION, S CORPORATION

If you hit the big time, it will be tempting for you to believe that forming a corporation is the next achievement required to prove your worth as a businessperson. The reality is that the LLC would still be the preferred way to go for most. In 1988, I formed my corporation, and I still operate it today, even though I have changed my line of business a few times. Because I have worked hard these many years to establish business credit and a reputation, it would not make sense for me to change my legal structure today; but frankly, were I to do it all over again, I would have formed an LLC.

A corporation (not an S corporation) is a fairly wild animal to tame. It is true that you can issue stock certificates and have an unlimited number of shareholders. Also, the corporation is its own entity and can live well after its founders have passed on. This is why major companies are still in business today well over a century after they were formed. The corporation can be bought and sold, and there are a lot of flexible benefits.

The downside is that the incorporation process requires a lot of paperwork, a burden that should not be undertaken by a small business owner. Incorporation also involves:

- articles of incorporation;
- bylaws;
- organizational board resolutions;
- stock certificates; and
- a stock ledger.

With a corporation, you can form a board of directors that has a general management duty to the business (kind of a steering committee). There are officers, such as the president, secretary, and treasurer, who handle the day-to-day responsibilities of the business. One person can act as the board and can also hold the positions of multiple officers. Again, however, this type of organization will probably never serve your best interests unless you get really huge as a company, and at that point, you will want to refer the process of setting up your corporation to a professional. That process is beyond the scope of this book. If being a Trading Assistant is your only business, I'm not going to suggest setting up a corporation.

With the filing of form 2553 with the Internal Revenue Service, you can elect to have your corporation (typically called a C corporation) convert to what is referred to as an S corporation. An S corporation will allow you many of the same benefits of an LLC. You can allow all of the profits to flow directly to the shareholders. The S corporation may only have a total of 100 shareholders (more than you'll need) and has the same protection from personal liability as the C corporation. This designation with the IRS allows you to treat the income pretty much the same as you would if you were a sole proprietor. However, you get the benefits of having a distinct, separate organization. The formation and operational documents, as well as administrative requirements, are the same as with a C corporation. You will still have to file separate tax returns for your company, and the professional fees will also be similar. Fewer and fewer businesspeople opt for the corporation status, because the LLC brings all of the same benefits to the table without the high costs of operating a formal corporation.

The upside to operating as a corporation (either type) is that the stock of the corporation can be transferred easily to other individuals and companies. This can make raising capital easier, as the investors can own a part of your company and also benefit from no liability in your operations. Single taxation is another benefit—because the profits flow directly to the shareholders of an S corporation, you do not pay the customary corporate tax in addition to the tax on your earnings.

It's worth noting as well that all of the legal structures, with the exception of sole proprietorship, require that you have a person or company designated and authorized to receive service of legal papers on your behalf (in the event of a lawsuit or other legal proceeding). Even though I seriously doubt that you will ever find yourself in court for any reason related to your business, you are required to maintain an Agent for Service of Process. If you don't know someone willing to do this for free, there are professional agents who offer this service. You can check the phone book or contact your secretary of state for some names.

TAKING IT TO THE NEXT LEVEL

If you want to form an LLC or a C or S corporation, you can contact an attorney in your area who specializes in setting up legal entities. A specialist will have the most knowledge and experience, and in the long run you will usually pay less for an expert's help than for the services of a general practice attorney. If you want to form the business entity yourself, remember that SCORE will be a big ally in your quest for fame and fortune as a Trading Assistant, so this is an excellent time to confer with a SCORE counselor.

The Company Corporation can help too. Founded in 1899 (yes, you read that right!), The Company Corporation helps with one in seven LLC or corporation creations. I have used their services, and they are outstanding. They are not lawyers. Rather, the company is a document preparation service, and they provide detailed instructions on how to operate your LLC or corporation properly. They are far less expensive than an attorney, the trade-off being a lack of legal advice that you may want. If you are on a budget and don't mind spending a bit more time up front, you can save a small fortune by using this company. Their Web site is *www.corporate.com*.

When you operate an LLC or corporation in one state and you want to set up shop in other states, you do not need to create a new organization for each state. You do have to apply for and register a Certificate of Authority to do business in the new state(s). And you'll have to file a state tax return for each state in which you have a physical operation. Although this will probably never apply to you, it is something to consider if you are planning on opening multiple stores in the future. The Company Corporation can also act as your Registered Agent and provide help filing for a Certificate of Authority to do business in other states.

There is a perception by the general public that a company with *LLC* or *Inc.* in the name is somehow better than a d/b/a. Although this may be very untrue, perception is so often reality, and thus this is a reality of business. Often as a sole proprietor, you will be treated as less serious, less credible, by prospective business associates, investors, banks, and clients. This is not to say that you should rush out and file for an LLC, but it is a reality that as you grow, your plans should include evaluating your legal structure at least once a year. Discuss the issue when you are working with your accountant at tax time. Closely related are the regular talks you should be having with your accountant about quarterly estimated taxes and tax planning throughout the year.

★ REMINDER

Once you have decided which way to go in terms of your business structure, be sure to update your business plan with the new information.

On a personal note, as a small entrepreneur, I started out as a sole proprietor. When my income began to grow dramatically, I sought professional advice from my accountant, and when the time was right, I made the leap to a more formal business structure. Believe it or not, that was way back when I was 18 years old! But don't obsess about your business structure if you are small. Keep everything simple and grow into your new business a bit before you get too fancy. You will sense when the time is right to form an LLC or corporation, as no one knows your business better than you. If you are feeling a little confused about which business structure is right for you, I encourage you to contact me personally for an opinion. Although I cannot give legal or accounting advice, I can certainly be a sounding board for your particular situation—and don't forget to seek help from a SCORE counselor!

4

WORK FROM HOME OR OPEN A BRICK-AND-MORTAR STORE?

I was an IBM executive working in Hong Kong and took an early retirement package in 1993 after 25 years of service. Upon returning to Florida, I wanted a steady addition to my retirement income but did not want to be locked into a storefront. I was looking for something I could do from my home. That's when I discovered eBay's Trading Assistant Program. It also seemed like a great opportunity to help the older folks in our community who are downsizing and finding that their children don't always want many of their old items. I recently sold a client's Civil War photo album on eBay for $1,650. I charge a flat 40 percent commission, and I pick up all items from my clients' homes.

Tom Murphy, Palm Beach Gardens, Florida;

eBay user IDs "pga-auctions" and "tfmurphhk"; trading on eBay since September 1, 1998

The question that I'll pose before diving into this next chapter is, "Do you have enough money—*cash dollars*—to open a brick-and-mortar store?" The question is simple enough, but there's another, closely related question: Just how fancy do you want to get with this new Trading Assistant business? You can start a store with little more than a small, cheap space and a sign that says you are in business, or you can invest a considerable amount of money to create a high-profile, corporate-looking, professional image. The latter will require a considerable amount of planning and budgeting on your part before you sign a lease and start talking to contractors to help you build your space.

When I started selling on eBay for my friend Mike Richards, I had a completely unrelated career, and I was storing items before shipping them wherever I could find the space. Eventually my eBay Trading Assistant hobby had grown to the point where I graduated to a tiny, 444-square-foot office. There I stored the items and handled the day-to-day operations of my eBay business in a dedicated, distinctly separate space. Having a separate space from my home and regular business allowed me some sanity. I sought out part-time help on one of my favorite Web sites, Craig's List (*www.craigslist.org*), where I found individuals with a desire to work an occasional day here and there. Craig's List is a worldwide group of Web sites, each based in a different city, which offers a bit of something for everyone, including help wanted ads. As my client base grew, my tiny space was stacked to the ceiling with merchandise, and I wanted to expand. I quit my day job and began planning my current retail storefront, where I now run a full-time eBay drop-off enterprise.

I thought of the transition from occasional seller to full-time store as a natural one. The money I earned from my business more than paid for the cost of leasing, renovating, and advertising my new business. Mind you, this happened over the course of *years*. I started selling in 1998, and by 2003, I had graduated to my very own retail operation. I didn't take out any loans or have any investors. This business was something I wanted to build gradually, slowly, carefully. I am an extremely cautious investor, and I looked at my eBay business as an investment. I wanted to make certain that this investment would be profitable for many years to come. I wanted to learn the ropes thoroughly before expanding and to devise a system that would ensure me long-term profits. It took me just over five years to make the transition from being small potatoes to actually hanging up my shingle.

The decision to stay small or go big is something you'll have to grapple with yourself. Some possible scenarios for you might be:

- Work from home
- Work from your office

- Have an eBay Trading Assistant business within your retail store
- Create a simple drop-off store
- Create a high-profile, professional drop-off store

YOUR COZY COTTAGE

This is your simplest and most inexpensive way to get started. As long as you can attract clients, working from home can be a great blessing, because you will have virtually zero start-up costs. If you have a personal computer with an Internet connection and a digital camera (or can borrow one, initially), then you are ready to start listing. You'll have to learn some basic accounting, because you will be collecting money for auctions, deducting your commission, and then paying your clients the balance. You will need an eBay account that is set up for selling as well as some basic office supplies. Because eBay provides an easy way to ship parcels via its integrated PayPal shipping system, and most shipping companies pick up packages (including the U.S. Postal Service), you can have a very efficient and streamlined business working from home. But there are drawbacks, and we'll cover them shortly.

★TIP

If you are a super cautious person, working from home will be your best bet when starting out. You'll want to discover if this new career is the right fit for you before pouring lots of money into a bigger project.

HANG YOUR SHINGLE AT WORK

If you work for another company, working from "work" may be very difficult—impossible in most cases. It is hard to convince an employer that your eBay Trading Assistant enterprise should take precedence over your duties as an employee. You might, however, be able to work out an arrangement with your boss by which you would do much, or all, of the Trading Assistant work over lunch or before/after your normal work schedule.

Why would any employer agree to allow this? Well, there are scenarios where this works. I have met individuals who offer to list their company's unwanted items on eBay for free in exchange for permission to spend breaks, lunchtime, etc., to list items for others. This arrangement is worthwhile for the company because it receives your services for free, and it's great for you because the company becomes a client. If you work for a business that sells a product, this might be a great fit. If you work at a job with any amount of idle time, you can make a fair argument that this is a logical fit to your job. If you work for a small, entrepreneurial company, you can earn the admiration and respect of your boss and make some extra money at the same time.

PIGGYBACK ON A RETAIL SHOP

Do you own your own retail store? If so, then offering eBay listing services is a smooth and easy fit. Think of a hardware store with hundreds or even thousands of customers passing through the doors on a monthly basis. Typically, weekend warriors like to have nice, bright, shiny new tools. I am guilty of this myself, because I'll be the first to go out and buy a new electric screw gun when mine gets a scratch. I know, I'm spoiled, but so is the rest of middle America. How does a guy like me justify the expense of a new air-powered nail gun? I sell my old one on eBay. If a hardware store offered to help their customers sell their used tools and equipment on eBay, they would stimulate the cycle of customer upgrade-ism.

This can be applied to almost any retail product store. If you own a store that sells products to consumers, you can offer eBay Trading Assistant services within that store. It would be a simple matter of obtaining the necessary equipment (computer, camera, etc.) and making up a flyer or other ad to get off and running. One clever way to present this service could also become a great marketing tool—offering to sell the items with no commission charged to the client/customer, so long as they spend the money that you obtain for them at your store. This could be in the form of a store credit or gift certificate. Offering a fee-free eBay listing service would generate quite a buzz for you, and the profits you made on the sale of new merchandise would make up for the free service.

THE SIMPLE DROP-OFF STORE

If working from home is out of the question and you do not have a day job, you might consider starting a cheap, small drop-off store. If you have savings, you may not need to borrow any money to get started, because you can probably find a small, suitable retail or office space to use for conducting business.

The idea here would be to keep your business and personal lives separate, while providing a reasonably professional environment to meet clients and handle the daily aspects of selling on behalf of others. You might work alone or hire full- or part-time help to keep up with the workload. In addition to possible one-time expenses such as buying a computer, camera, and lighting equipment, your recurring monthly expenses will include:

- Rent
- Utilities
- Telephone
- Internet
- Office supplies
- Salaries (if you hire anyone)
- Advertising expenses

Ideally, even in a low-cost office space, your landlord will provide some of the improvements, commonly referred to as leasehold improvements. If your landlord is providing a turnkey space, it will be painted, carpeted, and move-in ready. If you do not expect to depend upon foot traffic for attracting new customers, you can lease an office space or a retail space in a less than prime area. Commercial office parks can be quite inexpensive to begin with and less desirable for other types of businesses, so you may well be able to negotiate the rent down even further. You'll want to rent month-to-month or keep the lease as short as possible to give yourself maximum flexibility.

THE HIGH-PROFILE DROP-OFF STORE

So you have big bucks or a rich aunt, or you plan to borrow money from investors or a bank, and you want to set up a slick, professional looking eBay Trading Assistant store? A high-profile store requires a lot more planning. In addition to the requirements of creating a simple store, you will also need to think about leasing space in a high-traffic retail location. Along with a better location, you will not only pay a higher monthly rent, but you will also need to think about:

- Lease terms and conditions (a good location usually means a higher level of commitment to your landlord)
- Branding (the way your business looks)
- Store design and layout
- Renovation costs

If you have a tendency to think *big*, then this would be your strategy for making a splash as a Trading Assistant. But with bigger overhead, your need for ideas to bring in new clients will also be much more intense and urgent. You will need to sell a lot more merchandise to cover your expenses. I'll be giving you a comprehensive education about the entire process of opening a store in later chapters. Opening a high-profile drop-off store is not nearly as expensive or complicated as opening most of the popular franchise businesses. A new McDonald's franchise requires a minimum of $200,000 in cold, hard cash just to open the doors, and that is just the down payment! I think that a very fancy drop-off store would cost significantly less than that, and if you are in a part of the country with a low cost of living, your monthly overhead will be relatively low, too. The biggest overhead expense in any business is usually labor, with rent typically second. But if you become quite large—listing hundreds or even thousands of items monthly—then your eBay bill will grow proportionately, perhaps even becoming your single greatest expense.

WHO ARE YOUR CLIENTS?

A considerable amount of thought needs to go into answering this question. In my early eBay selling years, my first and only client was my best friend. As word spread that I sold unwanted items for others, new clients came into my life from all directions. I was taking in substantially more things than I could list in a day, and I was working seven 12-hour days a week. (Okay, I still work seven days a week, but I don't really have to.) Spending money on advertising never really crossed my mind, and until I opened my first storefront, I had never spent a dollar to place an ad to get new clients. Although my store is located next to a busy bank, I noticed immediately that the foot traffic walking by my store was not the upscale clientele that I was seeking; rather, it was mostly comprised of window shoppers and customers frequenting the various secondhand stores and antique shops near me. Attracting a client base with the high-quality merchandise that would generate the profits to keep the doors open posed a real challenge. I had to advertise, and still do today.

You might already have a list of eager people wanting your services, and if that is your situation, you can rent an office space or work from home. If you don't plan on being super busy, then you can open a simple store. The fancy store will require much more study—of the benefits of paying high rent for a good location. Quite a few of the successful drop-off stores I have seen are in the upscale strip malls common in Los Angeles. They are near other businesses that cater to the wealthy, such as dry cleaners, hair salons, or upscale supermarkets. The clients you want, as well as the level of activity you are seeking, will drive your location decision.

It would be a good idea to review your notes on how your competition is snagging their new clients. You should also consider the size of your town and cost of doing business. In Burbank, where I live and work, the cost of renting a prime retail space is a small treasure chest of money every month. And rent is just the beginning. We pay a hefty electric bill to cool and heat the 1,100-square-foot store. There is the annual insurance bill and, of course, other expenses, too. How important will your location be to reeling in the best clients?

HUNTING OR FARMING?

Many Trading Assistants survive with low rent because they provide high-touch customer service. Offering to pick up merchandise from your clients, instead of making them come to your place of business, accomplishes two things: You can get by without a fancy store, and you will be leaps and bounds ahead of any competitors who won't take the time or trouble to give this added level of client service. The catch here is that you simply cannot afford to make house (or office) calls unless the profit justifies the trip. You won't want to drive 15 miles to a client and spend time explaining your services—all for an item that ends up selling for $15. The value has to be there when making house calls.

If you have clients come to your place of business, you will have to maintain a neat, organized, and professional appearance to attract picky clients. Image is a large measure of your worth to a new client, because we live in a society where perception is reality. You also have to take into account that many wealthy individuals are busy. While high-income people always have unwanted things, it may be hard for them to find the time to come see you. You will have to be flexible to accommodate their busy schedules, and you may want to include evenings and weekends in your open-to-the-public hours for their convenience. My store is open from 10:00 AM to 7:00 PM, Monday through Saturday. I have employees to help greet customers and accept items, but bear in mind that if you run a one-person shop, you may not last long with such a strenuous schedule.

GRADUAL EVOLUTION

eBay has grown wildly popular with sellers across the world in great part because of the convenience of selling at will, and because, unlike most businesses, on eBay you can start making money without making a huge investment. When you sell from home and eBay is a supplemental source of income, you can take a break or a vacation from selling at any time, as long as your buyers and clients are happy. eBay is scalable, and there are no fees for using eBay unless you actually list and sell items.

But when you open a store, you no longer have the luxury of selling on eBay when and if it suits you. With the recurring bills associated with a drop-off store, you have to maintain a steady flow of clients and merchandise to meet your overhead. You can't simply lock the door and take a vacation without having someone to mind the store and take care of clients. Owning and running a business location is like a marriage, with tremendous responsibility, and you should give this reality careful consideration before making the leap. If you have never operated a successful business before, I must discourage you from making the move to a high-profile drop-off store immediately. Consider selling part-time from home at first, learning the ropes of being a Trading Assistant, before you get married to a lease and a long-term business. You can gradually evolve your business into an operation big enough to justify a full-time eBay Trading Assistant shop.

Having said all that, eBay is a dynamic marketplace, and as a Trading Assistant you will have numerous options available for operating a successful auction-based business. You will quickly learn that keeping up with the latest changes and enhancements that eBay launches in the e-commerce universe is hard work. For example, in addition to the several levels of features for its eBay Stores program, as this book went to press eBay had just introduced eBay Express (a no-auction, fixed-price/buy-it-now compilation of eBay listings) and ProStores (an e-commerce solutions service). Part of doing your research is to be aware of the venues and services that are available to you as your client's expert representative. You should not try to digest too much at once. You will peel the layers of eBay knowledge and discovery over time!

FAMILY MATTERS

Most everyone has a family life of one sort or another. If you live with other people, whether a spouse, significant other, or other family members, others will be impacting and influencing your business. Positive or negative energy will have the expected effect on your attitude, on your very plan to become an entrepreneur.

Working from home in an unsupportive environment is a recipe for failure. Without positive emotional support, your Trading Assistant business won't be fun. This could actually be one the reasons you might want to open a store—to separate your business from your personal life.

If you have the house to yourself during the day, then working at home will be much easier. But if others are around, it is only natural for the family magnet to drag you into this or that project and pull you away from your duties as a Trading Assistant.

Jealousy and envy are part of human nature, and if you live with anyone who is not completely in favor of your work at home, you may find subtle or obvious efforts to undermine your success. Try your best to rally support for your plans to start and grow a business. If you're getting positive vibes, you can give it a try and see how things go. But when you start spending hours defending your use of the kitchen as a packing and shipping "department," and explaining why the hall closet is bursting with clients' merchandise, it's time to consider separating your business from your home life.

You will know what is right for you. My philosophy in business has always been to seek the path of least resistance. If something is too hard, it's probably not the right way to go. Do what comes naturally and easily. I don't mean that this venture of yours will be a cake walk—I'm simply suggesting that your decision to work from home or not be based on your natural instincts and feelings.

★CAUTIOUS REMINDER

If you have a spouse or significant other in your life, they should be involved and committed to this new enterprise. As things grow, you don't want your better half to pitch a fit and cause the dominos to start falling over.

5

START-UP COSTS, CAPITAL REQUIREMENTS, AND BUDGETING

My son was born prematurely and weighed less than five pounds. I had to quit working and stay home with him. One of my first Trading Assistant items was an 1890s Nippon wall plaque that my client had tried selling at a local antique mall at $100 without success. After a year at the antique mall, my client wanted to try eBay, so I listed it with an opening bid of $99.99 and it ended up selling for $410! I have been so inspired by my eBay success that I now teach classes locally to help other people with eBay.

Tricia Hanley, Keyport, Washington;

Pacificquest Auction Services, LLC; eBay user ID "pacificquest"; trading on eBay since February 5, 1999

In the last chapter, I talked about the different ways to start an eBay Trading Assistant business. The start-up costs will depend on the direction you choose. If you are a risk taker with high ambition, are fairly savvy about borrowing money, and have a good personal credit score, you may well be considering the physical drop-off store. If you are not a risk taker and would like to take the more conservative route of working from home, your start-up costs will be the basics. Either way, you will still need to have some capital to start, and you'll want a budget to keep things moving along smoothly without the stress of a financial crisis due to poor planning. You will need to consider the source of your start-up capital before jumping into this new venture.

FROM DREAMS TO REALITY

By now, your business plan has begun to take shape, and although it is a work in progress, you can use your plan as a guide for creating your initial financial projections. In the Finances section of your business plan, I asked you to formulate a break-even analysis, to make certain that your venture's recurrent expenses will be covered. You will now want to refine this section of the plan to ensure that you will have both enough start-up and working capital. The start-up capital is the money you need to open your doors, and the working capital will be the cash you need to stay in business, paying your day-to-day bills, while you grow your business into profitability.

With a home-based business, working capital is much less important, because most of your overhead is covered. You may need funding for a computer, Internet account, a digital camera and lights for photography, and almost certainly for supplies. You might already have the first three or four items on the list, making your initial investment very, very small—perhaps $100 or less. If you will be working from your existing office or store, the start-up costs will also be nominal. You might want to add a few extra dollars to cover printing advertising materials and business cards, but for the most part, the budget is quite similar to that of a home-based enterprise.

The brick-and-mortar drop-off store will be quite a financial leap in terms of both start-up and working capital. Here are sample budgets for opening both a simple and fancy drop-off store in a 1,000-square-foot location, with a rent of $1.50 per square foot per month.

	Simple	Fancy
Security deposit and first month's rent ($1,500 rent plus $1,500 security deposit)	$3,000.00	$3,000.00
Computer, scanner, and printer	$1,000.00	$1,000.00
Telephone and Internet connections	$150.00	$150.00
Furniture	$500.00	$2,000.00

Leasehold improvements	$1,000.00	$20,000.00
Signage	$1,500.00	$5,000.00
Printing	$500.00	$2,500.00
Supplies	$250.00	$1,000.00
Camera	$500.00	$500.00
Lighting	$150.00	$600.00
File for a d/b/a	$100.00	$0.00
Set up LLC or corporation	$0.00	$1,000.00
Business license	$100.00	$100.00
Total	$8,750.00	$36,850.00
Contingency (25%)	$2,187.50	$9,212.50
Total start-up capital	$10,937.50	$46,062.50

Bear in mind that these figures are hypothetical, rounded-off examples. To keep things in perspective, rent of $1.50 per square foot might be very high in Geneva, Nebraska, but would be extremely inexpensive in Chicago, Los Angeles, New York, or San Francisco. You will have to survey rent levels for the type of space you seek in your particular locale. The same will be true for many of the other expenses. It takes a bit of research and a few phone calls to fill in all of the actual expenses of opening your own store.

The majority of the expenses of opening your simple store are rather straightforward, and you won't have much trouble determining them. Usually more problematic are the leasehold improvements and signage. These costs can vary not only from location to location but also depend greatly upon your store design. With your simple store concept, you will act as the store designer, but with a fancy store, you will want the services of a store layout expert to help with the entire design and branding package. You will also want to talk in more detail with the owners of other eBay drop-off stores.

CHAT WITH YOUR NEIGHBORS

You may recall that I had asked you to immediately write down everything you observed when visiting other Trading Assistants's drop-off stores. Take these notes out and review them carefully. Hopefully, you noted which Trading Assistants were friendly, and if so, this would be a good time to confer with them in detail about your own store design plans. It is always better to use proven concepts than to try to reinvent the wheel.

If the drop-off site visits you made did not yield enough warm and fuzzy people, you can always expand your search for Trading Assistant stores well beyond your immediate area. Try to set up appointments with the owners of at least three Trading Assistant stores that you felt were well run and professional. Don't be shy or hesitant—it is very common in business to ask peers for their opinions and to solicit feedback. You could ask to have this meeting on your very first visit, but a good drop-off store is busy by definition, and you don't want to impose on anyone while they are handling their daily routines. After you introduce yourself on your first visit—and if you feel the store is a model of elegance, professionalism, and efficiency—you could ask for an appointment at that time. But don't be discouraged if you are turned down. Not everyone is eager to help the competition, but if you are far enough away from this person's location, you can suggest that you will not be competing for the same clients. Polite, affable persistence will pay in the long run.

★**TIP**

Be armed with your questions about start-up capital and take notes. Ask about all of the expenses mentioned in the previous chart and add any additional items that might arise during your interview. As your knowledge and understanding of start-up requirements continues to expand, your business plan will also become more refined and clear.

PULL OUT THE PIGGY BANK

Working capital, the money you will need to stay afloat while you build your clientele base, the financial cushion to keep your lights on and your rent paid, will also vary greatly when you factor in the cost of paying employees.

If you have employees, their salaries may vary depending on the skills required. You may want to handle all your eBay listing and photography work yourself and add a part-time helper to assist with packing and shipping orders. If you have bigger plans for a high-volume operation, you will want to have employees handling nearly every aspect of your daily operations. To a great extent, your location will determine how much you will be expected to pay for good help.

Most of the tasks required for your business will be fairly repetitive and not really complicated. Making eBay listings and taking photos of merchandise can be handled in a systematic and almost automated fashion. Even accounting will be a fairly simple task, because you are simply calculating your commission and determining how much is owed to your clients. You will be able to train good employees in the skills you require.

★TIP

Reaching out to students and retirees can work well for you, because they can work part-time, affording flexibility and relieving you of any pressure to provide full-time employment.

Some of the general tasks that will be part of your day-to-day operation will be:

- Greeting existing and prospective clients
- Receiving items for listing
- Creating listings

- Photography
- Packing and shipping
- Accounting
- Filing

If the cost of living where you reside is low, you can expect to pay anywhere from $7 to $10 per hour for any of the above jobs. If you live in a part of the country with a high cost of living, the wages may be in the $10 to $20 per hour range. It is important that you do as much of the work yourself as possible, especially when starting out, so that you can keep your budget lean and trim.

When determining how much you will need for working capital, you can project all of your costs, including salaries, into a time frame comfortable for you. But I would strongly suggest an amount sufficient to fully cover at the very least three, and ideally six, months of *overall* expenses. In my sample start-up budget, I said the rent would be $1,500 per month. Here is a simple working capital projection.

	Monthly Cost
One full-time employee making $10/hour	$1,600.00
Rent	$1,500.00
Employment taxes	$200.00
Electric bill	$150.00
Office supplies	$100.00
Telephone	$65.00
High-speed Internet	$45.00
Bank fees	$15.00
Total	$3,675.00
Contingency (25%)	$918.75
Total monthly expenses	$4,593.75

This is a very simple monthly expense budget. Yours may be this simple, or you may have other expenses that pop up. You will notice that I did not add any line items to account for packing supplies or shipping costs. Those costs will be paid by the buyers of your clients' items, in addition to the cost of the items themselves. The shipping fees you charge may become a modest profit center if you are adding some extra handling charges to the actual shipping cost. (I suggest great moderation if you choose to do so, however. Most buyers expect or at least have no problem paying a minor handling fee, but you wouldn't want to be accused of "gouging.")

Of course, you will be offsetting some of your monthly expenses with the commissions you charge for your services. Initially, however, you will be playing a game of catch-up, because in the very beginning, until your client base has grown enough to consistently provide a profit, your expenses will exceed the fees you collect.

As previously stated, I urge you to plan on having six months of working capital to cover all your expenses during the initial growth phase of your business—and definitely not less than three months' worth. Below is a simple chart that shows our $4,593.75 monthly expense bill as accrued over a period of three to six months.

Monthly	$4,593.75
x 3	$13,781.25
x 4	$18,375.00
x 5	$22,968.75
x 6	$27,562.50

Holy cow! That's a lot of money. Starting a brick-and-mortar business will require some cash. You may be having second thoughts at this point about starting big, but the real kicker is that you also have to add in the total start-up capital that I mentioned in our sample start-up budget. If we use the start-up capital we calculated earlier in the chapter and add in a six-month working capital allowance, you will need approximately $38,500 in cash to open a simple store with one employee and as much as $73,625 to open the fancy store. Your actual cash requirements can be anything in between—even more, if you find that you want to spend a lot on the store design and your tastes are expensive.

These numbers may be enough to keep you at home, but if you are going to become a high volume Trading Assistant, you will need the professional image you can only achieve with a physical drop-off store. Your business plan will need to demonstrate to investors or a bank that you have given due consideration to both the start-up and working capital requirements of your proposed store.

RAINY DAY MONEY

Be sure to add the contingency allowance. A contingency is very similar to buying car insurance—you don't expect to need it, but when you do, you really appreciate having it. A contingency allowance will allow you a comfort level, a cushion, enabling you to handle unexpected variances in your start-up costs. You will notice that in my example of start-up and working capital, I allowed for a 25 percent contingency. This provides for the possibility of error and will help to cover any unexpected and necessary additional expenses. Do not try to skimp here. If you are the type of person who spends their last dime just in time for the next paycheck, you will really have to be disciplined in budgeting your new business.

6

LICENSING FOR
YOUR BUSINESS

I have been selling items for others on eBay as a Trading Assistant with great success. I sold a Catholic priest's lifetime collection of miniatures from all over the world and got over $11,000 for the collection. I sold a catering trailer to a film production company in South America, several motor homes, and many other high-quality items of all types. We will sell anything if asked. We are committed to giving professional service and do whatever it takes to make clients happy. Our state has some licensing requirements, which we researched to make certain we were in compliance with the laws in Arkansas.

Gary Puckett, North Little Rock, Arkansas;

eBay user ID "puckettauction"; trading on eBay since September 4, 2002

The government loves you. Usually they love you so much that they not only want to keep tabs on your daily business activities, but they also like to get paid to do so. Typically, this is done through a wonderful thing called a business license. There are all kinds of licenses out there for virtually every imaginable occupation, and it is important that you stay in compliance with local and state laws when performing your services as a Trading Assistant.

WHO WANTS YOUR BUSINESS?

How does your local government classify the business of a Trading Assistant? When you accept an item for listing on the eBay site, you are providing several services, including:

- Professional market value consulting
- Clerical work to create a listing
- Photography
- Storage
- Collecting the payment
- Packing
- Shipping
- Paying your client

In general, you are providing convenient assistance to anyone wanting to use eBay without committing the time and resources to create and manage their own listings.

Different states view business differently. Some states are quite aggressive about attracting business start-ups, and therefore are equally proactive in giving small businesses lots of breaks. Relaxed regulations and lower (or no) taxes are ways in which some states encourage business development. As a Trading Assistant, you are responsible for establishing your own fee structure and the range of services you offer, but some local authorities and states may have laws and/or regulations that affect the scope of the client services you provide. eBay does not check the laws for you; therefore, it is entirely your responsibility to determine not only the tax laws but also the licensing requirements for your business.

These laws may be very relaxed, or they may be quite strict. Either way, it is possible for you to operate a legal Trading Assistant business. Get the whole story before you spend a lot of money opening a drop-off store. If you live in a city with restrictive licensing rules, it might be prudent to consider a nearby city in which to hang your shingle—the commute may be worth it. If you are near the border of another state that has more relaxed and business-friendly regulations, the same suggestion applies.

KEEPING IT LEGAL

It's completely natural for many people to be apprehensive of anything even vaguely resembling a legal matter. But being in compliance with the laws of your city and state is just a routine matter. You don't have to pay a high-powered attorney to get the basic legal or tax advice that a Trading Assistant business requires. You will probably want an accountant's help if you operate a fairly good-sized business, but many sole proprietors choose to prepare and file their own taxes, and with today's robust tax software, doing so can be very straightforward if you have anything of a head for numbers.

Before you pay for legal help, you might want to reach out to SCORE again, this time for advice about licenses and taxes. And you will definitely want to give your state and local governments a chance to help you, too. In most cases, your local business license will be sufficient, but some states do require additional licenses.

The National Association of Secretaries of State (NASS) has a Web site (*www.nass.org*) that allows you to quickly locate the appropriate resources and contact information for your state. Click on the link for Business Registration and Filing Services, which will direct you to the appropriate page to learn more about your state's licensing requirements. Contact information is there, too, and a call to your secretary of state's office may be the best route to determining what state (not local) licenses are required to operate an eBay Trading Assistant business.

Talking with a government representative may be important, because eBay Trading Assistant businesses are still relatively new, as is selling on the Internet in general; and frankly, in some state governments, there seems to be some confusion as to the exact nature of a Trading Assistant. This is important, because some state governments want to classify Trading Assistants as consignment or auctioneering businesses, or secondhand dealers, and therefore want to require Trading Assistants to be licensed as such. Such licenses may be more restrictive and/or expensive than those more appropriate for a Trading Assistant, so you should clarify this distinction when speaking with your state's representative. We'll go into more depth on this subject later in this chapter.

If you have a little anxiety about all of this and don't mind paying for the help, you can engage the services of an attorney. Most attorneys are specialists, and you will want an expert in the field of business licensing. Try to obtain a referral from a colleague in business or by contacting your state's bar association, which handles the licensing of attorneys. You can locate the appropriate bar association on the Web site *www.findlegalhelp.org.*

But it is very rare for an entrepreneur to hire an attorney simply to handle a routine matter such as obtaining a license. I would suggest this only as a last resort. Generally you will want to work directly with your state and ask them for help understanding their requirements. If you are friendly and professional, you will no doubt succeed here and save yourself a bundle by doing it yourself.

Hopefully in your conversations with government contacts, you'll succeed in clarifying the important distinction between a Trading Assistant business and consignment and auctioneering businesses. Even so, it's a good idea to query your local and state governments with a follow-up letter asking for their specific regulations on a Trading Assistant business.

★TIP

A response in writing will be a good thing to have in your files as proof of your due diligence when communicating with regulators.

DO YOU NEED PERMISSION?

All states have special permits for businesses that buy products wholesale and sell them retail at a profit. When buying this way, most companies don't pay sales tax on the wholesale purchase, but they do charge their retail customers sales tax on the final sale. The sales tax is collected by the businesses, to be paid to a state agency that will then distribute these taxes to the state treasury and possibly the treasuries of the county and local governments. A permit is required if you are doing business this way. As a Trading Assistant, you may not need to acquire such a permit, but many Trading Assistant businesses find that they can make additional profits by selling boxes, offering packing and shipping services, and selling supplies or other merchandise from their store. If you own a drop-off store, you will really want to add packing and shipping services to your list of services—the increased shipping volume will allow you to negotiate discounts with the shipping companies you use. If you sell products, in this case packing materials, boxes, tape, etc., you will be collecting sales tax and then paying it to the state's coffers. You will need to get a permit to do so.

If your state does not have a sales tax, this is a moot point and you can move on to the next section. States call these permits by various names, but they all allow the collection and payment of sales taxes. Some of the names used for such permits are:

- Resale permit
- Resale license
- Resale certificate
- Sellers permit
- Certificate of authority
- Use and sales tax license
- Use and sales tax permit
- Application to collect and report tax
- Transaction privilege tax

These permits are also known by other names, depending on your state. And states may have different rules regarding the collection and payment of sales tax as well as other taxes. It would be a good idea to give your state officials a call and ask for details about the rules of the road where you live. You can use the conventional URL for your state as in this example: *www.state.ny.us*, where *ny* is the postal abbreviation for the state in question. This will take you to their Web site, where you can obtain contact information and information about state-specific regulations.

THE LOCALS MAY WANT A SLICE OF YOUR PIE

Your city may or may not have a licensing requirement if you work from home, but most will if you work from a drop-off store. Again, it's important to contact your local city licensing office and discuss your business, whether home based or office/store based. As discussed above (and below in more detail) with regard to state licenses, because Trading Assistant work is a rather new industry, your city may not have a business classification which exactly fits.

These issues should be settled early on with your local government through good communication. I suggest calling for an appointment with the appropriate city employee and speaking to them in person about your proposed enterprise. Don't be afraid to deal with these folks. They are usually quite willing to help any new enterprise and want to assist in making your new business a successful one. Remember: You are generating new sources of tax revenue and creating new jobs for this community.

Even if you are planning on working from home, a business license may be required. Be sure to get one and stay in compliance. You might be able to stay under the radar for a while, but as you become successful, you will be getting daily visits from UPS or the postman, and the volume of packages exiting your home will be a telltale sign of a home-based business. A nosy neighbor might turn you in, and you don't want to deal with the stress of possible fines for operating an unlicensed business. If you are a previous business owner or have worked in a small business, this will all seem routine and quite simple. If you are new to the business world, the mere thought of dealing with government types might cause you to break out into a cold sweat. Don't stress yourself out. It really is a routine matter, and you will take great pride—and be able to sleep well at night—in knowing you are running a completely *legit* business enterprise.

WHAT YOU ARE . . . AND AREN'T

Many lawmakers and regulators nationwide are trying to place Trading Assistants in the same category as auctioneers, pawnbrokers, secondhand dealers, or consignment stores. Because you will deal in both new and secondhand goods, for licensing purposes you may be pegged as a secondhand dealer, a business designation that may require additional licensing and regulatory red tape. Secondhand dealer permits or pawnbroker licenses usually require that you send a daily report of items received to the police or sheriff's department as well as hold the items for up to 30 days before you can sell them.

In some states, secondhand tangible personal property that bears a serial number, owner-applied number, or personalized inscriptions or initials or property such as jewelry and sterling silver utensils may be of concern to regulators. Contact your local police or sheriff's department for details on what is required to be reported to them.

Varying from state to state, some lawmakers are looking into the possibility of requiring Trading Assistants to fingerprint the sellers who drop off items for listing on eBay and to record transactions for possible inspection by police. Some state governments are proposing special registries and tracking databases to curtail trafficking in stolen merchandise. On a personal note, I have never seen a study from a reliable source that provides evidence that trafficking of stolen merchandise is a problem on eBay.

eBay's government relations folks oppose these concepts and reject the notion that Trading Assistants are analogous to secondhand dealers, auctioneers, pawnbrokers, or consignment stores. You are not the actual seller of the goods; rather you are providing listing services for clients. And because eBay is an open and transparent marketplace, there is no good argument for creating a separate registry or additional regulations, because anyone can find an item quickly and easily on eBay by searching for it.

When dealing with government offices, avoid using the terms *consignment* or *auction* when talking about your business. Your basic argument that a Trading Assistant is neither a secondhand dealer nor an auctioneer sounds like this:

A person who operates a Trading Assistant business provides listing assistance on eBay and cannot "recognize" bids made in an online auction. The auction-style listings on eBay receive bids through proprietary software owned by eBay, and you neither solicit bids nor do you gather bidders together to allow bids to be placed. You list items on behalf of the seller, who is your client. You provide them with some high-tech "secretarial" work. Your client is the seller and at all times retains complete ownership and control of their merchandise.

Whatever the regulations in your community, be in compliance at all times to avoid getting tangled in a web of legal troubles. Just as you pay your taxes and renew your driver's license, operate your business in a 100 percent legal way so that things will run smoothly.

7

SELECTING A SUITABLE LOCATION AND NEGOTIATING AND SIGNING A LEASE

One of my clients gave me a box of various Native American items. At the bottom of the box was a small, squished basket. I steamed the basket over a pot of boiling water, and it looked like new again. It ended up being a baleen basket from a Northwest Indian tribe, and we sold it on eBay for $950.

Mark Floersheim, Albuquerque, New Mexico;

The Platinum Store, eBay user ID "frostypaws$$$$"; trading on eBay since July 5, 2000

I trust that by this chapter, you are feeling clear and confident about your new Trading Assistant project. Now that financial issues such as start-up and working capital requirements have been settled, you may feel comfortable pitching your plan to potential investors. But many banks will require further explanation of your location selection, and you need a solid grasp of how to proceed with inspecting and analyzing prospective locations, selecting a space, and consummating a deal to rent or lease it. Many factors will affect your choice of location: Do you want a pricier retail location with strong walk-by traffic to generate potential clients or do you think your primary sources of merchandise will allow you the luxury of cheaper and possibly larger digs? You need to consider these questions very carefully, because not only will you spend much time and money opening the store, you will spend a lot of time working there, too. Your space needs to be a comfortable, pleasant, and productive environment for you.

Contact three or more licensed real estate brokers who specialize in leasing small- to medium-sized retail (or office) space. Explain your business and give them your budget. It's okay to work with more than one broker simultaneously, and try to maximize your appointments with them by asking to see at least three locations. Customarily brokers are paid by the property owner, and you will probably not have to pay anything more than your first month's rent, some form of security deposit, and possibly the last month's rent.

You should cast a large net when looking and scan the classified advertising section of your local newspapers. And use the Internet—localized Web sites such as Craig's List (*www.craigslist.org*) are good sources, and your local newspaper probably has a Web site for classified ads, too.

I found my current location by driving around. I love the Magnolia Park neighborhood of Burbank, and when I was looking to grow into a larger place I began to look for stores that had "For Lease" signs in the window. You should spend at least one afternoon each weekend looking, armed with a notepad and pen. Call on your cell phone whenever you see a promising sign and see if the broker is available. Good locations in nice neighborhoods will lease rather quickly, so the sooner you call the better. If you see a sign that has been up for a long time, you can bet it's either a bad location or the price and/or terms are unattractive. Call anyway and see what you can learn about the property. You will get a quick education by speaking to as many people as possible and looking at as many locations as you can.

CONSIDER YOUR CLIENTELE

You can run a successful Trading Assistant business by selling excess inventory from companies, in which case a commercial space, such as a small warehouse in an office park or retail space off the beaten track, would be fine.

But if your primary clients will come to you with their merchandise, it's important to have a clean, safe place to conduct business, ideally near other upscale retail businesses.

Your location needs available parking unless, of course, you live in a city like Manhattan. In virtually all other cases, allowing clients easy access via a dedicated parking lot or nearby public parking will be critical.

IS HEAVY TRAFFIC A GOOD THING?

Most probably yes. A location with constant foot traffic will be extremely beneficial to you—it's a great form of advertising. Your store will need good signage that grabs the eye and shouts the message, "I sell on eBay for you!" You can't survive without customers, and the less foot traffic passing your shop, the harder you will have to work to attract new business. Renting a cheap office with access from an alley will look like a great cost savings, but it will hurt your business and actually cost you more in the long run because of increased marketing costs. If you pay less in rent, you will ultimately have to pay more for necessary advertising. Your store should be easy to find, and being on a major street or near a major intersection is always a plus.

LOCATION, LOCATION, LOCATION

Strip Malls

Many of the Trading Assistant stores I have visited are located in strip malls (also called strip shopping centers). These stores depend heavily on the luxury shops and upscale supermarkets in their malls to draw in foot traffic, especially the well-heeled clients who likely have high-quality merchandise. The key is to find a location that will draw the right people to you. Look for busy strip malls with upscale stores, boutiques, and dry cleaners. But if you specialize in antiques, you may want to avoid placing yourself right next to an antiques shop, because it will be in direct competition for your clients' attention, pulling at their inclination to sell their merchandise outright.

One benefit of a strip mall is shared common area maintenance and a sense of safety. Clients like to visit clean, secure businesses, and professionally managed shopping centers and strip malls usually have good maintenance.

The downside of these locations is the cost. Typically, you will pay not only your own rent but also a customary additional charge for common area maintenance and possibly some of the owner's property taxes as well. And it's not unusual at very busy and successful locations for the mall to even charge you a percentage of your sales. You have to weigh the benefits of the foot traffic against these costs. But again, spending more money on the right location might save you thousands a year in advertising.

Business Park

A business park is typically located off the beaten track. The businesses in these mixed-use locations don't depend heavily on foot traffic and need larger, less expensive spaces. A business park may have offices, offices with attached warehouses, or just storefront warehouse space. If you already have a steady flow of merchandise and anticipate doing most of your deals by phone or by picking up the clients' items, you can locate in a business park and save a lot on rent. Ideally, your space would have an office with a warehouse attached, and this configuration is very common. You can conduct your daily business in the comfort of your office and receive, store, pack, and ship items in the warehouse. Keep an eye out for a warehouse with shelving already installed. Always check that high-speed Internet is available in the location before considering a lease. Some office parks are so much off the main drag that they have older telephone infrastructures, and it may be difficult and/or more expensive to get the fast Internet you will definitely need. This is less and less a problem as phone and cable companies improve and expand their Internet service—but be sure to check.

Look for clean, well-maintained locations. Because office parks are cheaper, their owners often have lower maintenance standards. Attractive and well-groomed landscaping is a sign that the owner cares for the property.

Security is also an issue. Because fewer people will be around the office park at night, you want to make sure that your space is safe and can be secured with an alarm and good locks. Check for any security weaknesses, such as older, vulnerable windows and doors, and ensure that there is no easy roof access for burglars. Office parks are often like a ghost town at night and can be easy targets for thieves. Most strip mall spaces have bathrooms in the units, but in a business park, you need to make sure that a restroom is included in your space or that common restrooms are close by and secure.

Free-Standing Building

In areas with a lower cost of living, you may that find a free-standing building is the ideal location for your drop-off store. A clean, attractive free-standing building will be inviting to your clients, especially if it has big windows (look for tempered glass windows for maximum security). Such buildings are usually equipped with bathrooms, but don't forget to check. Because your Trading Assistant business will need lots of different work areas, look for a building that can easily be configured for your use. Although you may be able to negotiate improvements with your landlord as part of the lease, you'll always get a better rate if you take the space as-is and do the work yourself. But keep a sharp eye out for anything that might become a money pit. Avoid former restaurants and buildings that would require a major renovation. Try to focus on spaces that are modern and up-to-date.

If you find a perfect spot that just needs a little cleaning and paint, grab it. A dirty location can be brightened up relatively inexpensively, but keep in mind that with a freestanding building, you will most likely have to maintain the landscaping and curb appeal yourself. Unlike with shopping centers and some business parks, maintenance is rarely included in a free-standing building lease.

BUY YOUR PANTS A FEW SIZES BIGGER

With eBay, your business's growth can be explosive, and you might actually become the victim of your own success. Outgrowing your space can be very frustrating and costly. If you become flooded with items for listing on eBay, you may find yourself bursting at the seams. It's critical that you carefully consider your growth potential and be very realistic about the room you will need to process and store items. Areas you need in your office include:

- A waiting area for clients, ideally with seating
- A work counter for evaluating and receiving items
- A staging area for cleaning items
- A comfortable area for listing items
- A photography area
- An item storage area
- A staging area for pulling, preparing, and packing shipments
- A temporary storage area for placing parcels that are awaiting pickup by your shipping companies
- A filing area for keeping important records
- An area for storing office supplies, packing materials, and cleaning products

Don't try to squeeze everything into a tiny space. Be practical and allow plenty of room to work comfortably. I keep lots of folding tables around to use as quick staging areas and as temporary storage for items I'm evaluating or listing.

CREATURE COMFORTS

In a mall, you will usually be leasing in a modern building with central heating and air-conditioning. Be sure to ask the leasing agent or owner if the property has separate temperature controls. My first office space didn't have its own control, and I would alternately be freezing or sweating. Having to constantly ask the neighbor with the controls to make an adjustment was a huge hassle. Separate controls are a must—don't compromise on this detail.

In older buildings, you may find that the space is heated or cooled with through-the-wall or window units. These units are often not large enough to heat and cool the space properly, and you will want to check their BTU (don't ask me why, but it stands for British Thermal Units) rating. I try to make sure that the units put out at least 25 BTUs of cooling and heating for each square foot of office or warehouse space. This means that a 1,000-square-foot location will need air-conditioning and heating units rated to put out at least 25,000 BTUs of cooling and heating. The ceiling height is a factor here, and if the location has very high ceilings and you pay for the utilities, you can find that your monthly overhead just took a big jump. I would avoid older buildings, high ceilings, and these types of wall or window units.

In office parks, it's not uncommon for the office portion of the space to be the only area with heat and air-conditioning, while the warehouse is neither heated nor cooled. Clearly this can cause very uncomfortable conditions for you and your employees. The comfort of your work environment will have a remarkable effect on your productivity—it's important that you feel good. It's also important to consider the storage needs of your merchandise: Some fragile or collectible items can be damaged if not stored properly.

If your lease does not include utilities and you have to pay for them separately, check with the different utility providers (gas, electric, and water) to see if they will provide you with some historical utility bill amounts for the property you are considering. I have found that many utility companies will provide this information by phone. Don't be shy—just be professional and ask. Add the projected utilities costs as a line item to your budget and update your business plan accordingly. Don't forget to ask if a deposit is required if you don't already have a business account with the utility companies.

SECURITY AND SAFETY

You will be handling other people's possessions, and some of the things you take in may be very valuable. The security of your space will be critical. When touring office or retail space, be sure to inspect the building's security features. As with a business park, look for strong, solid doors and modern, secure, tempered glass windows. Be sure no points of entry can be easily breached, such as access through the roof , and that all the locks and latches appear to be in good working order. Look for a location that is well lit at night. Consider an alarm system with live monitoring that will notify the police if the alarm is tripped. It is also possible to find old bank or jewelry store locations that might have an operating vault or at least the original vault room that can be made into a strong room.

Because you are an online business, you will have little or no concern about shoplifting. However, it's important that you store client items in a part of your space that is not easily accessible to unauthorized persons coming to your location. I keep the merchandise stored in the back of my drop-off store, far away from the public. I turn down requests to use our restroom, because it's located near the client items we are storing. I also have a firm policy of escorting/monitoring any vendors delivering supplies beyond my public areas. I prefer to have my own employees handle all deliveries from the front door to the back of my store. This minimizes the possibility of curious and prying eyes in our storage areas. I also do not permit clients to view other clients' items. This is for their own security and comfort as well. And I never discuss clients' names with others—I feel that confidentiality is a strong form of security.

Employee theft is retailers' number-one source of "shrinkage"— their term for loss of merchandise. But shrinkage comes in other forms, too, so when considering a location, look for configurations that allow you maximum control over your space. During office hours, we use only one entry and exit door. We keep our back door locked at all times, and if an employee is working alone, they are required to lock the store if they step out, even if only for a moment (putting up the good old

"Back in 15 Minutes" sign). Security is a top priority when choosing a location.

Lastly, walk the neighborhood. Take in the environment. What do you see? Are there classy people and nice businesses nearby? Are the sidewalks clean? Speak with neighboring businesses, tell them you are considering starting a business nearby, and gauge their response. Just as you visited with other Trading Assistants, you should now meet your future neighbors and learn about the area that you will call your second home for months or years to come. Ask questions about neighborhood safety.

You may also want to pay a visit to the local police department and find out about any burglaries or other crime in the area. The newspapers often compile and publish crime statistics as well.

WORKING WITH THE LANDLORD

Leasing your new store can be a nerve-racking experience if you are a first-timer. Be calm. Even though you may think that the location you have found is the most fantastic deal or the perfect home for your Trading Assistant business, don't let the owner or leasing agent sense desperation. If you are working through a leasing agent hired by the property owner, you will be in a good position, because agents are paid on commission and will work hard to earn your business. If you lease in a large office complex or mall, you will most likely be dealing with an agent and not the owners.

I prefer to do business with people who want to do business with me. When working out the terms of a lease, I am confident, relaxed, and comfortable. If the owner or agent makes me feel uncomfortable, as though I'm being rushed or patronized, or conjures up some complex set of rules or hoops to jump through, I simply walk away. There are always other spaces you can lease. Be professional and courteous at all times but ask for clarification of anything you don't understand.

Dealing directly with property owners has both pros and cons. Because the leasing agent acts as a buffer between you and the owner of the property, you will find that tempers rarely flare. But sometimes the owner of a property can be so personally (and emotionally) involved in their investment that they view you almost as an adversary, and you may find yourself being grilled about things such as your credit, your references, and the type of business you will be operating. Be extremely patient if this happens. Often owners soften up once they get to know you better. If the owner shows you the property personally, be affable, genuine, up-front, and candid, and try to build a rapport. You're proud of your business plan, and this is a golden opportunity to use it. A compelling business plan will speak volumes about your professionalism and ability to think through the requirements of your business.

Both the landlord and tenant have responsibilities. Normally, the landlord simply provides a space with a secure roof overhead. Unlike when renting an apartment, you won't find many commercial property owners plunging clogged toilets or fixing broken air-conditioning units, unless these services are specified in the lease. The landlord will probably want to get some or all of the following from you:

- An application
- A credit report (and possibly a fee to pull it)
- Business references
- An explanation of your business and a written assurance of your exact business use (but try to avoid getting too specific, or it may prevent you from providing other services down the road as your business grows)
- Their lease agreement signed by you

CURB YOUR ENTHUSIASM

You should ask the agent or owner if you can review a copy of their lease agreement, even if you will continue to view other properties. Even if you think you have found your perfect location, I strongly urge you to continue your search until a lease has actually been signed. So many factors can play into the lease negotiation process that it's always best to have options. Curb your enthusiasm about any particular location and carefully review your requirements before proceeding with the negotiation phase of the leasing process. When reading through the lease, be certain you fully understand all the terms and conditions as well as the security deposit and initial payment requirements (first month's and possibly last month's rent, etc.)

★TIP

Owners want to see that you are qualified to lease their property. Being prepared will improve your chances and put you ahead of others who may be interested in the same site. Credit reporting agencies will provide you with one free copy of your credit report each year. Besides a copy of your credit report, I suggest providing your prospective landlord with proof of your financial stability in the form of bank statements. Your business plan will also have your financial statement. I use *www.myfico.com* to obtain regular updates on the status of my credit reports from the major credit bureaus. The cost is nominal and includes notification when your report changes and tips on ways to improve your credit.

NEGOTIATIONS: THE FLOOR WAS GROSS, BUT THE PRICE WAS RIGHT

Negotiating a good lease can save you money. Establish what concessions your landlord is willing to make for you. When I leased my store in Burbank, the property owner would not agree to a lease term longer than three years. The location was fantastic for me, just walking distance from my home and next door to a busy bank and many retail shops. The rent was low, but the place was a wreck. Outside, it looked like any other retail store, but inside, the floor was gross, the paint was peeling, and junk and old furniture were everywhere. It was also dark and depressing. Because the price was extremely low, I didn't drive a hard bargain. It was very clear to me that I would be putting some elbow grease into the store to get it into good shape. But I did try to get a one-year term with the option to lease for up to five years with one-year renewal options. I really loved the location.

The landlord would not budge on the length of the lease so I ended up having to settle for the three years. I knew that I would be putting a lot of time and effort into marketing my business, and I wanted to make sure I had a secure and stable location. Because my rent was going to be very low, I paid to remove the trash and excess furniture. I then painted and carpeted. The results were dramatic, and the store looks great today. My current landlord is a very nice and very fair guy. As I expected, with the low rent came no assistance with renovations and absolutely no maintenance except for the roof.

KEEPING YOUR OPTIONS OPEN

The terms of a lease almost always favor the landlord, so be sure to keep this in mind when you review your lease agreement. With a little effort, you will probably be able to negotiate better terms—leases are, by the very nature of any business deal, nearly always negotiable. Your ability to gain concessions in any lease negotiation will depend greatly on the local rental market. In hot markets, you will be granted few concessions, because the landlord will have no problem leasing the property. In slower markets, however, you will be in a great position to seek concessions.

When you depend on walk-in traffic for your business, it's helpful to have long lease terms, which you can accomplish through renewal options, instead of one long lease term. But at the same time, you will want to have the shortest possible initial term, such as 6 to 12 months. In case the location doesn't work out, the last thing you want is to be trapped in a $3,000-per-month, three-year lease. Ask for renewal options that will extend your lease for additional years. If you are renting in a business park, on the other hand, you may want to seek a month-to-month lease. When you are not depending on a prime location for attracting clients, you can have a short lease.

NOWHERE TO GO BUT UP

Never assume the asking rent is firm. Looking at comparable properties will give you a good sense of the prices for similar space in your market. Keep good notes on the cost per square foot that each landlord is asking. Most landlords will ask for a moderate rent increase each year, so it's important to try to put a cap on the percentage or dollar amount that your rent can go up. Some landlords will tie this number to a cost-of-living increase, but I always prefer to stick with a fixed percentage. Paying an increase of 3 to 5 percent is fair. If the location is very desirable, the landlord may ask for more, or they may simply try to avoid specifying the increase method altogether. Try hard to get this locked in.

WITH LEASES, GROSS IS GOOD

There are several types of customary leases. Here are the most common:

- *Gross lease.* A property lease where the landlord pays all expenses normally associated with the ownership of the property, such as utilities, repairs, insurance, and taxes
- *Modified gross lease.* A property lease where the landlord pays the property taxes and building insurance and the lessee (you) pays for utilities, repairs, and maintenance
- *Net lease (also known as a triple-net lease or closed-end lease).* A property lease in which the lessee pays all expenses normally associated with ownership, such as property taxes, insurance, utilities, and repairs
- *Double-net lease.* A property lease in which the lessee pays rent to the landlord as well as all utilities, taxes, and insurance, while the landlord pays maintenance expenses

It would be in your best interest to try to obtain a gross lease. Though the rent will no doubt be higher with a gross lease, often it's better to pay a higher monthly rent that's fixed and predictable. Winter heating bills and summer cooling costs can really add up. With net leases and multiple tenants in a mall or building complex, each tenant pays a prorated share of the costs based on their unit's square footage. This can get complicated, and if this is your first lease, I advise sticking to simple lease agreements. I pay my own utilities and maintenance, but my landlord pays for maintaining the roof. It's pretty simple, and it's essentially a modified gross lease.

Renting It Again

Request a subletting clause in your contract. This means you have the right to rent the space to someone else in the event that you have too much space or if you want to move on to another location, business, or job.

Ask for a Hand

If the property needs a lot of improvements you should ask the landlord which improvements they would be willing to handle before you move in. For shorter leases, the owner may not be willing to do much, but if you are planning on staying for a long time, it will be a good opportunity to save a few bucks. Maybe you can ask for carpet or paint. These are basics, and many landlords will throw them in. Be fair with your requests—if you appear too demanding, you may alienate the owner.

WHEN TO WALK AND WHEN TO JUMP

When a landlord is completely inflexible on terms and you know that their price is not the lowest around, it's time to walk. You want to rent from someone who is professional, and a professional person is always willing to negotiate. Working out a lease is a give-and-take process, and if you aren't getting anywhere, don't worry—this isn't the right deal for you. Give yourself permission to move on. It's not a defeat to pass on a deal. It would be reasonable to look at 5 to 10 different locations and make offers on 3 or more of them to see which landlords are willing to work with you.

Once in a blue moon, you will be presented with an unreal opportunity—that perfect store location near the right mix of busy retailers. If the price is fantastic and you know you are getting a great deal, you need to move fast. Thinking too hard about a good deal may let someone else lease it instead of you. Landlords make killer deals for a variety of reasons. A smart landlord wants long-term tenants and no vacancies. A good tenant means few calls and little maintenance. A superior tenant keeps the property in as good condition as if it were their own. When you meet up with a once-in-a-lifetime deal, rent it. Don't bargain too hard, or don't bargain at all.

CHECK YOUR LIST TWICE

Here's a checklist to help you when reviewing your lease agreement. Never sign a lease on the spot when it is presented to you. Take the time to consider each clause carefully and ask questions if you don't understand something. This is a big decision, so you may want to discuss the lease with friends and family, or possibly an attorney if you can afford it.

- Rental amount
- Duration (lease term)
- Options to extend the lease
- Escalation amounts (rent increases) and how they will be calculated
- Any required security deposit and whether or not you will earn interest on it
- Any restrictions or conditions on your advertising signage
- Who will pay utilities, insurance, and taxes
- Any restrictions on the use of the space (can you change your line of business?)

- Any concessions such as paint, carpet, or other improvements that may be needed
- How the maintenance of the building, roof, and plumbing will be handled and who is responsible for paying these costs
- Who will be responsible for maintaining the heating and air-conditioning systems
- The amount of notice you are required to give before you terminate your lease and if it automatically renews if you do not
- Any rules and regulations you are required to follow
- Possible restrictions on your hours of operation

★ **TIP**

Check with other merchants in the area and ask if they would be willing to share a copy of their lease agreement with you. If they are willing, you can gain valuable insights (and experience) from them about the dos and don'ts when signing a lease of your own.

8

BUYING A COMMERCIAL BUILDING SPACE

We own a restaurant in Dubuque, Iowa, and we have a spare room in the back that we use for trading on eBay. A client had a vintage coffee pot that we listed with a starting bid of $2.99, and when the auction ended seven days later, it had a new owner who bid $380 for one of the very first mass-produced electric coffee pots from Silex. The client's wife had originally wanted to throw the pot in the trash, so he was really shocked by the final sales price we obtained for him.

Paul H. Connor, Dubuque, Iowa;

eBay user ID "ezsellusa"; trading on eBay since January 17, 2005

PLAYING MONOPOLY

eBay has been good to me. And so has real estate. My eBay earnings have allowed me to purchase a lot of it. I own my own home, numerous rental properties, hotel property, and raw land. I can honestly say without exaggeration that my eBay business has made me a millionaire. All of my real estate assets have made me money and earned me additional equity. I learned to buy and hold, and I don't intend to sell any of my valuable real estate assets anytime soon.

Why then do I lease a retail office space? Well, that's really a function of where I live. I have offered to buy the building from my landlord, and he has politely said no. There is very good reason why you rarely see a "For Sale" sign on commercial property in my neighborhood—values keep going up, and landlords keep collecting rents. Unlike homes, commercial properties don't sell frequently here unless they are lemons.

If I lived in an area where buying a building like mine didn't cost a million bucks (literally), I would have owned my own building long ago. When I was first starting out, it would have been easy and afford-able to buy a building in my area, and with the larger number of avail-able properties at that time, my landlord might have sold to me.

If you own your own home and understand property ownership re-sponsibilities, buying might be the right decision for you. You have to consider the possibility that you will own your business for a very long time, and you may prefer to be the master of your own destiny.

Unlike with single-family homes, you can expect to put up a pretty hefty down payment for a commercial property. Because a failed busi-ness can be abandoned rather easily, whereas a home is where you live, most lenders have a much higher down payment requirement on com-mercial properties. You can expect to put down between 25 and 40 per-cent of the total purchase price of a commercial property. But if commercial property is affordable where you live, and you have the cash, owning is better than renting.

My favorite book on real estate investing is *The Weekend Million-aire's Secrets to Investing in Real Estate: How to Become Wealthy in Your Spare Time* by Mike Summey and Roger Dawson. This book is a quick read and will be very helpful in making you an astute real estate nego-tiator and buyer.

TO BUY OR NOT TO BUY

The advantages of owning:

- Your rent will not go up based upon someone else's arbitrary decision.
- As you pay down your mortgage, eventually you will own the property completely.
- You can take advantage of tax breaks for renovations.

- You can lease the property to someone else if you decide to close your business.

The disadvantages of ownership:

- Your mortgage will most likely be of the adjustable rate type, and you may pay more or less each year based upon the current market interest rates.
- You have to pay all taxes, insurance, repairs, and maintenance costs.
- If you do not keep up with your payments, your credit will be affected.
- If you want to sell the property, it may be hard to do so quickly in a stale real estate market.

★ **TIP**

Never buy any property with your emotions in high gear. It is easy to overpay when you are in love with something. In both slow and overheated markets, it is always possible to make an excellent decision when purchasing real estate, if you take your time to study the market and learn as much as possible about the neighborhood, comparable properties, and prevailing prices.

THE BROKERS

Just as with commercial leasing agents (many of whom also sell commercial property), you want to find a real estate broker who is professional, patient, and courteous. Buying a building is a very big commitment, and it is imperative that your broker fully understands your business needs.

Start the process by showing your business plan to your broker. Engaging them in the nuances of your planned business operations will help them to weed out inappropriate properties, instead showing you just those most suitable for your needs. Use the same considerations discussed in the previous chapter on leasing. While working with real estate professionals, have a detailed checklist of your requirements on hand and have a budget in mind.

You will find that most real estate people will be aggressive in helping you to find property, if they believe that you are capable of meeting the financial requirements necessary to make the purchase. Meeting with a bank representative at this stage, with your credit report and business plan in hand, will give you an idea of your qualifications and how much you can afford. A prequalification letter from a bank will show the REALTOR® and the property owner, both of whom will want to make certain that you can actually qualify for the purchase, that you are serious.

Many REALTORS® will ask you to sign an exclusive representation agreement with them. I caution you to avoid doing this until you get a good feel for the REALTOR'S® qualifications. Most real estate is listed in the multiple listing service, also known as MLS. Any REALTOR® can show you property listed with the service, even if the property is not represented by them. Any REALTOR® can submit offers to the listing's real estate broker, who in turn can present such offers to their client, the owner of the property. Therefore, if you are dealing directly with the listing broker, you will be eliminating a middleman from the process. And if your REALTOR® is the listing broker on many commercial properties, it's fine to sign an exclusive representation agreement with them, provided that it has a reasonable term (not more than a month or perhaps two) and the broker has inventory that is suitable for your use.

With or without an agreement, when dealing with a REALTOR® it is important that your conduct be thoroughly professional. It is never appropriate to try to sidestep your broker by attempting to deal directly with the seller's broker when you have been shown the property by your REALTOR®. The two REALTORS® typically split commissions on sales when a seller and buyer are represented separately.

If and when you make a make an offer to purchase a property, your REALTOR® will submit the offer through a formal process as mandated by your state's regulatory agency for REALTORS®. Although there is a little latitude on how this process is handled, the initial offer will normally be prepared on a set of forms.

I encourage you to ask your REALTOR® to show you at least three properties with the features you need in your price range. Your REALTOR® will make a hefty commission on the sale, so don't be shy about asking to see many properties, as long as your expectations are reasonable and you are respectful of their time. Most real estate investors look at dozens of properties and make a lot of offers before they finally get the deal they want. This is a *process* that you should never rush.

You should work with a REALTOR® who is both patient and aggressive. They should be aggressive in trying to find suitable properties for you, but you should never feel pressured to make an immediate decision. There are certain tactics that a seller's REALTOR® may use to try to close a sale, but remember that many properties are usually for sale at any given time—make sure the one you buy is as close to ideal for your needs as possible. You most likely will be working in this space for a very long time, and you want to make sure it fits your personal tastes as well as business needs.

When reviewing properties, keep a written checklist of all the same basic requirements discussed in Chapter 7 and consider the following additional points:

- Age of the building
- Condition of the building
- Method of construction (wood, brick, etc.)
- Location (you want your property to appreciate in value, and a better neighborhood will help to ensure this)
- Taxes and utility costs
- Adjacent uses

"Location, location, location"—it's so important in valuing property, and the old saying holds true for you, too. The location and quality of the neighborhood where you buy should be conducive not only to your business needs but also to appreciation—you want a property that will increase in value over time. Your local chamber of commerce may have economic studies and statistics that could be valuable in location decision making.

When going out with a REALTOR®, ask them to line up as many properties as possible for you to see. Carry a notepad and jot down anything that may jump out at you, especially problems. There's no need to share any of this information with your REALTOR®, until it comes time to assess the value of the property. Then you'll discuss any deductions you may want to make for problems. You should also sketch a floor plan of each property, indicating any problem areas. The floor plan will help you later in your evaluation of the space and its suitability for your eBay drop-off store needs. If the list of issues is substantial, try to imagine at what point, looking at other properties, you would simply rule this building out.

TAKE YOUR TIME, BUT DON'T BE A "TIRE KICKER"

Your REALTOR® may ask you to consider making an offer right away, but I caution you to look at many properties and review your notes before making any offers. If you own a digital camera already (and you will need one soon!), be sure to take photos of the exterior and interior of each building, and pay attention to details. During and after viewing properties, don't show your REALTOR® much emotion. Avoid selling yourself on any one property and take time to digest the pros and cons of each building while reviewing your notes and photos. Talk to other business property owners before making any decisions so you benefit from other people's experience.

You may want to have a building with a loading dock and a big warehouse area if you foresee listing a lot of large items. If you will handle expensive items such as jewelry, you want a building that is secure and can be protected with an alarm. There are too many possible variables to list—you'll have to try carefully to project all your possible business scenarios and needs.

Be sure to thank your REALTOR® after they have shown you *each* property, and let them know you will get back to them *if* you are interested in making an offer. Be relaxed—you aren't in any rush—and let the REALTOR® know that you are considering all possible options before making your final decision. Be respectful of the REALTOR'S® time—if they sense you are a "tire kicker" or a window shopper, they may well stop returning your calls or simply be too "busy" to meet with you again.

PUT YOUR MONEY WHERE YOUR MOUTH IS

If you look at a building that seems absolutely perfect for you in every possible way, you will still want to make certain that it's in good condition. A building that appears to be in great condition may have problems lurking behind drywall or under a subfloor. There may be dry rot that you can't see, or maybe termites are munching away.

Most offers are contingent upon later inspection. It is illogical to pay someone to inspect a property before you make an offer to purchase it, because if your offer is not accepted, you have wasted your money. Prior to submitting your first offer, you will want to have a professional, licensed property inspector, and probably a termite extermination company, lined up for inspections of the building if your offer is accepted. These inspectors should be in place prior to your offer, because if your offer is accepted, the time window for the contingent inspections is typically only one to two weeks.

The property inspector will look at every single nook and cranny of the building; check the roof, plumbing, structural aspects, etc.; and submit a comprehensive written condition report, including, of course, any problems they found. Professional inspectors are experts in evaluating the condition of equipment as well. Most termite companies will conduct an inspection for free in the hope that eventually it will result in some extermination work. If you have any trouble finding a good termite company and/or property inspector, you should contact the chamber of commerce in your city for referrals.

Once you have made a decision on the suitability of a property, it's time to make an offer for purchase. Normally making the offer will require a good faith deposit that you pledge toward the deal if the offer is accepted. This shows you are serious, and most sellers will not consider an offer without this deposit, called earnest money. The earnest money can be $500, $1,000, or a percentage of the property's value. I have seen it all over the map, and I have given up to 3 percent of the property's value when making an offer. Customarily, your check is not cashed until your offer is accepted.

THE OFFER

The offer will be a rather long document and may have some terms or concepts that are new to you. As part of the offer process, this document states whether you are asking the seller to pay the costs of handling certain aspects of the transaction. Below are some of the costs that are often associated with the sale of a property.

Escrow fees. In some states, a separate, third-party company holds all funds during the transaction and manages all of the paperwork in conjunction with a sale. Although an escrow company is not required for cash purchases of real property, lenders will require an escrow company or, alternatively, a property title company, to handle the money; file legal documents with the county to confirm the transfer of the property from the seller to you; pay all fees to various parties, such as the appraiser, etc.; and to make sure in general that the sale process runs smoothly. A "title" is the property ownership, in effect proof that you are the owner of the property, which can be evidenced by a deed. Don't worry about all these terms—your REALTOR® and your lender will ensure that all documents are filed properly. The escrow fees are often split equally between buyer and seller. You can ask the seller to pay all of them, but that would be very unusual.

Appraisal fees. Most commercial lenders will require that a licensed property appraiser assess the property's value. This will involve a physical inspection of the property and research to determine what other similar properties have fetched recently. The recent sales of similar properties are called "comps." The lender will usually bill you, the buyer, for the appraisal. If the property has had a recent appraisal, you should let your lender know, and asking about this detail may save you a large sum of money. I suggest that you don't allow the property to be appraised until you have a formal approval letter from your lender. Your offer's time frame should allow enough time for you to accomplish this task, and if you were able to get prequalified by your lender, this process should all move very quickly and smoothly.

Survey. A property survey is essentially a formal statement from a licensed surveyor that shows the property boundaries. The survey is important in making certain that everyone (especially you) knows the actual physical boundaries of the property you are buying. If the seller has a survey on the property already, this is a moot point, and you can use their survey. If the seller doesn't, it's not unusual to ask them to pay for the survey.

Termite work. Virtually all commercial lenders will want to have a termite inspection of the property. This is crucial. You may want to have your own company do this, because often sellers or their REALTORS® have close relationships with their own companies. I am not saying that your seller or their REALTOR® will assert undue influence on this inspection either way, but in the past, I have found extensive infestations of termites after I'd purchased property, even though the seller's termite inspection had come back with no evidence of infestation. It's appropriate to have a truly neutral person handle this. It is also normal for a seller to provide a property that is free of infestations, and the seller should, and typically will, pay for any termite eradication or termite-related repairs. Because the building you are buying is probably 100 percent commercial use, it is practical to "tent" the building to exterminate any infestations. In tenting, the termite company will cover the entire building with a special tent and then pump gas into the property to kill all of the termites. This is the only truly reliable way to kill all the termites, and you should try to negotiate with the seller to pay for this type of treatment if infestations are found.

Loan costs. The lender you select to finance this property will normally charge some fees. These fees are completely at the lender's discretion and vary greatly. Some lenders will charge no up-front fees, but the interest rate they charge may be a bit higher to compensate. Almost all lenders pay their loan agents some form of incentive or commission, typically paid for through "points." The points are a percentage of the total loan and are charged to you in return for the loan's origination. These fees can be negotiated, and if you shop your loan around to various lenders, you may be able to avoid paying points and still obtain a favorable interest rate. Remember that an appraisal fee is paid to an appraiser, but the loan origination fees are paid to the lender itself, so the lender may have a lot of discretion with these fees. If you are dealing with a direct lender, these fees are typically very low. If you deal with a loan broker (i.e., someone who sends your loan package out to a number of lenders), you will most certainly pay points to compensate this broker for their commissions. Many lenders may charge a loan application fee as well, and this fee is usually nonrefundable. With a loan broker, you may be able to avoid this application fee, but you will probably end up paying a bit more in the long run. An aggressive loan broker will increase your chances of obtaining financing, but you will most likely pay more for the money. You need to weigh these factors. For first-time borrowers, I suggest you work with a loan broker.

Title insurance. The property's title (ownership records) can be guaranteed by an insurance company through what is normally called title insurance. Lenders will require title insurance to assure that there are no liens against the property or other problems. Normally, the seller pays for title insurance. If you plan on adding a second (or even a third) loan to the property at some later date, you can pay an additional fee to obtain a buyer's title insurance policy, which will save you money on future title insurance for these additional loans.

Property insurance. Lenders will also require that the property have hazard insurance in place at the time of closing. You should shop around for this insurance to get a favorable rate. However, you should always get a policy from a highly rated company—you will be glad you did if you ever have the need to file a claim. Include the cost of hazard insurance when estimating your total costs for acquiring the property. It would be a good idea to obtain estimates from this same insurer for the policy you will need to cover your business operations as well as worker's compensation insurance (if you intend to have employees). An insurer will give discounts for multiple policies, including your auto and homeowners' insurance. I have saved a lot of money by carrying all my insurance policies with one company.

Property taxes. The county where you reside will charge you an annual assessment for property taxes. You may pay taxes to your city for municipal services as well. These taxes will be paid twice a year. I suggest you ask your lender to impound or escrow both your property taxes and hazard insurance. The lender can spread the tax bill over your monthly mortgage payments and make it more digestible. You need to consider your tax bill as part of your overall overhead when buying a building, and at the time your real estate purchase is consummated, you may see an adjustment for prorated taxes.

Miscellaneous fees. Other fees associated with the purchase of real property include government fees for the filing of the deed as well as fees charged to you by the escrow or title company for preparing various documents and mailing or sending them via express courier. You will incur an additional fee if you live in a state which requires an attorney to prepare your deed. These fees are usually rather nominal, but they can add up.

Before you make an offer, you should ask your lender to review your credit and your income to estimate both what you can afford to buy and also the total cost of making the purchase, including the down payment. Make sure you have the cash necessary before you start making any offers.

Study your floor plans. Does the building have enough space for you to handle listings, photography, storage, packing, shipping, and future growth? Once you have compiled a list of which properties will work well for your new eBay drop-off store, it's time to start writing offers. I would never offer full price for any property. There is no need to make offensively low offers, but all sellers expect to receive offers below their asking price. The exception would be if you are in a very hot real estate market, when it is normal for offers even to exceed the asking price, especially if there are multiple offers. But if a REALTOR® tells you there are multiple offers on a property, it's not necessarily an indication that you should make an offer above the asking price. Your REALTOR® must submit any offer you present, whether or not they believe it will be accepted. You should expect to make many offers, on numerous properties, before getting a great deal on one you want. You can pay full price for any property and get it fast—or, with a little patience, you can wait until you find a great deal. This simply depends upon how quickly you need to start your business. When I am investing in property, I am always patient, and I never overpay.

When writing your offer, remember to determine who will pay for each of the above anticipated costs, and remember that all this is totally negotiable. There is no right or wrong way to make your offer. You can ask the seller to pay for all the closing costs, or you can agree to split them. In your offer, indicate who pays for:

- Property inspection
- Termite work (if any)
- Repairs to the property (if you found problems after a property inspection)
- Title insurance
- Escrow fees
- Survey
- Any other costs for closing

Your REALTOR® will have forms to use for making the offer. Read these over carefully and be sure to indicate in every instance whether you or the seller will pay for a particular cost. You will also want to allow ample time for the property inspection, termite work, and loan approvals. These items should be written into your offer in the form of contingencies, which will state that the offer is subject to inspection of the property, a clean termite report, and approval from your lender with terms that are acceptable to you. All of this will protect you from losing your earnest money in the event you cannot secure financing or if you discover something drastically wrong with the building after the inspections have been completed.

HAGGLING

Once you submit your offer, the seller will have a period of time specified in the offer in which to respond. If the seller fails to respond within that time, your earnest money check will not be cashed. If the seller agrees to your offer as-is, the earnest money will go to the title or escrow company mutually agreed upon by the buyer and seller. Many REALTORS® have in-house escrow services, which can speed up the closing process.

If the seller comes back to you with a counteroffer, review the counteroffer with your REALTOR® to understand the terms that have been modified and/or added by the seller. It's not uncommon to go back and forth a few times before settling on final terms and conditions that are acceptable to both parties. Rarely will a seller accept the initial offer.

Remember at all times that your REALTOR® and the REALTOR® representing the seller are paid on a commission basis. They have a strong financial incentive to sell the property to you. And it is important that your mind is clear and that you very carefully think through the terms of the sale before making a final agreement.

Be prepared to walk away from an unfavorable deal. Keep your emotions under control and understand that you are making a business decision. Often, a seller will come back to the bargaining table when a buyer walks away from a deal. Being prepared to say no is a powerful negotiating tool for you, because it shows that you are not desperate. Play it cool and relax. No deal is ever a once-in-a-lifetime opportunity.

If you plan to make offers on more than one property, you should bear in mind that more than one offer may be accepted. If you provide earnest money toward the purchase of more than one property at a time, be sure to watch your timing for contingencies. You will want to have an easy "out" in the event you are presented with the difficult decision of having more than one accepted offer—you don't want to lose your earnest money.

OTHER PEOPLE'S MONEY

As previously stated, your down payment requirements can be as low as 10 percent and as high as 40 percent, depending upon the loan program. The Small Business Administration (SBA) has loan guarantee programs that allow making a lower down payment. The SBA also offers programs that will guarantee your financing for the entire business, including your leasehold improvements, so it's smart to ask your lender if you qualify for one of these programs. And you may want to show your lender your business plan and determine if you can obtain financing for your new building and your eBay business at the same time.

Each lender will have their own loan application guidelines, and they will look at your financial strength and the feasibility of your project before agreeing to lend you money. They will also want to see that you have sufficient working capital to keep the business operating during your initial start-up and growth.

Work closely with your lender and establish a strong rapport with them. If they feel very positive about your proposed business, they will go above and beyond the call of duty to make certain you have every possible chance of obtaining financing.

Many sellers have owned their buildings for a long time and often have a very small mortgage or own the property free and clear. Because of this, on several occasions I have been able to purchase property with seller financing. This means that the seller, instead of a commercial lender, carried the note on the property. These deals are rare, but they do come up. And when they do, it's a wonderful thing, because the seller won't charge you fees and points as a bank will, and typically their guidelines for lending you the money will be much more relaxed than a bank's. If the seller is highly motivated to sell, they may be willing to help you with some or even all of the financing.

You should ask the REALTOR® if the seller would consider financing the mortgage. If you are short on cash, you can also structure offers

★TIP

You can hold title of real property with any legal business entity or under your personal name. Chapter 3 discussed the various legal entities that you can use to operate your business. You can take title of a property as an individual, jointly with another individual (or individuals), through an LLC, a partnership, a corporation, or one of various other legal entities. It may be a logical decision for you to hold title as an individual and then lease the property back to your new company for a nominal sum (such as $1 a year). This will help to create a layer of protection for your property against potential liabilities such as lawsuits or liens in the event your business fails (but we don't think it will!).

in which the seller carries a second mortgage as part of the purchase agreement.

The terms of the financing will vary from lender to lender, and your payment terms could range from 5 to 30 years. Your payment will be determined by the amortization period: If the loan is fully amortized for 30 years, the payment will be lower than if the same loan amount were amortized over 15 years. It is important for your financial projections to know what terms the bank can offer you. Many seller-financed properties will have a long amortization period, but the seller may want a balloon payment in a shorter period of time, such as three to five years. A balloon payment is the lump sum of the original loan owing, less principal payments you have made. A balloon payment is the result of a short-term loan where the amortization period is longer than the loan term.

Closing the deal on your new building may take as little as a few weeks (with seller financing) to as much as a couple of months. You will end up with a deed to your new property, and you will be the proud owner of your own building. Then the real work begins—now you have to get your doors open and your new eBay venture off the ground.

I haven't attempted to make you a real estate expert in one chapter. However, this chapter is a good primer for understanding the mechanics of purchasing your own building to start your eBay drop-off store.

YOU'RE THE LANDLORD NOW

When you are just starting out in a new business, having cash coming in is very helpful. If you have decided to purchase a building with lots of extra space, you might be able to sublet parts of your space to help pay your bills. You can rent office or storage space, or you might offer to handle warehousing for other companies.

If you have extra space with secure and separate entries, you can attract other businesspeople who are seeking temporary digs within which to conduct their small businesses. In my store, we offer parcel shipping services to increase our revenues. Be creative and think of ways to benefit from being the landlord.

You can put out the word to leasing agents and offer them a commission to help you sublet parts of your new building. You can attract tenants with ads in local newspapers or on the Internet. You might even rent meeting space or conference rooms by the hour. You own the building now, so if you are trying to stretch your dollar, find creative ways to bring in the extra revenue.

9

INSURANCE

Someone we knew told us that the engine in his 1993 Mazda MX6 had seized and was headed for the junkyard. He had been offered $250 for scrapping it. We talked him into letting us sell it on eBay, and it ended up going for $2,550. The winning bidders were a couple in Oklahoma. The husband was a former mechanic, and his wife needed a reliable car to attend college classes. They towed the car away and, even though it needed a new engine, they were pleased with the bargain price they paid—and my client got more than ten times what he was offered by the junkyard.

Andy and Deb Mowery, Fort Collins, Colorado;
eBay user ID "debnroo"; trading on eBay since October 1, 1999

THE REASONS FOR INSURANCE AND WHY YOU CANNOT OPERATE WITHOUT IT

If you are a work-at-home Trading Assistant and don't handle a lot of expensive items, buying extra insurance may not be necessary. You will probably already have theft coverage with your homeowners' policy, and if you don't own your own home, you should have a renters' policy that serves the same purpose. Be sure to check your policy to see if it provides sufficient coverage, and ask your insurance company if a work-at-home business will be covered.

If you operate a drop-off store, you will need to plan your insurance coverage carefully to make certain you and your clients will be protected in the event of loss due to theft, fire, or acts of God (referred to as *force majeure*).

You can get into a lot of financial trouble if you don't have insurance to cover a loss. Don't take excessive risks by running your new business without insurance. If you hire employees, you will also need to have workers' compensation insurance in the event of an on-the-job injury.

BROKERS—PART DEUX

Most insurance companies sell their policies through authorized agents or brokers. Some sell insurance directly by telephone without using brokers. So many insurance companies provide all types of business insurance, it may be confusing, so it's helpful to shop around to learn about the various companies and their offerings.

You can talk to your auto, homeowners', or renters' insurance company and see if they also offer business insurance. You will get better service (and often a better price) from a company when you have multiple policies with them. You can also reach out to friends, family, and your chamber of commerce for referrals to a great insurance broker.

Explain to the broker that you will be operating a business where you handle and store items on behalf of others, and that because you will probably rarely handle cash, most of the liability will concern your equipment and business records and the clients' items. Also, if you own your business's building, you may have to buy separate coverage for it. Because your insurance rates will be determined by the amounts of coverage, your location, and the policies of the insurance company, it is important for you to be classified as the correct business type. Insurance companies' rates are based on the severity of the risk they are insuring. Being a Trading Assistant does not normally involve a lot of dangerous activities or unusual risks.

Ask the broker if they specialize in insuring businesses, and if they have a variety of carriers to choose from. You may do better working with a broker who is an independent agent and can shop your policy to more than one company. Ask the broker to shop your policy only to companies with a strong financial rating. You want an insurance company with a solid financial base that can make prompt payment on claims. You also want to avoid any companies that may have government regulatory actions pending.

REPORT CARDS

AM Best (*www.ambest.com*) provides ratings of insurance companies' abilities to meet their obligations to their policyholders. Below is their rating system:

- A++ or A+ (superior)
- A or A- (excellent)
- B++ or B+ (very good)
- B or B- (fair)
- C++ or C+ (marginal)
- C or C- (weak)
- D (poor)
- E (under regulatory supervision)
- F (in liquidation)
- S (rating suspended)

This is Standard and Poor's (*www.standardandpoors.com*) rating system for insurers:

- AAA (extremely strong)
- AA (very strong)
- A (strong)
- BBB (good)
- BB (marginal)
- B (weak)
- CCC (very weak)
- CC (extremely weak)
- R (under regulatory supervision)
- NR (rating suspended)

Moody's (*www.moodys.com*) is another company that rates insurance companies:

- Aaa (exceptional financial security)
- Aa (excellent financial security)

- A (good financial security)
- Baa (adequate financial security)
- Ba (questionable financial security)
- B (poor financial security)
- Caa (very poor financial security)
- Ca (extremely poor financial security)
- C (lowest financial security)

Ask your broker to look at companies with a great or superior rating from one of the above companies. Stick to insurance companies that have a rating from any of the above three ratings firms that starts with an *A*. Don't be seduced by the lowest price quote—it may be from a financially unstable insurance carrier, and you need to be sure that your claim will be paid, promptly, in the event you need to use your insurance policy.

RAISE THAT DEDUCTIBLE

Your insurance broker, just like a real estate broker, is paid by incentives (commissions), and they will want you to be a customer for a very long time. It is in their interest to sell you good insurance and offer you coverage that will protect you both personally and in business—not just sell you cut-rate insurance.

The price of your insurance depends upon a variety of factors, including:

- Your deductible (the amount you have to pay on each claim before your insurance kicks in and starts paying)
- The number of policies that you have with the insurance company
- The insurance company's financial strength (rating)
- The amounts and types of coverage
- Your location
- The type of building and its construction
- Your security system
- Your claims history

Insurance is really designed to cover you in a catastrophic situation. If you break a client's $50 lamp, you will pay for it out of your own pocket; not file a claim against your insurance. Most likely, the deductible would be higher than the value of that item, and the insurance company wouldn't pay anyway. You will want your insurance to cover something big, like a runaway truck smashing into your store, a tornado moving the building to a new zip code, or an earthquake leveling the shop—this is what insurance is for.

You will find that the rate you pay will drop substantially as your deductible goes up. I suggest you go for a high deductible, such as $1,000 (or more if possible). You want your business insurance to be affordable, so in the event of a loss, you want your deductible to be the largest amount you can reasonably pay out of your own pocket without putting a strain on your finances. Ask your broker to give you a variety of quotes based on different deductible amounts so that you can compare the rates and see what makes sense for you.

PEOPLE, PROPERTY, AND UMBRELLAS

★ TIP

If you cannot find a single insurance company to handle all your insurance needs, be sure to read each of your policies carefully to make certain you do not duplicate coverage.

Your insurance should cover both people and property. Here are the different types of insurance and what they cover.

General Liability

- *Bodily injury.* This covers your liability when someone else is injured at your business location. Examples would be slip-and-fall injuries or injury as a result of a box falling on a customer.
- *Property damage.* For damage claims to the property of others, such as damage caused by *force majeure.* If something happens to your clients' items while in your custody, you will be covered.
- *Personal injury.* Coverage for things such as libel, slander, false arrest, or wrongful entry. These situations will probably not occur in your type of business, but this coverage is often automatically included in a general liability policy.
- *Advertising injury.* This covers your legal liability for damage to others caused by your wrongful advertising of your business' goods and services. In the unlikely event that you misrepresent yourself, such as making exaggerated claims about prices you can obtain on eBay, you will be able to get legal defense from your insurance company.

Commercial Automobile Protection

- *Liability.* This will cover you in the event you or an employee are sued as a result of an auto accident while using a vehicle in connection with your business, such as when picking up items from a client's home or running errands.
- *Collision.* Pays for physical damage caused to your business's vehicle as a result of an automobile accident.
- *Comprehensive.* Covers damage to your business's vehicle as a result of fire, theft, or glass breakage.
- *Rental reimbursement.* Special coverage to pay for a rental vehicle for a specific length of time while your vehicle is disabled due to a covered loss (such as while it is being repaired after an accident).

Business Property Protection

- Protects your building and its contents in the event of physical damage or loss.

Umbrella Excess Liability Coverage

- An umbrella policy will provide very high limits *in excess* of your other coverage. Individuals with a high net worth should invest in this type of additional coverage to protect their primary residence and assets in the event of a major lawsuit or personal injury claim arising out of the business's activities.

Workers' Compensation Insurance

- This coverage is legally required in most states and covers employees and their medical expenses in the event of an on-the-job injury. The rate you pay is normally a percentage of your estimated payroll. Some business insurance packages will also include worker's compensation insurance.

Be sure to discuss all of the above coverage options with your insurance broker. Don't skimp on insurance—you want to be sure you have sufficient coverage to meet the conditions of your business activities. To help take the bite out of the insurance bill, virtually any insurance company will give you a payment plan if requested, so that your payments are spread out in monthly installments.

But you also don't want to be overinsured, paying for policy limits far beyond anything you'll need. Because the average eBay listing duration is seven days, you won't have a lot of items lying around, so your exposure for other people's property will generally be limited, unless you get behind on your listings or have very expensive items in your care.

You will want to get a policy in place before starting any property renovations so your protection is in force right away, even while you are getting ready to open your doors.

> **★ TIP**
>
> Frame a copy of your insurance policy and hang it in the lobby of your business along with your business licenses. Clients will appreciate knowing that you are an insured business.

BONDING WITH YOUR BUYERS

Bonding is not insurance, but it is related, and buyers on eBay prefer to purchase from bonded merchants.

A bond on an eBay listing is a guarantee of the seller's performance. Bonding provides buyers with financial protection in connection with the transaction in the event a dispute arises.

My company uses buySAFE (*www.buysafe.com*) bonding on every transaction. buySAFE requires the seller to pass through a comprehensive business inspection to make certain that the seller has the ability to perform all commitments made in connection with eBay transactions. The bonding gives buyers a very high level of confidence that the seller will ship within the time frame promised in the listing and that the order will arrive as it was shown and described on eBay. The seller pays a 1 percent bonding fee on every listing they put on eBay at the time that the item actually sells—there is no fee if the merchandise does not sell.

Bonding your listings will encourage business from buyers, and buyers will pay more for a bonded listing, because they know they can request repayment from the bonding company in the event of a dispute or problem with the order. Bonding is not insurance, because you, as the seller, will have to repay any monies paid by the bonding company if they pay a valid claim—that is, a claim where you have been determined to be at fault in your performance or representation of the item you listed on eBay.

Bonding is very, very good for your business, and I strongly encourage you to offer it on your eBay listings. Because I complete all my eBay transactions as promised, I have never had to pay a claim on my bond, but the bonding has definitely created more business and higher bids for our company. We receive many positive e-mails from buyers who thank us for bonding the listings, and we also see comments in our feedback profile from buyers who have included appreciation for our bonding in their feedback comments.

10 STORE DESIGN AND CONSTRUCTION

I deal mostly with corporate clients, because corporations are much less attached to their goods and have little time for handling their own sales on eBay. I have a major account who asked me to move a bulk lot of over 2,000 pairs of shoes. I'm using eBay's Reseller Marketplace, with the client assuming all of the fees, to move larger lots through eBay's wholesale marketplace. My daughter is getting married soon, and I'm using eBay to help pay for a spare-no-expense wedding.

Robert O. Sachs, Memphis, Tennessee;

eBay user ID "rosachs"; trading on eBay since September 21, 1997

Let's assume that you have made the decision to open a drop-off store. (If you are planning to work from home or from within an existing business, you won't need to design and build a store as we'll discuss here.) Though you have secured your location and are eager to get going, it would be very unusual if you could simply open your doors. There is work to be done, including laying out your work space—your daily working environment must be comfortable and functional. At my drop-off store, I like to have lots of staging areas where I can place merchandise while I work on it. I have a work counter for greeting customers that doubles as a shipping center, for the packing and shipping services we offer to the public as well as our own Trading Assistant work. Photography and listings are done at the front of the store for all to see, and from the street you can see our bright photography lights— a beacon that often draws potential customers into our store out of sheer curiosity.

Your plan at this point calls for either a simple or a fancy drop-off store, and either way, you will need to have a plan—a *design*—to organize the store to make it work. You will need about 30 to 45 days to get your doors open if you plan to have a fancy store. A simple store may take less time to get started, but you should be realistic about your timeline, which will also depend upon the existing condition of your space. Also, don't forget that many municipalities will require a final "sign-off" from the fire department or possibly some other agency. Be sure to have your local business license secured before setting a firm open date.

BUILDING BLOCKS

A good store design includes some basic elements:

- Functionality
- Atmospherics
- Visual merchandising

Functional Elements

These are the basic tools of the trade—desks, staging areas, work and photography tables, storage, etc. Don't underestimate the value and necessity of these elements in your design. You will need elbow room and lots of it, because a successful drop-off store will be receiving tons of items to list, and you will need to be able to manage them easily without working around piles of clutter. Be generous with the square footage you allocate for working space.

Store Atmospherics

The interior decoration of your store is critical for making you, your employees, and clients feel welcome and comfortable. The lobby of your store should have a place to sit down, some warm, attractive artwork on the walls, and possibly plants. It's really up to your personal sense of style. Overly sanitized, cold, or sterile atmospherics will turn off clients, even if they don't realize it, while a pleasant environment will be important to your mental well-being as well as that of your employees.

Visual Merchandising

Any successful business has to attract customers, and your eBay Trading Assistant store is no exception. Having a good exterior sign is a must. If you have a retail storefront, you will also want to put something in the windows to draw the eye of passers-by. You might be able to set up a display area in the windows of your store displaying items that you presently have listed on eBay, with a sign that says "Presently on eBay" or something similar. Inside your store, you might have a "menu" of your services similar to those found in fast food restaurants. Even your listing and photography areas should be in plain view to serve as visual merchandising of your business. The point of visual merchandising is to appeal to potential clients and spark their curiosity, drawing them in and motivating them to buy your service. Selling your service involves not only excellent customer service but also the entire visual and emotional experience created by your functional, elegant store design. Your store's appeal to clients starts with the exterior façade and window displays and continues with the interior merchandising.

PEER GROUP TREASURE

By now, you have already made a visit to one or more other drop-off stores. In this more advanced stage in developing your new operation, it is important to go to the well again—by reaching out to your peers. Again, don't be shy—no doubt you have already made some friends among your colleagues in the Trading Assistant business, and it's time to network with them on the subject of store layout. You want to avoid repeating others' mistakes, and you will need all the help you can get. Study your notes and carefully consider the other stores you visited. Did any particular store strike your fancy? What was your initial reaction when you walked in? Did something appear particularly clever or interesting to you? Another visit to your favorite Trading Assistant stores might help you formulate your final plans for your own layout. Call for an appointment with your peers and ask if you can seek their advice about store layout. Make several copies of your store's floor plan so that you can try different ideas while you talk with others.

Remember that the shortest path to success will come with the help of others. Most people have a good heart, and you will usually get the help you need.

SOMEONE HAS TO DESIGN IT

Your store layout and design will be based on your planned operations, as discussed in the previous chapters.

You will also want to consider your target customers so as to create an ambience that will attract the right type of people for your business. If you are seeking high-quality items from an upscale clientele, you will need to create upscale, as well as professional and attractive, visuals.

If you are comfortable with computer software, you may want to try your own hand at designing the store. I recommend a program called SmartDraw (*www.smartdraw.com*). This software has more than 1,200 templates and wizards to help you design your office (including a home office) or virtually any other sort of floor plan. It comes with a free trial so you can give it a test drive before buying it. The program includes graphics for desks, computers, and just about anything else you may need to lay out your new store. But software is no substitute for a creative eye and experience, so use it only if you feel comfortable doing it yourself or if you are planning a simple store.

Basics you will need to think about include:

- Materials (wood, Formica, tile, etc.)
- Access for electrical and Internet wiring
- Cost
- Time for construction
- Permits from your local city to complete the work legally

The physical areas of your store should include the following:

- A customer counter for meeting and consulting with clients
- A temporary staging area for placing items before they are listed
- An area for cleaning items before photographing and listing them
- A desk with plenty of elbow room so that you can research and evaluate the items prior to listing them
- A photography booth or table where the photos are taken
- A storage area for placing items while they are listed
- A storage area for boxes, foam packing peanuts, bubble wrap, and other shipping supplies
- A storage area for keeping office supplies such as printer/copier paper, pens, cleaning supplies, and anything else you may need for your daily operations
- A shipping counter with a computer for handling shipping tasks
- A storage area for placing packed, outgoing boxes awaiting pickup by the respective shipping companies
- A comfy table and chairs for eating lunch and relaxing at break times (optional, but important if you have employees)
- A bulletin board for reminders, staff schedules, and anything else you may need out in plain view
- A place to hold unsold items that require pickup by clients

If you are not a naturally creative person, and especially if you are opening an upscale store, it may be time to engage the services of a professional store designer. If you are opening a fancy store this will be money well spent, because you will be investing quite a bit of cash in the store construction, and a designer doesn't have to be expensive. Ask owners of other drop-off stores for a referral if you like their store design and layout. And if you are buying off-the-shelf furniture and fixtures, many of these retailers now have in-house design services to help you put together a floor plan. Reach out again to your chamber of commerce for referrals.

Interview at least three designers and ask to see their portfolios of other store designs, with photos. Insist on this. Any designer will have a portfolio, and they should be happy to share it with you—this is their visual resume. You should hire someone who has actually designed stores similar to the look and feel you are seeking. If you are having difficulty finding the right person who shares your creative vision, walk through upscale retail shopping districts, and when you see a store design you like, simply ask who designed that store. This is an outstanding way to get the look and feel you want.

You may also want to pick up a copy of *The Budget Guide to Retail Store Planning and Design* by Jeff Grant to get some additional information on the entire store design process, including how to clarify your expectations with design firms, sample contracts, and much more.

When you seek the services of an outside professional, be sure to share with them your business plan and budgetary expectations regarding the entire renovations project. You may also want to have an installment payment agreement with the designer to ensure timely delivery of their work. You should ask them to allow some time for revisions of their initial design, so that you can make minor modifications as you see fit. And before you ask them to show you any designs, you will want to find a contractor. Your designer and contractor will need to work hand-in-hand to establish the look and feel of your store, the materials used, and the overall cost of making it happen. Get the contractor on board before the designer puts anything to paper, and I suggest holding off on paying out any money until you have had a chance to meet with both of them.

WHO WILL BUILD IT?

Your designer will most likely know qualified contractors. Consider using them, because the designer will be familiar with their work, reliability, and ability to adhere to a budget. Meet with the designer's contractors and get a feel for your comfort level with them.

As with finding store designers, use other businesses in your area whose look you admire and your chamber of commerce as potential sources for contractor referrals.

A few questions to ask when interviewing contractors:

- Are they licensed and bonded contractors? Surprisingly, many are not, and you can check with the state to confirm their licensing status.
- Do they carry workers' compensation insurance for their employees? Liability insurance?
- How much money will they require up front, and how much more money will they require during the construction of your store?
- Do they guarantee their work against defects? For what period of time?
- Do they guarantee that they will complete the job in a specified period of time?
- Would they provide at least three references? Visit these people and see the contractor's work in person.

Don't feel pressured to go with any particular contractor. You should have two or three to choose from, and each will have their own particular style and way of doing business.

WHEELING AND DEALING AGAIN

My user ID on eBay is "borntodeal," and I like to think that I was born to deal (perhaps a completely misguided thought, but my own thinking nonetheless!). I like to negotiate the best deal possible when I hire a contractor.

You must establish a firm budget. Custom construction, flooring, lights, fixtures, and everything else you will need for your new store can add up quickly. You may spend a lot or a little, but either way you must have a firm financial plan—you don't want a runaway budget.

Get estimates. Set up meetings with your store designer and prospective contractors. Be diplomatic, because busy contractors may dislike competing for your business. Specify your budget and determine what elements of your store are critical and which are flexible (or optional).

You may be able to reduce the cost of your project by using off-the-shelf furniture and fixtures rather than asking the contractor to build everything to order.

The curb appeal of your store will have the most impact on your ability to attract clients, so focus on such things as the exterior paint colors, signage, and the lobby. The rest of the store will be functional, and you may want to have the open space beyond the front counter set up in such a way that you can reconfigure it at will. Perhaps you want the ability to move your photography table from one end of the store to another, or maybe you want to option of adding or removing storage shelves.

Having a flexible floor plan will reduce the amount of work that your contractor will do, because these areas can be set up with movable furniture instead of fixed counter and work space. You can set up your own shelving units using inexpensive, readily available boltless systems. We chose these systems because they can be dismantled in a matter of minutes. We also use inexpensive plastic folding tables for instant staging areas and work spaces. Although this may sound a bit cheap, actually these tables are actually rather attractive—and they allow us the luxury of flexibility.

Here are some tips on what to talk about during the meetings with the designer and contractors:

- Establish whether the contractor will be installing your signage and who will create the graphics for that sign. Do you need a separate sign contractor to bid this job and install it?
- Does the contractor handle every aspect of the job, or will they require you to get separate bids for such things as electrical work and plumbing?
- Is the contractor familiar with the permit process in your town? Will the contractor obtain all the necessary permits from the city, and will their bid include these permit costs?
- Does the contractor offer financing of the project? If so, at what interest rate and repayment terms?

Find out from the contractors you interview about their current workload and schedule, and get some idea of the speed of their work. You want to avoid hiring a contractor who has poor planning and

> **★TIP**
>
> Always ask to be able to see the completed work of any subcontractors. If you are hiring a tile installer to tile your front lobby, ask if you can see other projects this installer has completed. When you hire a sign company, ask to see two or three of their signs at actual installed locations. Visit the locations at night and be sure the sign is bright, crisp, and easy to read. Be picky—it is your money, and you want quality work for your store.

scheduling skills. I prefer to deal with people who are highly confident about their ability to complete a job in a specified amount of time. That alone may be worth paying a bit more for, because a job that takes too long can cost you a tremendous amount of extra money in the form of lost business, additional rent, or loan payments—and the domino effect of everything else falling out of place while you anxiously attempt to get this business off the ground.

A MILLION DOLLARS A DAY

I also like to discuss early completion bonuses with contractors. I would never work on a time-and-materials payment arrangement with anyone doing a job this big. I prefer to get a flat rate for completing the agreed-on work, and I would suggest offering a completion bonus for each day the job is finished early. After the 1994 earthquake in Los Angeles, the contractor who was repairing the freeways was paid a bonus of one million dollars a day for each day the completed project was ahead of schedule. This is an extreme example (also quite controversial), but it seems perfectly reasonable to me, considering the immense expense the city was racking up due to police overtime for diverting traffic and the general inconvenience to the public due to the traffic congestion. If your mortgage (with interest and taxes) is $1,000 a month, you could offer the contractor $30 to $40 a day for each day the project comes in early, because that approximately matches your daily cost for the building. If your mortgage is $3,000 a month, paying an extra $100 a day for early completion would be a savings to you. A contractor may work night and day until your project is finished, knowing this extra money is on the table. It is always in your best interest to pay more (within reason of course) for a faster job, as late work is no bargain.

PEN TO PAPER

It will come as no surprise to you that I suggest you take notes during your meeting with each contractor, and that you be sure to write down your thoughts about each one after the meeting is concluded. Gather the ideas from each one and see what strikes your fancy. Use these notes in formulating your final plan for the store layout, before you write a check to start the process with your designer. And again, please seriously consider making your work space flexible and configurable, thus avoiding a marriage to one specific floor plan.

Give your store designer some final guidance and work out their final fee for the design with the contractor budget as a top priority. Create a written agreement with your designer that specifies your expectations, their fee, and your contractor budget. Establish a deadline with your designer for the first draft of their design plans.

Remember to put in writing how many revisions you can expect to request before being charged an additional fee. When agreement in writing has been reached, both you and your designer should sign off on the design fees. As a rule of thumb, I would pay the store designer no more than 10 to 15 percent of the total contractor budget. I am not saying you should offer them a percentage; I am suggesting you limit their fees to what you can afford to pay on the overall project.

Although it may be fine to operate with verbal agreements, I suggest you always get everything in writing the first time you hire someone. I rarely leave this to chance. Unless you have the luxury of an unlimited budget or time frame, you should establish all expectations in writing. This does not have to be a complex or fancy contract—just something to establish a meeting of the minds.

With your first design plan in hand, review it carefully and talk it over with friends and family. Did the designer execute on paper what was originally in your mind? Does it faithfully resemble what you and the designer discussed at your meetings? Take the initial plan to other, experienced retailers, and especially to your fellow Trading Assistants who own drop-off stores, and discuss it with them, too. As always, take notes.

If you want changes, go back to your designer and ask for the revisions you feel are needed. Be respectful of their time, and don't expect more than is reasonable for what you are paying them. You establish a successful business relationship when everyone involved feels they are getting what is just, and creative people can have a higher sensitivity to what is fair or unfair than a hardcore businessperson.

Once you have settled on your initial plans, submit them to all of the contractors for written bids. Ask them to review the required materials and to identify in their bids any aspects of the design plan that they are not qualified to complete. Often this may be the exterior sign. Sign design and construction is a specialized field, and I have seen more than a few bad ones. A great sign will not be cheap, but it is a high priority—be prepared to pay in proportion to its importance. If the contractor gives you a list of items on your plan that will require additional contractors, ask for referrals and bid those jobs out separately. Be sure to account for these separate bids in your final budget.

Ask for confirmation as to whether the cost of permits will be included in the bid or if they will be charged separately. And don't forget sales tax! Materials, and sometimes labor, may be taxable items, depending on your state. Ask if the tax is included in the bid or if that will be charged separately. This can be a huge additional cost, so don't forget to mention it. Finally, be sure to ask the contractor for their first available date to begin the work and an exact number of days required to complete it (weather permitting, etc.).

A MATCH MADE IN HEAVEN

First and foremost, don't take the lowest bid automatically. This may be tempting, but consider all available information, including your gut feeling about the contractor. Check their references and ask each reference if the contractor was clean, professional, and timely in the completion of their project. I once hired a roofing contractor who was the highest of three bids, because he provided me with over two dozen references, and each of them spoke very highly of the quality, timeliness, and professionalism of his work.

Consider your feelings about the contractor from your initial meeting. Did they arrive at the appointment on time? Did you feel they were professional and attentive to you during the meeting? Did they make you feel completely comfortable? What were their payment terms? Did they require a lot of money up front, or were they willing to defer the majority of your payments until the project was finished?

My most trusted and faithful painting contractor's name is Ernesto. I recently hired him to do some work for me that involved well over $2,000 in materials alone. He is so confident in the quality and satisfaction he provides to his clients that he agreed to wait until the job was 100 percent completed before he received one dime! His work for me has always been even higher quality than I expected. He is punctual and highly professional and always asks questions about how I want the completed project to look and about the small details. Every job he touches turns out perfectly.

Most contractors will require a deposit, often 25 percent (or possibly more) of their total fee before the work starts. For large jobs, a contractor will require progress payments, to cover their materials and labor costs, as they complete various stages of the work. These payment arrangements are negotiable and may help in determining who you hire.

Once you make up your mind, agree on a start date (in writing), sign off on the estimate to indicate your approval, and pay the contractor's advance.

NOSY IS NATURAL

When working with someone unfamiliar, it is critical to be present for the start of the construction. Do a walk-through on the first day of the work to discuss any minor details and to show your new contractor that you are "hands-on"—available to confer and answer questions.

Develop a friendly rapport with your contractor, and make certain that your plans are being followed. Make an appointment to return at the end of each working day, if possible, to review the work in progress. Make a note of any issues and report them immediately to the contractor to avoid costly delays or major changes later. Being hands-on will pay off for your vision and expectations.

Be mindful of the relationship between your design and construction contract. Be aware that changes to your design plans may translate into extra costs in your final bill. Be fair about this, and if you do want to make on-the-fly changes to your plan, establish in advance the amount of any additional charges so that you can budget for them. Perhaps you realize that your store's bathroom has a small sink and you really need a larger one for washing and cleaning items, such as china. Maybe you notice that the front counter is too low and you need it a couple inches higher. These kinds of things should be relatively easy to fix along the way, but be prepared to foot the bill for the modifications.

If you have established a payment schedule, be prompt in meeting your deadlines as well. You will obtain the best service when you are prompt in paying for it as agreed.

GIVING YOUR STAMP OF APPROVAL

When dealing with people in general, it's best to trust but verify. As with supervising the work in progress, you should also make a final inspection of all work completed before you sign off on the construction of your new store and make your final contractor payment.

If you are using money from a third party such as a bank, you may be required to provide them with photographs of the work or even arrange for them to make their own inspection of your project.

Be sure to review your written agreement with the contractor carefully and walk through and inspect each and every item on your agreed-upon list. If the city is required to approve any of the work that has been completed, it is important to have these inspections finalized before you make your final payment to the contractor. If for any reason the city disapproves the work, it is the contractor's responsibility to make certain that the work meets local codes and regulations.

★**TIP**

You may be able to get creative and cut some corners if you are on a limited budget. An upscale look for your store, without the high cost, may be possible by checking the newspapers for auction sales of businesses that are closing. If you want to go for an antique look, you can visit the weekly auctions in your area and look for fancy old wood counters to use in your shop. If you want a modern look, drive around and look for signs that a business is closing its doors and see if you can pick up any of their furniture, fixtures, or storage racks. You may be able to get lots of great equipment cheap this way, saving yourself a bundle. Having a flexible floor plan will also allow you to use secondhand furnishings and equipment easily in your new business.

11 SETTING FEES FOR YOUR SERVICES

I listed and sold a wonderful cowboy Western oil painting by a local artist, J.A. Kirkpatrick. He has exhibited artwork at prestigious galleries nationally, and his paintings hang in the Smithsonian Institute and the U.S. Senate building. My client was selling it to help pay for his daughter's special schooling needs. The minimum bid was $300, and 10 days later it sold for $2,705 with 27 bids. I collected a $20 listing fee and a 20 percent commission on the final selling price.

Michael J. Ellingson, Fargo, North Dakota;

eBay user ID "phonomike"; trading on eBay since October 18, 1998

Let's do a quick reality check—what type of business will you be operating? Yes, it's a Trading Assistant business, but ask yourself—what is it, exactly, that you do? Think of yourself as being in the *unwanted item liquidation business*. Your clients have things—unwanted things—that they want out of their lives. Therefore, when setting your fees, you have to realize that you are providing an extremely valuable service. If you seek out clients who want new channels to sell brand new merchandise or want to maximize recovery of their original investment in their unwanted items, you are bound to have trouble justifying your fees. Your ideal client is someone who has things for which they have no further emotional or financial attachment, things that can be sold for whatever price the market will bear.

Keep this concept in mind at all times when discussing your fees—fees that reflect the high value of your service.

TIME IS MONEY

What is your time worth? How much were you making on an hourly basis at your last job? If you owned or presently own a business, how much money do you keep at the end of each week, month, or year? Many new business owners fail because their businesses do not collect a sufficient amount of revenue to pay expenses and leave a tidy profit. A common pitfall for many new business owners is a failure to realize and value the importance of their time.

Not only will you have to evaluate each item you might list, to determine if it can make you a reasonable profit given the time you spend handling it; you will also have to confront the true costs of doing business and create a schedule of fees that will return the profits you need.

I have set a standard for myself. I decided that I want to make no less than $80 per hour while I am working at my office. I know this may seem high, but my services are worth this much. So I have had to reverse engineer the revenue at my business, establishing fee rates for my clients that will provide this value for my time.

When you advertise your business, you will receive many inquiries from people interested in your services. Such inquiries will flow in from having a retail store as well. If you accept items worth $5 each for listing on eBay, you will find yourself quickly losing money regardless of what percentage you charge your clients. The reality will quickly become apparent—it takes the same amount of time to list an item worth $5 as it does to list one that is worth $100, $500, or even $5,000.

When you set your rates, you should also remember that your client is paying not only for your time, but for your staff, rent (or mortgage), insurance, office expenses, and any other costs associated with operating your business. You have also made substantial investments in equipment and in creating your business.

LET THE MARKET SET THE PRICE

At my store, we charge no up-front fee for listing items on eBay, but we also rarely accept items for which a minimum price is required by our clients. There is a good reason for this: We are in the unwanted item liquidation business. We are neither profit maximizers nor distributors for manufacturers or dealers of new products. The fees that eBay charges are dependent on both the final selling price and on the starting price of any item—the lower the starting price, the lower the fees eBay charges us for the listing. We have learned the hard way that, for the most part, when you agree to take an item at a minimum starting price or reserve price, the likelihood of your selling that item decreases dramatically. A reserve is a secret "hold back" number that you establish to ensure that an item will not sell below this pre-established figure.

The eBay site is still predominantly an auction-style listing venue, with less than one-third of items being sold at fixed prices. For many people, there is a certain excitement in bidding. Items that start at low opening bids generate this excitement, and some bids bring in more bids. We have seen this phenomenon literally thousands of times in our own listings. We want to sell *every* item we accept for listing, and taking items with minimum prices or reserves means that we might spend our valuable time creating a listing with no guarantee of profit, because the item may not sell.

Although you can charge an up-front listing fee for taking any item, in practice you will find a tremendous amount of resistance from clients when asking them to pay more money on an already depreciating asset with no assurance that they will get a return. Most clients feel this is throwing good money after bad. Though up-front fees are common in the Trading Assistant business, it is my strong belief that having such a fee will reduce your chances of getting an item submission.

You want every item to sell, and at my shop we encourage a lot more business by having no up-front fees for listing items (except in extremely rare cases). It is also my general policy that we do not accept items for which the client demands a minimum selling price. We use auction-style listings and start most of them at $0.99 with no reserve. The eBay marketplace sets the price by competitive bidding, and the items end up selling for what they are worth to the highest bidder. I have listed items starting at $0.99 that sold for thousands!

DON'T SECOND THAT EMOTION

I want you to contemplate very carefully the type of items you want to attract and the type of people you want coming through your doors. How you present, and how you price, your service will determine both of these.

I prefer the upscale client with quality, brand-name items that they no longer need or want and to which they have no emotional or financial attachment whatsoever. These well-to-do folks don't really care how much they will recover from their sale, but at the same time, they realize that with a yard sale, they will end up giving their things away for virtually nothing. When they receive their checks, most of my upscale clients are amazed at the prices I have realized for them on eBay.

WHAT THE OTHERS ARE CHARGING

Your name may not be Bill Gates, but it is possible to run a monopoly. Trading Assistant businesses are still a rather novel concept, and you may find very little competition in your area. If no other Trading Assistants are near you, then you can pretty much call the shots as to how you charge for your services.

If you live in a bigger town, as I do, you will find Trading Assistants and eBay drop-off stores all over the place. It is important to know how they run their businesses and charge for their services. You are already armed with quite a bit of knowledge about their operations because of your previous fact-finding visits to them, including, hopefully, their rates.

At my store, we charge a 38 percent commission on the first $500 of any individual sale. If the item sells for more, we charge 25 percent of the next $500 (from $501 to $1,000) and 15 percent of any amount over $1,000. Holy cow, you may be thinking, that's a huge piece of the pie! Not really—when you consider that the industry standard commission for consignment shops is 50 percent, if you are not paying the shop rent. Some consignment shops might charge a much lower commission, but they will also charge you rent for any space you use in their shop. I have a client who routinely brings in high-end collectibles and antiques for us to list on eBay. He has been paying $150 a month to rent a small display case in an antiques mall. He sells a lot of items there and pays only a 15 percent commission, but the antiques mall clears a guaranteed $150 a month from him, regardless of his sales.

In the rare event that we do list a client's item at a minimum price, my store charges the client an up-front fee of $9.99 per eBay listing. This nonrefundable listing fee helps us defray the cost of the eBay fees and the handling of the item if it doesn't sell. I have seen other stores charging up-front fees ranging from $2.99 for a basic auction all the way up to $500 for listing a piece of real estate on eBay. But of course, these fees don't guarantee the client a successful outcome.

NICKELS AND DIMES

Having the lowest percentage commission of all your competition is not your goal. You should always remember that you are a highly skilled and specialized consultant. You bring additional value to the transaction, and if you can net your client more money because of your expertise, the quality of your photos, and your excellent service, the percentage you charge becomes quite irrelevant. Having a good sense of your competition's practices and routinely checking the other shops' rates will empower you with the knowledge you need to be in the ballpark with them. Also, being the lowest-cost Trading Assistant in your market will tend to attract a lower grade of clients. Someone who chooses to go with the cheapest Trading Assistant will be a picky, thrifty individual who will likely also try to nickel-and-dime you to death—asking for even further reductions of your fees.

CLEVER BUT FLAWED

Take your survey of the other Trading Assistants and review it. Do you find their fees confusing or easy to understand? I have found that many stores appear to have low fees, but in the fine print, they charge the client all the eBay and PayPal fees in addition to their commission.

This may appear to be a clever sales practice. A client will believe they are getting a low commission, until they receive their check and realize that the eBay and PayPal fees add up to a rather large bite out of their net proceeds. In the long run, this is probably not the best way to keep good clients coming back.

In considering your commission percentage, you should realize, too, that your average item will be of bread-and-butter quality. Unless you have great luck or tremendous connections, the average person bringing you merchandise will have items valued at between about $50 and $500. We sell a few items here and there for more money—we recently sold a rare photo of Abraham Lincoln for $5,000—but the high-ticket items are fewer and farther between.

★TIP

Many Trading Assistants offer their services to the competition. If you have an area of specialty that your competitor does not, you can help them write a winning description for their auctions and take a fee, either a fixed amount or a percentage of the sale, for helping them evaluate something they aren't familiar with.

"HOW MUCH WILL YOU CHARGE ME?"

In general, you should charge as much for your services as the market will bear. But rates can be adjusted depending upon the amount of business coming in the door. You may have noticed that popular hotels will charge more for busy weekends, holidays, and special events than they normally charge the rest of the year. I once called to book a room at The Venetian Hotel in Las Vegas in connection with one of my eBay speaking engagements, which happened to fall on Valentine's Day. The city was so booked up that The Venetian wanted $900 a night for the room, although I have stayed there many times for as little as $99. I ended up staying at a lowly motel, because I am too proud to pay that much to rest my head. Your fees can also vary depending upon the final price of the sale, your level of expertise in a particular field, and other factors such as your current workload. If you find yourself constantly backed up with weeks of work, as is often the case at my store, you can either raise rates or become more selective about the value of the items you accept for listing.

Nothing should be set in stone, but you do not want to change rates too frequently. I suggest giving your fees much thought, coming up with fair rates that the market can bear, and sticking to them.

Here are some questions to ask yourself:

- Are you offering to sell items for which a special skill or knowledge is required? If so, you can command a higher fee.
- Do you plan to sell vehicles or real estate? Doing so may also require special licenses, and the eBay fees are higher for these types of items. Before establishing your fees, be sure you understand eBay's fees for listing items and PayPal's for receiving payments.
- Will you charge an up-front listing fee for each item you accept? Will that fee be charged only if the client wants to start off the item with a minimum listing price or reserve? Will you refund this fee if the item sells or apply it to the commission?
- Will your commission include eBay and PayPal fees, or will you charge your clients those fees in addition to your commission?
- Will you accept virtually any item, or will you require a minimum item value or other criteria for acceptance?

Because the fees charged by eBay and PayPal may change over time, you should always be sure to keep up-to-date on any changes, to be able to change your rates accordingly.

Flat Fee Finito

I have seen some Trading Assistants charge only a flat fee for each item they list, with no commission at all if it sells. One such company, not far from my store, couldn't make a profit this way and discontinued their operations. I firmly believe that you must share in your clients' success by charging a percentage-based fee. This will give you the incentive to give the time and care appropriate for each item, and hopefully it will also keep your business in the black.

EBAY'S SIDE OF THE COIN

Now let's get a detailed perspective on the costs you will incur when you list an item on eBay. First, for each eBay listing, you will pay eBay a nonrefundable fee called an Insertion Fee, whether or not the item sells (but you will not be billed until after the auction ends). As of this writing, the eBay Insertion Fees for general merchandise (what you will mostly be selling) are between $0.20 and $4.80, depending upon the starting or reserve price of your listing.

An eBay listing that makes available a quantity of identical items, and through which a buyer can purchase any number of the quantity available, is called a Dutch listing. In Dutch auctions, Insertion Fees are based on the opening bid, or starting price, multiplied by the quantity of items. For example, if you list ten identical sterling forks as a Dutch auction, with a starting price of $10 each, your Insertion Fee will be based on a listing with a starting price of $100. But the maximum Insertion Fee for any multiple item Dutch listing never exceeds $4.80.

Listings in which items are sold at a fixed price without bidding are appropriately called Fixed Price listings. The Insertion Fees for Fixed Price listings are based on the set prices of the items.

The Insertion Fee for capital equipment, such as a farm tractor or metalworking machine—anything considered capital equipment—is $20. The Insertion Fee for vehicles is between $3 (for pocket bikes) to as much as $40 for autos. Real estate Insertion Fees are between $35 and $300, depending on the listing format and duration.

In addition to Insertion Fees, eBay charges an additional fee for using a reserve, a protected figure you can place on a listing to prevent it from selling below a set price. For example, you might list a rare sterling pitcher with a $200 reserve but with a $9.99 opening bid, or starting price. Even though the starting price is $9.99, there is no chance that your client's rare piece will sell for that price, or for any amount less than $200. No bidder can have the item until bids reach at least $200. Up to that point, the listing will show "Reserve not met"; when the bidding reaches $200, the listing will read "Reserve met" for the bidders' information. The Reserve Fee can be up to $100 for a single listing of general merchandise and up to $250 for a capital equipment listing. The Reserve Fee is charged only if an item does *not* sell, and this is important to keep in mind when dealing with clients who may want to set unrealistic reserve prices. Remember that, with rare exceptions, your business should be liquidating *unwanted* items, those to which your clients have no emotional or financial attachment.

IN THE GALLERY

You can also add enhancements to your eBay listings to provide more visibility on the eBay site, such enhancements being designed to create more bids and higher sale prices. These listing upgrades cost more, and there are a lot of them. But there is one that I feel is very important and always use—the Gallery feature. The Gallery contains small photos, "thumbnails," one picture for each listing using the enhancement. With Gallery, those searching for or browsing eBay listings will see a catalog-like view of items. This feature only costs $0.35, and I consider it mandatory on every listing. As a buyer on eBay, I do not even click on listings that have not paid for this feature. The Gallery photo allows buyers to see your item and determine immediately if it is what they are seeking, before even going to your listing itself.

If the listing sells successfully, eBay will take an additional fee, called the Final Value Fee, which is a percentage that ranges from 1.5 to 5.25 percent of your item's final sales price.

If you accept PayPal as a method of payment for your listings, you will pay an additional 1.9 to 2.9 percent of your item's final selling price, plus $0.30 per transaction. The rate depends upon your gross monthly volume, with lower rates as your volume increases.

These are just your eBay listing costs and PayPal payment processing fees. Within the fees you charge your clients, you not only have to recover all of these fees but also your overhead, and you need to provide a profit for yourself. Make sure that your rates are sufficient for you to realize the profit margins you deserve—you are providing a valuable service.

To recap the fees you can expect from eBay and PayPal:

- *Insertion Fee.* The cost you pay eBay for your listing, based on the starting or reserve price of your merchandise
- *Listing Upgrade Fees.* The cost you pay for enhancing your listing with special features such as Gallery
- *Final Value Fee.* The percentage of the final sale price or fixed fee you pay to eBay when an item successfully sells. With some types of merchandise, this fee may be a fixed amount or have a cap (e.g., motors, real estate, and capital equipment)
- *PayPal Fee.* The amount you pay to PayPal for receiving money from buyers (buyers do not pay a fee to send money)

Here are the eBay and PayPal sites with their fee information:

- For eBay: *http://pages.ebay.com/help/sell/fees.html*
- For PayPal: *www.paypal.com/us/fees*

$0.99 TO $100

Here is an example of the total of all eBay and PayPal fees you will incur if you successfully sell an item for $100. This example assumes an auction-style listing with a starting price of $0.99, using the Gallery feature, with a winning bidder who pays with PayPal.

Insertion Fee	$0.20
Gallery	$0.35
Final Value Fee	$3.56
PayPal Fee	$3.20
Total Fees	$7.31

The $7.31 in total fees is 7.31 percent of the item's $100 selling price. Keep in mind that in this example the starting price is $0.99, and, therefore, eBay's Insertion Fee is very low. If I were to list the same item at $100 and if it then sold for $100 to one bidder, your Insertion Fee, based on eBay's current fee structure, would be $2.40 instead of $0.20, increasing the total cost of listing and selling this same item to $9.51 or 9.51 percent of the sale value. I can't emphasize enough that clients who insist that you list their items at high starting prices can significantly increase your own costs, while not necessarily changing the outcome of the sale itself.

I believe you can reasonably charge your clients whatever the market will bear. I have seen other Trading Assistants charge fees of up to 50 percent of the final sales price, and clients who gladly pay this rate to get rid of unwanted items. But of course, markets vary, and yours may not bear this rate. In general, though, I think you will find it hard to charge this price for higher-ticket merchandise. I have found that a sliding or graduated scale commission structure makes the most sense, charging lesser percentages for higher-value items.

Ultimately, setting rates is a rather fuzzy mix of math, market research, and gut instinct. You want your clients to feel that they are getting their money's worth for your work. At the same time, I want you to go home every day feeling that you have been paid very well for what you do. You deserve it and should be able to enjoy the fruits of your hard work, expertise, and high-quality services.

YOUR FEES—RECAP

To reiterate key points about how you set and structure your Trading Assistant fees:

- If you do not charge an up-front listing fee for your services, you will attract more clients, but you will also need to be extremely diligent about accepting only items that will sell successfully—at a price that will make you a profit.

- When charging an up-front fee for minimum or reserve price listings, be certain you recover not only your eBay Insertion Fees but at least enough in addition to justify your time spent on unsuccessful listings. Items that don't sell are time bandits, taking you away from other clients for whom you can make successful sales, with a profit for everyone.
- The simpler and easier to understand your fee structure is, the fewer fee-related questions clients will ask. Charging eBay and PayPal fees separately may be logical, but it can easily confuse clients who don't understand these fees.
- If you include all eBay and PayPal fees in your commission, use this as a selling point. On the surface, you may appear to be charging more than the competition, but in reality, you are charging less once you account for the eBay and PayPal fees you are paying out-of-pocket. Be sure you explain this to your clients.
- Try using a graduated commission scale. I charge 38 percent of the first $500, 25 percent of the next $500, and 15 percent of any amount over $1,000 in any single sale.
- Type up your fee structure in a simple, easy-to-understand, single-page format. You can then provide not only a detailed explanation of your services but also of your fees when a client asks about them.
- Remember to publish your current fees on your Web site.
- If you are going to sell vehicles, real estate, or capital equipment, be sure to check your local and state laws first regarding any regulations for sales of these items. You may also want to charge an up-front fee, because the eBay Insertion Fees are substantially higher. Study the fee structure for these items carefully.

Your fees may spark a debate with some clients who feel every business transaction is a negotiation. You may find yourself being questioned or even chided about your fee structure by those who don't understand the work involved in selling for others on eBay. Many will attempt to negotiate down your fees. I can't say that we never negotiate our fees, but rarely do we make concessions. The item in question would have to be a very, very rare piece indeed and/or something of extreme value. In general, stick to your guns and don't cave in.

★TIP

I have found that, if you set a fair fee structure and stick to it, regardless of whom you may lose along the way, you will attract the quality, upscale clients you need. And their referrals will bring you even more fine merchandise.

---

12 CONTRACTS AND OTHER PAPERWORK

One of my clients asked me to sell a 1950s Italian Gamma camera. After doing some research, I knew it was rare and of great value. I listed it at a minimum bid of $0.99 with no reserve. It received several bids immediately but hovered at just over $200 for most of the week. Within the last 30 seconds of the auction, the price escalated rapidly, and it sold for $1,425! I earned $427.50 on the sale, which was my 30 percent commission. After my sixth child was born, and with my Trading Assistant sales growing by leaps and bounds, my husband decided to quit his full-time job and spend more time with the kids. I love the fact that my children have so much more time with their daddy. If I can be a successful eBay seller with six kids running around the house, then anyone can do this.

Teresa D. Bankston, Madison, Mississippi;
eBay user ID "teresab_foundvalue"; trading on eBay since March 24, 2005

Frankly, in my life I've had more than my fair share of legal disputes with people. I've been to court a few times to collect personal and private debts, among other things. But I've been very lucky with my eBay Trading Assistant business—I have never had a legal dispute. Or maybe, to a large degree, I've made my own "luck"—with rock-solid contractual practices.

I feel it is very important, in any business, to formalize agreements between people. There is solid logic here—we all tend to forget things over time, and you will want to avoid the possibility of miscommunication or a misunderstanding at some future date. Because you are a professional Trading Assistant, you fully understand your services and how they work. But your business may be completely novel to someone else, who, even with your clear verbal explanation, may not fully understand all of the obligations of both parties within the transaction. Selling items for others on eBay is a fairly simple process, but it helps to get a formal, written agreement between client and Trading Assistant.

I once had a client who brought us a collection of *Star Trek* memorabilia to sell. We listed all of her items, and virtually all of them sold. Some of the merchandise that had sold was still sitting on our shelves awaiting buyer payment. And one day while I was away, she barreled into the store and frantically demanded of John, my photographer, that he turn over all of the remaining items because she had an important job interview and the prospective employer was a huge *Star Trek* fan. She wanted the items as gifts, to help persuade the employer to hire her. John was so caught off guard by her urgency that he actually did give her the items. And no sooner was she out the door with a box of *Star Trek* collectibles, than John realized to his dismay what he had done. Those items were now the property of a new owner, the eBay buyer, and the client had no right to the memorabilia. We did have a written agreement with the client, which would have legally entitled us to damages for her actions, but our staff was partly to blame. Fortunately, the eBay buyer took the situation in stride and agreed to release us from our obligations. We sent a token payment to the buyer as compensation for their time and trouble.

It's not good enough simply to get someone's signature on a contract; you also have to explain the essence of that agreement and make certain your client fully understands it. A contract is a formalization of an agreement, not just a piece of paper that you hastily sign simply to have a written document.

> **★ TIP**
>
> Contracts should be simple and easy to understand. Avoid complicated language. A contract in plain English is just as binding as a contract with complex and obscure wording—possibly even more so, because the client will have a harder time arguing that they misunderstood the agreement when it is articulated in nonlegalistic language.

DETAILS, DETAILS, DETAILS

There are a couple of ways to go about the process of handling client contracts:

1. Create a single document that serves as an individual item listing agreement
2. Create a master agreement for each client and a separate item submission form for each of their items

If you routinely receive a small number of individual items from one person or company, having an all-in-one document would create the least amount of paperwork for you in the long run. To save more time, you can use no-carbon-required (NCR) paper for your agreements, so that you can quickly hand your client a copy of the contract without having to make a photocopy. If you use a separate item submission form, triplicate works: one copy for your files, one copy for the client, and a copy that can sit on the storage shelf with the item itself until it ships out.

For each client, you should create a folder to be filed alphabetically by last name or company name. If you use separate item submission forms, you can file the master contract in this folder along with one copy each of that client's item submission forms. You should be able to access the master contract and/or an item submission form for any particular client in a matter of seconds if you need to refer to it.

By having the additional copy of the item submission form with the item itself, you can quickly pay your client from this form when the item actually sells and ships.

MAKING IT ROCK SOLID

Contracts are the basis upon which business is conducted, and well-drafted contracts can help avoid unnecessary problems. A contract is created when two or more parties (people or entities, such as a corporation) mutually agree to exchange property (including money) or the promise of future performance. Contracts can be verbal or written, but a verbal agreement is risky, because one or both of the parties may later fail to remember the terms and conditions of the agreement. And a verbal contract may be unenforceable if its terms aren't executed within a specified time (such as one year) or if the agreement involves more than a specified amount of money. In many cases where disputes arise, proving your version of a verbal agreement can be difficult.

Having a good written contract is so important that you will want to hire an attorney to review your contract. I urge you to author the initial draft of your contract yourself, but some legal nuances may require professional wordsmithery by an attorney.

I am deliberately avoiding giving you sample contract language because every state has different laws, and the contract should be reviewed by a competent attorney anyway. The good news is that if you perform your Trading Assistant responsibilities diligently and honestly there is only a remote chance that a legal issue with a client will arise.

Here is an overview of the basic elements of a good contract.

Names

The contract should include the names of each party signing the agreement. Give full names for individuals and proper legal names for organizations (such as an LLC or corporation), for which you should also specify the state within which the organization was formed.

Competence

A contract should only exist between competent parties, and your client should be at least 18 years of age, or the contract may become unenforceable. Your contract should have a space to write down their identification information. You may want to provide a check box on your contract that indicates you verified that your client is at least 18 years of age.

Definition of Terminology

In this section of your agreement, it would be prudent to define any terms that might not be used in everyday language. The term *Trading Assistant* should definitely be defined in your contract. As an example, you may wish to define yourself according to eBay's definition of a Trading Assistant. Trading Assistants are experienced eBay sellers from throughout the eBay user community who sell your items for you for a fee. You may also wish to add to this definition that you provide listing, clerical, and administrative support to the client in order to help them sell their items on eBay.

Obligations

This section of the contract must clearly outline the obligations and expectations of both parties. It should include details such as what services you will perform as the Trading Assistant, the costs of your services if the item sells (and if it does not), and your rights as well as those of the client. You should also specify the time frame within which the obligations are to be performed. Some time frame items can include:

- How long you will be permitted, from the day you receive the item(s), until you must list it on eBay
- How long the item should be listed on eBay (there are one-, three-, five-, seven-, and ten-day listings, as well as longer ones for eBay Stores listings)

- Whether or not you are required or permitted to relist unsold items
- How soon a client must pick up unsold items
- What you will charge for storage if the unsold items are not picked up promptly (you do not want to offer unlimited and indefinite free storage)
- If items are not picked up after a specified period, how you can dispose of them (donate to charity, etc.)

Try to think through every possible scenario. Much of what is important in your agreement will become clearer as you actually start to list items as a Trading Assistant. Even having read this book, no doubt you will learn something from trial and error. My foremost problem when starting out was the issue of unclaimed unsold items. Most unwanted merchandise really is unwanted. Paying for actual storage is expensive, and some clients will have no problem using your store as a free, secure storage facility if they can. In my agreement, I give my clients seven days from the date their listing ends on eBay until I have the right to donate the unsold item to charity. Before I added this clause to my agreement, there were items remaining in my store for months on end despite phone calls and reminder letters.

Force Majeure

This section of your contract provides you with partial or total excuse from performance of your Trading Assistant obligations as a result of acts of God (earthquake, hurricane, etc.). Such clauses are common in contacts and referred to as force majeure.

Liquidated Damages

In the event that either party fails to perform their responsibilities in the agreement, this section will serve to define the consequences for that nonperformance. The amount of damages can be defined in advance when actual losses may be hard to determine. For example, if you have sold an item that was not stored on your premises, and the client is unable or unwilling to deliver the item to you for shipping, your contract can call for liquidated damages equal to three times the current market value of the highest-priced eBay sale for the same item. This is just a hypothetical example to give you an idea, not necessarily the actual language you will use.

Jurisdiction

When you are doing business with clients who may not be located in the same state as you, or if they are on the other end of the state and your state is a big one, you will want to determine where disputes will be settled. The jurisdiction clause should specify which state's laws will govern the dispute and the location in which the dispute will be settled (where the parties are to appear in the event of a dispute, such as Los Angeles County, etc.).

Legality and Severability

Naturally, for your contract to be enforceable, it must be legal. If any portion of your contract is found to be illegal, the entire contract may be null and void, unless you provide language that states that any such provisions will become severable. This means that a clause in your contract would specify that any portion of the contract deemed to be unenforceable would not affect the validity of the rest of the contract.

Arbitration Clause

Arbitration is a less formal way to resolve legal disputes than using the courts, and arbitration does not necessarily require attorneys' involvement. Arbitration procedures are much less formal than those in court, and the costs are far less. Because Trading Assistant work is fairly simple, a clause making arbitration an option would be advisable. However, more complex disputes are more difficult to arbitrate.

Attorney's Fees

If you wish to recover your attorney's fees and costs as the prevailing party in a dispute, your contract will most likely need a provision for this. In most states, you cannot recover these fees unless your contract specifies it.

Personal Guarantee

If any party to your agreement is not an individual person, you may wish to indicate whether you want the individual officer(s) of the organization(s) (corporation, LLC, etc.) to be personally responsible as well. If so, you will require that all parties sign both in their capacity for the organization and personally. Normally, however, this is to be avoided, because one of the purposes of most organizations is to shield the principals from personal liability.

I suggest that you take a first crack at your contract by typing up the above sections yourself. If you are planning to use a separate item submission form, be sure that this document states that it is a master agreement that will govern the submission of items using these individual forms. Once you have a first draft of your agreement, you can run it by an attorney, who can then make any necessary modifications. Generating the first draft of the contract yourself will make the attorney's task much faster and less expensive. I caution you not to simply write up a contract and start using it without first having it reviewed by a legal professional. There is never a substitute for qualified legal advice. If you can't presently afford an attorney, you may have to start off with verbal agreements backed up by a simple written item submission form that defines your terms as clearly and completely as possible. If you are opening a drop-off store, however, you really should budget for an attorney, because the stakes will be much higher than if you work from home or do Trading Assistant work part-time.

ITEM SUBMISSION FORM

As noted earlier, your item submission form and contract can be one document. This would work best if you normally receive a small number of items from each client. If you expect to be handling lots of items from individual clients, a separate form for each item may be helpful. If you have huge numbers of items being listed for individual clients, you may also want to have an item submission form that covers multiple item submissions.

The item submission form should contain this basic information:

- The date that the item was submitted
- The client's full legal name or company name
- The client's address (for correspondence and payments)
- The client's telephone number
- The client's identification information (such as driver's license or state identification card number)
- A check box that indicates you have verified your client's age (as being 18 or over)
- A space to describe briefly the item that you are accepting
- The minimum agreed-upon starting price (or reserve price) for the item
- The type of listing you will be creating (auction-style or buy-it-now)
- The fee you are charging for accepting the item (if you charge a fee up front)
- The fee you will charge if the item sells successfully
- Some brief terms and conditions (how soon the item must be picked up if not sold, etc.)

You can create your item submission form using a word processor or spreadsheet program. It doesn't need to be fancy. You can also try one of the many form creation software packages on the market. You can find plenty of them by searching the keyword forms at *www.down load.com*. You can use your own printer to create copies of the form, or your local commercial printer can print them in triplicate with NCR paper, as discussed earlier.

Because the submission form contains everything you need to know to pay your client, it's also a quick way to handle your accounting at the end of the sale. You can lay out the form in such a way that the client's name and address will show through a standard window envelope when folded into thirds like a letter. This way, you can stuff that extra copy of your submission form into an envelope along with a check, speeding payment to your client.

TESTIMONIALS—HIGH-OCTANE FUEL

Testimonials are a powerful way to convince prospective clients to use your services. Initially there will be few, but as your business grows, so will the potential for gathering compelling client testimonials about your high-quality work and services.

To solicit glowing client testimonials, you can create a simple letter:

Thank you very much for your business. We truly appreciate your giving us the opportunity to serve you, and we would be very grateful for your help in spreading the word about what we do. We would like to get your comments about our company's services. Please tell us what you think by writing your comments in the blank space at the bottom of this letter. Can we also have your permission to quote your comments and use them as part of our testimonials? If so, please simply say so at the end of your comments. As a token of our appreciation for providing us with your feedback, we would be delighted to give you one free listing just for responding.

Warmest regards,
Christopher Matthew Spencer

A form letter similar to this should be included with every client payment. Over time, you will build a huge library of testimonials that you can use for your Web site, printed literature, and even when asking banks for additional loans. Be sure to include a self-addressed, stamped envelope if you expect to get a response. You can also direct clients to fax the form back, so be sure to include your fax number as well.

Testimonials are one of the most compelling and effective forms of advertising ever. And very few clients will turn you down when you ask to print their words on your marketing messages. Most individuals will feel honored to be included. Your testimonials will have much more credibility if the client will grant permission to use their full name as well as their city; they no doubt would be pleased to have their Web site address included if they, too, run a business. You can see the mutual benefits of a testimonial such as this:

I was astonished! I turned my entire excess inventory over to the folks at XYZ Company, and they turned it all into cash in less than two weeks! I received a check for more than two times the amount I was offered for the same items by a local liquidator.

John Doe, Sioux Falls, South Dakota (*www.johndoeautoparts.com*)

You can correct any spelling or grammatical errors, but don't polish or edit the testimonials you receive. Let them speak for themselves.

★TIP

When you are new in business, until you build your list of clients, you can seek out testimonials from friends and colleagues who can speak about your honesty and integrity.

PUTTING THE CARDS ON THE TABLE

One of the most common questions you will be asked from day to day will be, "How much do you charge?"

Having a simple printed rate sheet that quickly explains what you do and how much you charge for doing it will help:

> Thank you for your interest in our services. We are eBay Trading Assistants, and we help you sell your high-quality, unwanted items on eBay. We specialize in selling antiques, cameras, car parts, and electronics, but we can help you sell anything of value on eBay. We will handle all of the work, including photography, listing, storage, shipping, and accounting. All you have to do is drop off your items, and we'll do the rest! Our fees are based on the final selling price of your item. Here is a chart of how much we charge for our services . . .

Most people have rather short attention spans. You are catering to busy, upscale people, and you want to get your information across quickly, so keep the text of your rate sheet nice and lean—don't overdo it. Include your name, address, telephone number, Web site address, and hours of operation on the document. Don't forget to specify whether you include all eBay and PayPal fees in your fee or charge them separately. You might also want to include a few of your strongest testimonials on your rate sheet—but keep it trim!

TO THE LETTER

I have already suggested a form letter for soliciting testimonials. No doubt there will be other times when you will communicate with clients, and it's a good idea to save this correspondence in a folder on your personal computer, for reference and repurposing.

Some of my clients don't have e-mail, and many are slow to respond to phone calls. The latter is natural: they are busy people—that's why they called on me to handle their eBay sales in the first place. Communication with such clients can be challenging, but nevertheless you will need a quick way to get additional information from your clients, update them, and inform them of your actions or decisions.

Letters you may want to develop immediately include:

- Request for additional information on an item (provenance, original cost, certificate of authenticity, chain of title or ownership, etc.)
- Request to your client for a lower minimum bid price or reserve (when you feel, after further research, that their original price is unrealistic)
- Notice of delay in listing their item (if the item requires additional research or for some other reason)
- Request that a client pick up their unsold items, with a deadline and a reminder of your company's policy regarding unsold merchandise unclaimed after the deadline (donate to charity, discard, etc.)
- Notification of delay in making a payment (due to a customer service problem, buyer return of merchandise, or other reason)
- Notice to a client that their item is prohibited for sale on eBay and therefore cannot be listed

Incorporate your letterhead into the document so that your company's logo and contact information appears. For information on business correspondence formatting, go to *www.writing-business-letters.com*.

Personalize your form letters by typing in your clients' names and addresses in the proper business letter format and by adding a few personalized words pertinent to the specific client. You want to connect with each client, making sure they feel like a person, not a number.

13 TECHNOLOGY

A client brought us an advertising handbill for a 1967 concert featuring Jefferson Airplane and the Grateful Dead, which was held in Toronto. It measured a mere 4 inches by 7 inches. We received 13 bids and ended up selling it for $4,057.53—for one little piece of paper!

Kevin McGinnis, Berkeley, California;
eBay user ID "pictureitsold"; trading on eBay since July 19, 2003

It might seem a contradiction, because eBay itself is so technology-rich, but I think of an eBay Trading Assistant business as a fairly low-tech proposition. A plethora of software, services, and equipment are available to operate an eBay-related business. But though much of it could indeed make your life easier, be cautious—many of these products and services are designed primarily to make their inventors wealthier. An eBay Trading Assistant business can be operated entirely without any additional software. For instance, if you use the item submission forms discussed in Chapter 12, you can easily track hundreds of items a month manually without complex or expensive software programs.

I have been a Trading Assistant for many years now, and have never used a third-party software application other than that offered directly by eBay. The software I use to manage my eBay listings is called Blackthorne Pro (formerly Seller's Assistant Pro), and in 2004 I was granted the honor of creating and hosting all the official eBay online training videos for their seller tools.

The temptation to keep changing and upgrading software is a time bandit, eventually leading to your being in the software learning business instead of the eBay selling business. Your goal is to spend your entire time acquiring new clients and selling their items, and if you can stay organized, you will be able to keep your technology requirements simple.

You should plan your technology requirements carefully, before spending money on them. This is particularly true of software. I never buy any software program until I have fully tested it. Most software manufacturers offer a free trial, and I maintain that if you can't try it, don't buy it! And I never implement any new technology into my actual business until it has been tested in a nonoperational environment. We call this our beta testing process. If you have employees, any technology changes you make will cost you even more money because of the additional training required to get the staff up to speed.

YOUR TECHNOLOGY TOOLBOX

Basic equipment you will need:

- Modern computer system (with an Internet connection)
- Printer
- Copier
- Scanner
- Digital camera
- Tripod (optional)
- Backdrop or background for photography
- Photo lighting equipment

Things you may want:

- Shipping software for each shipping company you use (United Parcel Service, U.S. Postal Service, etc.)
- A shipping scale that "speaks" to the above software, automatically entering the weight of your parcels
- A label printer for printing shipping labels (oh so handy!)
- More advanced lighting equipment
- Internet telephone service (Voice over IP or VoIP)

I could devote an entire book to technology and equipment, but what really matters is that you are comfortable using it. And equipment for your Trading Assistant business doesn't need to be expensive. I have purchased a lot of my office equipment used on eBay, but be wary of buying personal computers or printers used—both of these become obsolete fairly quickly, and purchasing them used is really false economy with the vast array of low-cost new options available.

COMPUTER ANALYSIS

Hopefully, you already have a computer and don't have to invest in a new one. You can use an older computer to run your business. The shipping computer we use for preparing our parcels is a five-year-old laptop that I used for presentations as a speaker for eBay and then re-purposed for shipping tasks because it still works great. Most of the computers we use for listing items on eBay are not new, either. In selecting a computer for use on eBay, whether it's new or used, you may want to determine first if you will be listing items directly on eBay without the aid of additional software. If so, any Internet-ready computer should be fine for your purposes. A more powerful computer will probably only benefit you if you want to use high-powered software, such as certain photo-editing programs. We do virtually no editing at our company, because we shoot eBay-ready photos and do not retouch our images. And the reality is that, for listing on eBay, the speed of a computer is really moot. You won't benefit greatly from a superfast computer, simply because the speed of your Internet connection will be far more important in terms of your efficiency.

There is no reason to buy a new computer if you have a perfectly good one that does everything you need. Lots of nontechie people are duped into thinking that they have to spend thousands to get a computer that will do basic tasks such as browsing the Internet or authoring documents. I suggest making do with what you have until it no longer serves your purposes. Don't feel pressured to constantly upgrade.

But if you do need to buy a new computer, I would strongly suggest that it be a Windows-based machine. I know that Apple makes fine computers that are aesthetically pleasing and work wonderfully—but the reality is that most business software applications are written for computers that use a Windows operating system. And if you are planning to use any of the software that eBay provides for listing items, it only works on Windows machines. (I am just the messenger—don't shoot me!)

★ TIP

Set a budget and determine what computer features and software you will need for your Trading Assistant business—this will help you define what you want and need for your system. If you will need Quickbooks or Quicken accounting software, for instance, you might look for a system with this software already installed. Most systems do not include the pricy Microsoft Office programs, and you will want to have word processing and spreadsheet functionality on your machine.

With every passing day, computers become cheaper and more powerful. Recently, I saw an ad for Dell computers in which they offered a brand new system with a 17-inch flat panel monitor for under $400. At this writing, I would certainly not spend much more than $1,000, which should buy you a top-of-the-line machine for your eBay business. The last two computers I purchased for my business were both under $500, with a monitor. Because we really don't need tremendous computing power, these machines served our purposes well.

Another consideration might be a desktop replacement—the laptop. Many computer users are buying widescreen laptops instead of desktops, because they are extremely powerful and portable. Most laptops will work splendidly in your office environment and can be taken with you when you are traveling. I caution you to keep backups of your important files if you do go laptop, because a stolen or dropped laptop can mean the end of all your precious data if no copy is stored securely somewhere else.

TIPS ON BUYING

Your computer's processor, the part that does the work, is important. You'll want to buy a computer with an Intel Pentium 4, Intel Pentium D, or AMD Athlon 64-bit processor. The Athlon 64-bit processor will support the newest version of 64-bit Windows and thus would be a sound choice if you plan to upgrade to this new Windows version. When buying a Pentium 4 computer, look for one with Hyperthreading Technology (HT), because this is a true multitasking computer processor, better designed to handle multiple software tasks simultaneously. Pentium D processors have dual computing cores and will handle your computing tasks fast as well.

Here's a quick check list of things to look for when comparing computer brands and features:

- *Processor.* Pentium 4, Pentium D, or AMD Athlon 64-bit
- *Processor speed.* 2GHz or higher
- *Front-side bus.* 800MHz or higher
- *Memory.* 1 gigabyte (GB) or higher
- *Hard drive space.* 60GB or higher (the bigger the better if you plan to have a lot of images stored on your computer)
- *Networking.* 10/100 or 10/100/1000 base (using category 5 cable). Wireless networking is fine for browsing and sharing on the Internet, however, the current 802.11g networking products do not provide the capability to move large amounts of data quickly through the air. If you are networking your eBay listing software or planning to transfer large numbers of images via your wireless network, you will want to look into the new 802.11n networking products, which can achieve speeds up to five times faster than the older "g" networking products
- *Modem.* Only if you plan to use a dial-up connection or computer faxing—otherwise skip it
- *Speakers.* Optional but nice to have and very cheap
- *Monitor.* Flat panel (don't waste money on older CRTs—thrift stores don't even accept them as donations anymore)

- *Optical drives.* Try to get a dual drive, one DVD reader and one DVD/CD burner—helpful if you need to make large file backups
- *Media readers.* Depending on your camera, you will find it helpful to have a computer with a built-in media card reader that will accept the type of media card your camera uses—saving your camera batteries and allowing you to work with picture files while still using your camera for other things
- *Sound card.* The built-in sound cards for most computers are perfectly fine, unless you are a serious audiophile and plan to use this computer for multimedia and games—but you need a business computer, right?
- *Ports.* You will want the fast Universal Serial Bus (USB) version 2.0, because most up-to-date external peripherals use it
- *Mouse.* Always select an optical mouse, because a cheaper mechanical mouse gets "gunked" up fast and will need regular cleaning
- *Keyboard.* Your computer's keyboard is important because you'll be using it a lot. If you are a fast typist as I am, you will want a keyboard that has a great tactile feel. The keyboards sold bundled with most computers are not very good, and I suggest looking at spending an additional (small) amount on a better one. Test drive a lot of keyboards before you decide—pamper your fingers with the best one you can find

Regarding computer brands, I always prefer to buy preconfigured systems from major manufacturers. They are nearly always cheaper than building your own computer and many of the bigger companies offer customization when you are ordering a system anyway. Avoid buying a lot of unnecessary software and hardware add-ons that you aren't sure you will need. I won't recommend specific brands because everyone has their preferences, but a major company will stand by its products, and most computers will perform reliably for a long time.

When pondering an extended warranty or service plan, consider the added cost carefully. In all my years of owning computers, nothing has gone wrong except for a couple of faulty power supplies and one bad hard drive. Largely because they have moving parts, power supplies and hard drives can fail, but only rarely. For the most part, unless you have a lot of power surges in your area, you should never have a problem. Getting a good surge suppressor would be smart if you expect lots of lightning storms or inconsistent power. If you back up your data regularly, you can consider extended service plans a luxury and avoid them. They are pricey, and if anything goes wrong with a computer, it will usually present itself within the manufacturer's warranty period.

SURFING THE WORLD WIDE WEB

You will be spending much of your time online, and you always need to have the absolute fastest Internet connection that you can reasonably afford. The cliché "time is money" is incredibly relevant to the use of the Internet as a business tool. Each minute you waste waiting for a slow Internet connection is time you could be spending on other profit-making tasks. Even if fast Internet is costly, it's worth it! When I first started selling on eBay in the late 1990s, broadband (fast) Internet was just becoming available in my area. The fastest Internet connection I could obtain from my phone company was $179 a month—and I gladly paid it! Today, you can get blazing Internet speeds for prices ranging from $30 to $60 a month, with the higher end of the price range providing speeds that were once available only to big corporations spending hundreds or even thousands a month.

GETTING CONNECTED

There are many ways to connect to the Internet. The primary ways for a small business are analog, ISDN (faster analog), DSL, and cable. Analog connections to the Internet, including ISDN (integrated services digital network), require dial-up access over a telephone line. This means that the true cost of using analog Internet access is higher than just the cost of the Internet service—you have to tie up a phone line, and pay for it, too. And you can't receive telephone calls on that line while you are online—very inconvenient!

DSL and cable modem services are permanent connections to the Internet that are always on, which means no chance of losing your Internet connection due to bad telephone connections or someone picking up an extension telephone in your home or office. These services provide immediate Internet access without having to dial a phone number. DSL and cable services are both broadband connections and are substantially faster than analog services. They used to be much more expensive than they are now, but competition has made digital broadband a viable option for small businesses.

The following are summaries of each kind of Internet connection:

- *Analog.* Good old dial-up! It's fine for sending e-mail, and it's pretty cheap, too, but for sending and receiving files such as pictures, it's the pits. You will quickly begin to hate your dial-up connection, because it has so much in common with molasses—it's extremely slow. The only advantage of dial-up is that you can use it anywhere: on the road, in hotels. But with the growing prevalence of wireless broadband Internet hot spots across the country and broadband in virtually all hotels (free in many), dial-up is a dinosaur. Forget it!
- *ISDN.* An ISDN is about twice as fast as dial-up and is available throughout most of the country. This is the service of last resort if you cannot obtain DSL or cable in your area. It works on a telephone line in the same way as dial-up, and it's relatively inexpensive.
- *DSL.* DSL provides extremely fast connectivity over an ordinary phone line with a special modem that allows use of the phone and the Internet simultaneously. DSL is a great way to get superfast Internet service without having to add additional wiring to your home or office. DSL can reach speeds more than 140 times faster than dial-up. And DSL has become inexpensive. If you are no more than 18,000 feet (3.4 miles) from the phone company's offices, you can probably get it. Rural telephone customers may be unable to obtain the service, but most everyone else has access to DSL these days. DSL comes in a few flavors: ADSL (the most common) allows you to download faster than you can upload.

This is an ideal service for people who are browsing the Internet, and I use it at my office. SDSL has the same upload and download capabilities, possibly useful if you expect to be uploading huge volumes of data such as images. But if you are not uploading a lot beyond your eBay auctions, SDSL is not really worth the added expense. Check the rates with your local provider (usually the phone company).

- *Cable.* Cable Internet is provided by your local cable television provider. Therefore, residential neighborhoods will usually have a higher availability of this type of service than commercial areas. Theoretically, cable is capable of much higher speeds than DSL, but it is a shared connection with other users on the cable network, which means its speed can depend on how many people are using the network at the same time. This is rarely an issue, but it can come up.

There are other ways to connect to the Internet, such as through a satellite dish, but if you can get it, DSL will be your best bet. It's a totally dedicated circuit and will provide you with consistent high speeds and reliable service. Do everything in your power to get a broadband connection—it will have you speeding around eBay.

One thing to remember about all permanent Internet connections, such as DSL and cable, is that they can make your computer vulnerable to attacks from hackers. It will be necessary to make sure that you have an Internet firewall (discussed later in this chapter) on at all times to prevent unwanted people from accessing your computer.

DIAL-UP—THEN THE EARTH COOLED

This chapter is pretty darn long, but I want to mention the tremendous value of Internet telephone services. Vonage (*www.vonage.com*) is an extremely cool tool that I use to make telephone calls via the Internet. Vonage sends you a special router that integrates your Internet connection and a standard telephone. For a low monthly fee (currently $24.99) you can make unlimited calls anywhere in the United States and Canada with no additional charges. International calls cost pennies. The call quality is outstanding, but if you have poor Internet connectivity, you may experience some erratic quality, and you really will need a broadband Internet connection to get the most from this service. Check with Vonage to see if it is available in your area code.

Lots of other Internet telephone providers are on the market, including an eBay company called Skype (*www.skype.com*). Skype is a small software program with which, after downloading and installing it on your computer, you use a headset or special telephone device to make calls. Using Skype is a bit more complex, because it's similar to using a chat service. After signing up for the service (which is free), you can call others on the Internet by knowing their e-mail address or Skype user ID. Calls to other Skype members are 100 percent free, and calls to conventional telephone numbers cost pennies. I love Skype for talking to customers across the globe. To make totally free calls, the person you're calling does have to be online and signed into their Skype account. Skype's partners are regularly coming out with new Skype-compatible telephones and other devices, and it's fast becoming a popular way to communicate.

NAVIGATION TOOLS

Microsoft's Internet Explorer (IE) is the world's dominant browser, used by just about everyone on the Internet. The reason is simple—IE is embedded in the Windows operating system. I find that the browser does the job of surfing the Internet quite well. Some eBay features, such as their Picture Services, with which you can crop, rotate, and enhance your photos directly on the eBay site, will only work with IE.

Even so, I prefer to use a free browser called Firefox (*www.mozilla.org*) that was developed by some very bright programmers who believe that people should have an alternative to IE. The feature I like best about Firefox is a unique system of "tabs" that allows you to open multiple Web sites without having to open new windows, as with IE. With Firefox, you can quickly navigate among multiple sites without closing or opening windows, and I find this feature very handy when using eBay, PayPal, and other sites I need all at the same time. Also, it's generally believed that Firefox is a more secure browser than IE, with better defenses against Internet security threats.

SLAMMING THE DOOR ON NOSY PEOPLE

A firewall protects your computer from Internet outlaws who may be trying to ruin your day. Some of these pesky hackers roam the Internet doing wrong just for fun, but many will try to steal your passwords so they can hijack your eBay, PayPal, or other secure accounts. Having a firewall installed on your computer will prevent unauthorized access.

I have used my laptop computer, using a shared network, on planes and in hotels countless times, and I am always amused when I can "see" the contents of other people's computers—they aren't using a firewall. When you are online without the protection of a firewall, you allow the world to see inside your computer.

There are almost as many firewall programs on the market as there are fish in the sea, but before you spend any money, be aware that Windows XP has a handy firewall utility built into the operating system—all you have to do is turn it on. So if your operating system is XP, you are married to Windows—and you might as well love the one you're with!

INTERNET EXTERMINATORS

In the early days of Windows and the Internet, most people purchased antivirus software to help protect computers from infiltration by malicious scripts and programs. These programs are written by hackers, jokers, and fraudsters who create them to do harm, but usually with no apparent motive other than to piss us all off.

These days, it is typical to install a complete Internet security suite that contains many tools to help prevent these programs from finding their unwelcome way onto your computer. Currently I use eTrust Internet Security on my office computers.

Take some time to review the features of these programs before making a purchase. Here is a list of the most popular security suites:

- BitDefender Internet Security: *www.bitdefender.com*
- eTrust Internet Security Suite: *www.ca.com*
- F-Secure Internet Security: *http://f-secure.com*
- McAfee Internet Security Suite: *www.mcafee.com*
- Norton Internet Security: *http://symantec.com*
- Panda Platinum Internet Security: *www.pandasoftware.com*
- PC-cillin Internet Security: *www.trendmicro.com*
- ZoneAlarm Security Suite: *www.zonelabs.com*

GOODBYE SPIES

Spyware is software that covertly mines user information through an Internet connection, usually for advertising purposes. Spyware applications often piggyback on freeware or shareware applications that you may have downloaded. Once spyware makes its way onto your computer, it can secretly monitor your activity and transmit your personal information, such as e-mail addresses, login information, credit card numbers, or bank accounts, to someone else.

Spyware can be introduced into your computer through e-mail or when you are browsing Web sites. Sometimes, these programs reside on removable media when you share files with someone else; therefore, it is important to have antispyware software installed on your computer. Currently, I use Microsoft's Windows AntiSpyware on my office computers.

Here is a list of popular antispyware programs on the market:

- Aluria Anti-Spyware: *www.aluriasoftware.com*
- Microsoft Windows Defender: *www.microsoft.com*
- NOD32 Antivirus System: *www.eset.com*
- Outpost Firewall Pro: *www.agnitum.com*
- SpyCatcher: *www.tenebril.com*
- Spy Sweeper: *www.webroot.com*

- Spyware Doctor: *www.pctools.com*
- Trend Micro Anti-Spyware: *www.trendmicro.com*
- ZeroSpyware: *www.zerospyware.com*

EVERYBODY LOVES FREEBIES

I love free stuff. Maybe it's genetics, because my mother grew up during the Great Depression, but I am by nature an enthusiastic cheapo. And there is a vast community of software programmers who love to create fantastic software and give it away for free. Many of these individuals and companies make their money by providing support for their free products, but a lot of them just design software because of their passion for their art.

OpenOffice.org

OpenOffice.org (*www.openoffice.org*) is a free, multiplatform (works with more than one operating system) office suite program that's compatible with other major office suites such as the dominant Microsoft Office. This is useful, because with OpenOffice.org, you can author and view all of the same files that are created in Microsoft Office without paying Microsoft's hefty price tag. OpenOffice.org creates and edits documents, spreadsheets, presentations, Web documents, and graphics. If you plan to purchase a new computer, try to avoid paying for an office suite and download OpenOffice.org instead.

IrfanView

IrfanView (*www.irfanview.com*) is a small, freeware graphic viewer and editing program. Although it's not a full substitute for the expensive but feature-loaded Photoshop program, it accomplishes all the picture manipulation tasks you'll probably need as an eBay user. Working with pictures in IrfanView, you can rotate, crop, resize, adjust color and brightness/contrast, and more. My favorite IrfanView feature is the batch conversion function. The program will allow you to change a large group of files at once (be sure you make copies first!). I find this very helpful, because, for instance, I can quickly resize hundreds of image files with a few mouse clicks. IrfanView also plays movies, enables scanning and printing, and converts files from a large number of supported formats. It's a very handy tool to have on your computer.

SUPERCHARGE YOUR BUSINESS

Listing tools are designed to help you put items on eBay faster. eBay provides some great free tools, and numerous commercial listing tools are available from third parties as well. Software can be either a great ally or a tremendous burden. If you struggle when learning new software and are listing only a few items at a time, then a manual system may be the best solution for you. Before eBay (or anyone else) had auction and listing tools, I managed my business for the first couple of years with no such software, and I was able to pay clients accurately and efficiently using a manual system. It was extremely tedious and time consuming, however, so if your listings come more than a handful at a time, I strongly suggest using software. And if you are running a big business (I mean really big), a software solution will be mandatory because of the large volume of data you will be processing.

The eBay tools described below can be found at *http://pages.ebay.com/ sell/tools.html*.

Blackthorne Basic

You can download and install this software program from eBay to your computer. It is designed for small to medium sellers, who will be able to do the following with it:

- Create and edit listings in bulk
- Use free eBay Listing Designer templates (a nice feature and a savings over that on eBay's Web site)

- Create templates to automate data entry and listing format/design
- Automate relisting of large numbers of items
- Track sales
- Automate e-mail and feedback
- Export sales data
- Permanently archive sales data

The program has a 30-day free trial and thereafter costs $9.99 per month.

Blackthorne Pro

This program is the more enhanced version of eBay's Blackthorne product and is designed for higher-volume sellers. It is a complex program, but in many way, it's designed to help Trading Assistants run their businesses. This program has all the functions of the basic version plus these additional features:

- Consignment sales management (this is the primary reason to have this program)
- Product inventory management (you will need this!)
- Free scheduled listings (save $0.10—eBay's charge—on every scheduled listing, adding up to big bucks over time)
- Bulk printing of invoices and shipping labels
- Profit and loss as well as sales tax collection reporting
- Support for multiple users and multiple eBay user IDs

Blackthorne Pro is free for 30 days and costs $24.99 per month thereafter. Before you spend hours trying out different software solutions, I suggest you consider Blackthorne Pro. It's not easy to learn, especially for a computer novice, but once you master its steep learning curve, the program will manage your entire eBay Trading Assistant business. From personal experience, I can tell you that neither of the Blackthorne products works well on older computers, because the programs are resource and memory hogs. You will need a computer with a fast processor and lots of memory (at least 1GB) to get the best possible experience from this software.

Selling Manager

A supercharged version of the My eBay feature, this online program provided by eBay allows sellers to organize and track their listings better. The program shows the status of your sales so that you can manage payments, shipping, and feedback more efficiently. It provides e-mail and feedback templates, bulk relisting, invoices and shipping labels, and downloadable sales history reports; and it allows you to process unpaid items and feedback in bulk. It has a 30-day free trial and costs $4.99 per month thereafter. It comes free with your subscription to either Blackthorne product and with a basic eBay Store subscription. There is no software to download, and you can access this program from any Internet computer.

Selling Manager Pro

This program has all of the same great features as Selling Manager and adds inventory management, listing statistics, additional reporting, and free listing designer templates for dressing up your listings. With this program, you can fully automate e-mails and feedback, and it allows you to set automatic relisting rules for your item inventory. Entirely Web-based like Selling Manager, it also has a free 30-day trial and costs $15.99 per month thereafter. The program is free when you have a Fetured or Anchor eBay Store subscription. Because both Selling Manager products work entirely online, they work well with older computer systems.

Turbo Lister

eBay's free bulk listing tool is an application you download and install on your computer. It is not a listing management program; rather, it is designed to help you create listing templates and bulk load items, and it's ideal for anyone wanting to sell quantities of the same product. With the templates it lets you create, Turbo Lister stores information so that you can avoid repetitive data entry tasks. It won't handle consignment equations, but if you sell media in quantity (books, videos, etc.) Turbo Lister allows you to quickly enter thousands of items by author, title, ISBN number, or UPC code, using eBay's prefilled item catalogs. For media sellers, this program is an extreme time saver. Plus, if you add a bar code scanner, listing these items will be incredibly fast, because you can scan the bar code on the book, video, or other supported item directly into the program. This program's templates can be handy for sellers listing many products for the same person or for lower-volume Trading Assistants. It can be used effectively in conjunction with eBay's online Selling Manager programs to both list and manage your sales. Turbo Lister works very well on older machines because it doesn't require a lot of processor speed or memory, and it works well with dial-up Internet connections because you can work offline.

If you want to consider third-party products or services to help with your sales on eBay, visit *http://solutions.ebay.com* to browse the offerings of various Certified Providers. These companies' products are designed to help high-volume sellers with listing and post-sales management, and you should browse this rapidly changing directory for software designed specifically for Trading Assistants. Always request a trial version of any software or a trial password for any online solution before you sign a contract or make a commitment. Third parties charge for their services in a variety of ways, including subscription fees, percentages, and per-transaction fees, and these fees are in addition to your eBay and PayPal fees. If you decide on a third-party tool, you will need to do some math, add these fees to your profit projections, and update your business plan accordingly.

A plethora of other software is available to help you with your eBay Trading Assistant business. eBay publishes a directory containing many of these solutions. Because the universe of software designed to help Trading Assistants is expanding rapidly, it would be a good idea before you buy to evaluate solutions from the directory and perhaps post questions on eBay's Community Boards (*www.ebay.com/community*) to solicit feedback from other eBay members.

★TIP

A really cool do-it-yourself application called Contribute 3 for eBay can be purchased from Macromedia (*www.macromedia.com*). This software has helped many novice computer users design award-winning eBay Stores, and it only costs $99. If you prefer, you can delegate your Store design to a third-party company such as Pixclinic (*www.pixclinic.com*), which charges fees based on your specifications and needs.

A SHIPPER'S BEST FRIENDS

If you are a low-volume Trading Assistant, you can use eBay's shipping system, which is integrated with PayPal. When your item sells successfully on eBay, a link on the listing will appear that enables you to print a shipping label for either UPS or the U.S. Postal Service. The label will print directly on plain paper, and you can then apply it to your parcel. If you do not have a daily UPS pickup, which carries an additional charge, you can drop your UPS parcels off at any nearby UPS location, UPS store, or UPS authorized shipping outlet. You can save a tremendous amount of time with your U.S. Postal Service parcels by arranging a carrier pick-up on their Web site—your regular postal carrier will pick up all of your mail without additional cost. (Wondering how you can get insurance for your parcels and still have a pick-up? See below.) Both services will conveniently deduct the shipping fees directly from your PayPal account!

I use UPS WorldShip software (*http://ups.com*), available free by calling 800-742-5877. This handy program will print shipping labels on a variety of printers and works in real time with many different shipping scales. I bought my label printer on eBay for under $50 and found a high-quality surplus scale for under $30. The UPS customer service representatives can help you with a list of supported label printers and scales, and then you can hunt for them on eBay. I use an Eltron printer (now owned by Zebra) and a Fairbanks scale. Be sure to check model numbers on the compatible list of supported devices before buying a printer or scale. For the supported printers, UPS also provides free labels that you can order on their Web site (registration is required).

For my shipments through the U.S. Postal Service, I use DAZzle software by Envelope Manager Software (*http://endicia.com*). DAZzle makes preparing your U.S. Postal Service shipments much easier, and it supports the same printers used by UPS WorldShip, so you can print labels for both services on the same label stock. Because parcels insured by the Postal Service require a visit to the long lines at the post office and preclude carrier pick-ups, their insurance is not a cost-effective option for Trading Assistants. DAZzle has its own insurance, however, so that you can insure your parcels at your place of business, even with U.S. Postal Service carrier pick-ups.

IMAGE IS EVERYTHING

A digital camera is a must, and ultimately this may be your single most expensive purchase (assuming you already own a computer). Keep in mind that digital cameras come in all sorts of flavors, sizes, resolutions, and prices. We have been in business selling on the Internet since 1998, and we have always used a standard point-and-shoot, consumer-grade digital camera. We have tried digital single lens reflex (SLR), professional grade cameras but found them heavy and difficult to use. You are not shooting for the cover of *Vogue*—you simply need clear, well-lit, and in-focus pictures of your items. If you browse eBay for a few minutes and study the listings, you will see that the vast majority of sellers have pictures that are not professional looking or particularly excellent.

This doesn't mean that your pictures can't be excellent. Many sellers get by with pictures that are just adequate. You must be better. We have always used Nikon Coolpix cameras because they are quite simple, they take superb pictures, and they are relatively inexpensive. We found ours (new) on eBay for under $150. I would not suggest buying used camera equipment, even if you can save a little money. Your camera has to work all the time and a camera with a warranty will allow you to sleep soundly. Also, stick to major brand names. You may save a little money buying an off-brand camera, but in the long run you will be unhappy. The major companies have invested millions of dollars in research and development, and they know imaging. Their cameras will work best.

You don't need to have a fancy-schmancy camera with lots of bells and whistles. Here's what to look for:

- Light weight
- Simple features
- At least 2.0 megapixels
- Built-in macro feature (avoid digital macros, make sure the macro function is optical)
- Manual white balance
- Uses standard batteries (AA, AAA, etc.) and rechargeable batteries—proprietary batteries are much more expensive and, of course, can't be found everywhere

The key to buying a camera is to try it first. You might want to speak to friends and family and, if possible, borrow several cameras to try out before purchasing a new one. I have tried many different brands and models, including expensive ones with high ratings from various consumer reporting organizations, and I always came back to my trusty Nikon Coolpix.

Fight the urge to buy the most expensive camera you can afford. Digital cameras get cheaper and more powerful by the day, and you won't really benefit from a fancy camera in the long run. The pictures you use on eBay will be relatively small, normally shot on the lower settings of your camera (e.g., 640 by 480 pixels or 800 by 600 pixels). You won't need a high-end camera to capture these shots. Shooting anything above a 2.0 megapixel image would be overkill for eBay listings.

LET THERE BE LIGHT

You will need to light your items for photography, and actually, lighting is usually a much more important factor in taking excellent photos than is the camera itself.

I use professional lights these days—a Novatron professional lighting kit (strobes with photo umbrellas) and a pair of Arri 300-watt fresnel tungsten lights on stands. We have a special silk screen in front of each of the Arris to diffuse and soften the light and prevent harsh shadows. We bought the Novatron V240 Fun Kit recently, and it requires a camera with a hot shoe for synchronization with the strobes (most consumer-grade digital cameras don't have a hot shoe). We have been testing the Novatron kit, and it does give amazing results—we will have to buy a digital camera with a hot shoe if we decide to use these lights on a regular basis.

We also use a device called a Cloud Dome to photograph highly reflective items such as sterling silver and glass objects. This is a half sphere made of translucent white plastic with an opening in the center through which the camera shoots. The dome is placed over the object to be photographed, between our regular Arri lights, further diffusing the light and minimizing harsh reflections. The cloud dome is relatively expensive, but you can make a quite effective substitute (for very small items) from a plastic gallon milk container.

Both of these lighting setups are expensive, but I didn't buy expensive lights immediately—at first I made due with cheaper solutions. Initially, you can make a simple and inexpensive lighting setup yourself with items you can find at a local hardware store or camera shop. Indirect natural light can provide great lighting initially, too, but eventually you will want to invest in the best lighting equipment you can afford (after you make some sales first, of course!).

Quite a bit of trial and error is involved in learning to use lighting equipment effectively. You should spend the time needed to learn how to white balance your camera. And you can pick up quite a few tips on photography and lighting (and HTML) on the eBay Discussion Boards. You can post questions and get answers from other eBay members on the Photos/HTML Discussion Board—from the eBay home page, click Community > Discussion Boards > Photos & HTML.

RENAISSANCE MACHINES

I "killed three birds with one stone" when I bought a multifunction machine that is a combination printer, fax, and scanner. This is much cheaper to operate than a separate fax and printer because the all-in-one machine uses the same print cartridge for both faxes and printouts. I use the fax a lot more than I ever imagined, and having a fax machine handy is a good idea. These machines are typically very cheap, with manufacturers actually selling them below cost because they make their profits on the ongoing supplies you will need. If you foresee a lot of printing, it will be cheaper to use a black-and-white laser printer than an ink printer. Stick to the major brands—the supplies will be easier to find and cheaper in the long run. Also, I never use recycled or remanufactured cartridges, because they nearly always produce inadequate or poor print quality.

You may also need a separate printer for making high-quality client statements and possibly printing checks and a cheap (but good) color scanner for making scans of flat items you list on eBay.

14 BUILDING YOUR NAME ONLINE

An elderly Swedish man asked me to list 11 decks of old playing cards for him. One deck was quite nice—over a hundred years old with hand-colored illustrations of Swedish royalty from that time. We could find very little information about them, but we decided to start the bidding at $19.99. Several bidders asked for additional close-up photos, and by the end of the auction, the deck of cards sold for $2,575 for my client. The buyer was a man in the Netherlands who indicated that he had not seen this particular deck offered anywhere in over 27 years!

Sally Milo, Tucson, Arizona;
eBay user ID "going1nceamc"; trading on eBay since April 29, 1999

We live in an Internet world. You are starting an Internet business. Selling yourself with a Web site will help promote your new business, and you will want your Web site to explain your services to, and thus reduces the number of questions from, prospective new clients. Creating a Web site can be simple, inexpensive, and fun.

Much of this chapter assumes that you are HTML-familiar and Net-savvy enough to design your own Web site. However, I will try to help you find your comfort zone, even if you are a complete novice. Many domain registrars, Web hosting companies, and online services offer build-your-own Web site templates. However, they are not particularly "portable" if you change hosting companies. That's why it's a good idea to learn how to build your own Web pages from scratch.

TELL THE WORLD (LITERALLY)

As your business grows, more people will want to know about what you do. Having a Web site that outlines your services, terms of service, and fees and includes testimonials from happy clients and buyers, compelling examples of items you've actually sold for others on eBay (with pictures), and other company information will give your firm credibility and generate more business for you.

You will be busy running your company and juggling many tasks. Giving prospective clients the opportunity to read up on your business before walking in the door will reduce the amount of "sales" time you have to spend articulating your business processes and fees. A simple, easy-to-understand Web site will shorten the time needed to convince people of the benefits of your valuable Trading Assistant services.

Your site should have the following basic elements:

- A home page that greets the visitor when they arrive at your Web site
- A page that explains the process of what you do and how you do it, selling the client on the convenience and value of your company's services
- A page that outlines your fees
- A page with some testimonials from other clients (the number of testimonials will grow as your business grows)
- A page that shows some examples of items you have sold and their selling prices
- A link to your eBay listings
- A contact page which includes your company name, address (and e-mail address), and telephone number

Home Page

The home page of your site can be simple or very fancy. Either way, it should engage and grab the attention. Maybe your home page can have some *wow* stories such as, ". . . this old film camera sold for $550!" Your Web site's first impression really needs to sell you and your business, and it must create enough interest to keep visitors reading. The links to other pages should be easy to locate, and the colors and fonts should be clear and easy to read.

Services Page

This page explains your company's overall process—how you handle the clients' items from start to finish. Just like a dry cleaner or car wash, you provide convenience and value. Remember that you provide a service that anyone could provide—anyone can sell on eBay. What sets your company apart—what makes it more professional, trustworthy, reliable, and efficient—will sell you as the right choice for listing a client's items on eBay. I caution you to avoid making your service seem complex. You are simply providing convenience to your clients and helping them use eBay, not offering some arcane techie service. Also, you are providing a personalized service, with a high level of integrity and expertise, and your services page should fully and forcefully express this. You need to make certain your clients trust and believe in you—this page should accomplish that.

Fees Page

We discussed fees in detail in Chapter 11. This section of your Web site should address the cost of doing business with you. And this page should be decidedly simple. Non-eBay users do not normally understand the fees charged by eBay (and PayPal), and it is critical that you don't turn people off by making your fees page complex in any way. Most successful eBay drop-off stores have a very simple fee structure.

Testimonials Page

Success breeds more success and a page of testimonials will sell your success: "'Apple Drop sold my set of china for $650! I thought it would never bring more than a few dollars at a yard sale . . . I'm amazed,' Candy Johnson, Sioux Falls, South Dakota." Your testimonials page should only include individuals who have given you written permission, by letter or e-mail, to use their name and quote. The testimonials page will grow and grow as you add more people to your list.

Hall of Fame Page

This page could be called Hall of Fame or Items We Have Sold. This is a showcase of photos, sale dates, and final prices of actual items you have sold for clients. When creating this page, try to show examples of not only your highest-priced sales but also the types of items you would like to see clients bring in to you. If you are an expert on numismatics, then show the sale of a rare coin. If you know clothing, show some high-end shoes.

My eBay Listings Page

Clients will want to see the quality of your work. Having a link to your listings is invaluable in convincing people to use your company. This link will serve double duty, because some clients are also eBay buyers, and you may pick up some extra sales along the way.

Contact Page

On this page, provide your full company information. Make it easy to reach you. Provide your name (and possibly a list of employees' names and what they do), your company name and address, telephone number(s), and e-mail address. Your contact page should include your hours of operation so that clients can know when they can reach you, and if you observe specific holidays, mention them on this page as well.

With a high-quality yet simple Web site, you will attract more clients. Start simply and develop your site over time, just as you did your business plan. You'll see fairly quickly what works and what needs improvement. If you are not an Internet expert, don't worry—there are plenty of ways to get a Web site up and running with zero programming knowledge.

A HAPPY HOME FOR YOUR WEB SITE

Your Web site must be fast and reliable. The Web hosting company you choose will determine the speed and uptime of your site. The uptime is the percentage of time that your Web site can be expected to be available and working properly. Most Web hosting companies will tell you their uptime statistics, and this figure should be very close to 100 percent. The speed of the hosting company's services will affect the time it takes for a Web page to load. The server (the computer upon which your site will reside) should be a modern, fast computer. Most major Web hosting companies have state-of-the-art equipment, and you can expect great service. Choosing a good Web host is not complicated, nor should it be a difficult decision.

Here are some of the factors you will need to consider when selecting a Web hosting plan.

Domains

Your Internet domain name is the address used by anyone wanting to visit your Web site. Although the Internet is really run by the numbers (like telephone numbers) called IP addresses, people find that the numbers are hard to remember and, well . . . boring. The purpose of a domain name is to point a Web user to your site quickly and easily. A memorable name, typically the exact name of your company, will make the process of finding you easy. Domain names are cheap these days, and you will probably get a discount on your domain name registration and annual fees if you buy the domain name along with a hosting package. My absolute favorite domain name registration company is GoDaddy.com. They provide extremely low-cost domain names, high-quality Web hosting, e-mail, and many other services. If your company name is Acme Auction Listing Helper, you might want a domain name called *www.acmeauctionlistinghelper.com*. On the other hand, this is long, so shortening it to *www.acmeauctionhelper.com* will make it easier on the fingers. A domain name from GoDaddy.com can be registered for $8.95 per year (as of January 2006) or just $1.99 if you purchase a domain name in conjunction with their Web hosting services.

Setup Charge

This is usually a one-time charge for setting up your account with the Web hosting company. These days, this fee should be close to zero because of the stiff competition among hosting companies.

Monthly Fee

This is the fee you will pay for the Web hosting plan, and rates will vary greatly, depending on the amount of disk space (see the next section) and level of service you want from your hosting company. At this writing, the monthly fee for Web hosting ranges from about $4 to $20 per month.

Disk Space

This is the amount of physical space you are allocated on the Web hosting company's servers to store your files. For an information-only site, this can be a very small amount of space—as little as a few megabytes. Most hosting plans offer gigabytes of storage, far more than you will need for an information site. If you plan to host images (more on this later), expect to need more, but you can always upgrade to a larger plan later as your storage space needs increase. Keeping your site clean and free of unwanted or unused files will also help in managing disk space (e.g., if you host images for your eBay listings here, you can delete the images from the server after an item has sold to conserve disk space). Remember to keep copies of your files on your own personal computer as a backup—always!

Monthly Data Transfer

A Web hosting plan is like your car—the more you use it, the more it costs to operate. Data transfers are uploads (pictures or other data you are sending out) and downloads (instances of people accessing your Web site and/or any of your stored pictures). Most hosting plans place a limit on the maximum amount of data you can transfer each month. For a simple site, this figure will be very low, probably well below the host's maximum. If you plan to use eBay's own picture hosting service for your listings' pictures, rather than your Web host, this number can be extremely low; but if you intend to host your photos using this server, your transfers may get rather large. For example, in September 2005, our company's server had 76,982,190 kilobytes of transfers. This means that more than 73 gigabytes of data were transferred into and out of our host's server. This is a lot, but we do host our own images (to save money on eBay's picture hosting fees), and we list a heck of a lot of stuff. You can start off much smaller, and for most sellers, the lowest-cost hosting plan with a major hosting company will usually suffice. You can always monitor your usage with your hosting company and decide when it's time to upgrade your plan.

E-mail Accounts

Your hosting plan should have free e-mail accounts, which will allow you and your staff to have branded e-mail with your own company's domain name. These e-mail accounts should have built-in spam and virus protection as well as a Web interface that allows you to check your e-mail from anywhere in the world on any computer.

SSL Certificate

You probably won't need one, but if the Web hosting plan includes a secure sockets layer (SSL) certificate, you can allow users of your Web site to transmit personal information securely. This is typically used when sending credit card or other sensitive information via the Internet.

With most buyers now paying via PayPal, the SSL certificate may be superfluous, but if it's free with your hosting plan, why not?

Databases

I'll discuss content management scripting later in this chapter, but for now, I'll just mention that you'll want to have database capability with your hosting plan. This is usually offered as part of the hosting package, and you will want to have at least a handful of what are called SQL or MySQL server databases (see below) with your hosting plan to maintain and update your Web site. These databases are easy to install and use, working with simple and automatic Web interfaces, and they will be useful in creating content, image galleries, blogs, message boards, and other features that you may want to add down the road.

Server Operating System

Typically, your Web hosting company will offer two types of servers, Linux and Windows. I myself use a Linux server, but many people prefer Windows. (We're not talking about the Windows operating system that may run your computer. Most of the free software that will help you develop your site is compatible with a Linux system, and you will find that Linux is the economy choice without compromising the features you need. I would suggest using Linux. If you do so, your hosting plan must support a computer language called PHP, as opposed to ASP for a Windows-based hosting plan.

Forums

This is a great service that's free with most hosting plans, allowing you to set up community boards for users of your Web site to share ideas and make comments. Having a forum, as well a as a page hit counter, lets you check your Web site's "pulse."

Blogging

Blog is a shortened term for *Web log*, and is a (usually) frequently updated journal intended for reading by the general public on the Internet. This popular format is typically informal and personal and can be a great way for you to "chat" with your public.

Photo Galleries

Your hosting plan may include photo gallery support, and this would be helpful for you in setting up your Hall of Fame page. You can use a photo gallery to keep visitors to your site up-to-date on your sales. Normally, galleries are not used for hosting your eBay listing images, as that can be better automated using software (more on this later).

Dedicated or Shared Hosting

You may see the terms *dedicated* or *shared hosting* when selecting a hosting plan. You won't need a dedicated server to run your eBay Trading Assistant enterprise. A dedicated server is a computer at the Web hosting company's location hosting only a single client, while with a shared hosting plan, as the name implies, your Web site resides on a computer shared by other users and maintained by the hosting company. A dedicated server is more expensive and requires an administrator (you or someone else outside the hosting company) to maintain it.

When comparing Web hosting plans look for a company that won't charge a set-up fee or require a minimum annual commitment or contract. GoDaddy.com's basic $3.95 Web hosting plan includes 5 gigabytes of storage, 250 gigabytes of monthly transfers, a choice of Linux or Windows operating systems, 500 e-mail accounts (with antispam and antivirus protection), 10 MySQL databases, forums, blogging, photo gallery, and more. This deal, for the price of a premium coffee drink, is hard to beat. Don't let the low price fool you; this total package will run your business with great bandwidth and uptime. But shop around—there are thousands of Web hosting companies out there.

> **★ TIP**
>
> Avoid expensive Web design packages. Keep yourself on a tight budget and keep things simple, until you become proficient in setting up a site for yourself. You'll want to be able to update your site quickly, so don't delegate too much control (if any) to others.

MORE FREEBIES

Content management is a concept that has become very popular as the Internet has attracted nontechie people who want to set up Web sites easily and quickly. A content management script allows you to create and update your Web site without a single bit of computer code or programming knowledge.

After installing a content management program such as FrontPage or Dreamweaver, you will be able to design your Web site rapidly, adding pages, images, and links with a bit of typing instead of complex coding. If you want the capability to maintain your Web site from anywhere in the world, allow user-level access for your employees to contribute content, create e-mail, generate your own "press releases," and a lot more, you will want a content management program.

Many of these programs are free, and among the best is Mambo. Mambo is feature-rich and can be installed automatically from your GoDaddy.com Web hosting account. If your Web hosting company does not provide automatic installation of a content management script, you can find Mambo at *www.mamboserver.com*. You will need PHP and MySQL support to run this program, both of which should come with your hosting plan.

There are many great free (and low-cost) content management systems available. Mambo is my favorite, but you can easily find more free programs simply by going to Google.com and searching for "free content management software." The software development community has really stepped up to the plate with these free systems, and you will get an almost overwhelming list. As long as the content management software is easy for you to understand and use, any program will do the trick. GoDaddy has an inventory of free content management scripts that you can install instantly with zero programming knowledge.

THE DARK SIDE

The reality is that the Internet is teeming with questionable people. Hackers seek out and try to exploit Web sites with security vulnerabilities. Some viruses come in e-mail, install themselves on your computer, and then log your keystrokes to capture the passwords that you use to log onto your accounts on Web sites such as eBay or PayPal.

Fraudsters send out phony *phishing* e-mails (known as "spoofs") by the millions. A spoof looks like a legitimate e-mail from eBay or PayPal (or some other well-known company site) and is designed to convince you to click a link within that e-mail that will compromise your eBay, PayPal, or other password. The term *phishing* was coined because the illegal practice is designed to "fish" for your password. As a rule, you should never click any link in an e-mail to sign in on a Web site. eBay has a secure system called My Messages, part of their effort to combat fraud. This system allows you to see any e-mail sent to you by another eBay member or staff person right on the eBay site, without an external e-mail program. And eBay offers a free toolbar that works with Microsoft's Internet Explorer and will warn you if you are about to give up your precious eBay or PayPal password on a fraudster's Web site.

Your Web hosting company should provide spam and virus protection for your e-mail, and (if they are a big company) have systems to thwart hackers from attacking your Web site. It is critical to understand, however, that nothing can stop a con artist if you accidentally give up your password to them. Having a good antivirus software program on your computer will help to identify and delete dangerous viruses that may attempt to steal your login. Microsoft lists its partners who publish antivirus utilities: *www.microsoft.com/security/partners/antivirus.asp*.

Keep in mind that most security problems are caused by lax security policies. Your Web hosting company will do much to protect you by handling the security of their (shared) servers themselves. If you choose dedicated hosting, however, you will be on your own, because the hosting company will not take measures to prevent hackers from breaking into your server. This is one of the benefits of shared hosting.

SECURITY CHECKUP

Here is a quick security "checkup" review to make certain you remain safe on the Internet and that your business information is secure:

- Ask your Web hosting company about their security and anti-hacking procedures
- Determine if your hosting company has redundancy (if a server goes down, a backup machine should automatically kick in) and daily backup of files, in case they have an equipment failure or a security violation that results in the loss of or damage to your data
- Find out how much your Web hosting company will charge to provide automatic daily backups of your data and the cost of restoring your data in the event of data loss
- Keep a backup of all files on your own computer
- Activate the firewall feature on your personal computer to keep intruders from hacking into your computer while you are connected to the Internet
- Install an antispyware program on your computer (Microsoft offers a free one on their Web site, or use Google to find available free or low-cost programs)
- Install an antivirus program on your computer
- Keep all passwords secret and do not share passwords or user IDs with others
- Change passwords frequently and keep a written record of your passwords in a secure place (but not on your computer!)
- Maintain constant physical security of computers at your home and office (if you share computers with others, you increase the risk of accidental—or intentional—data destruction)
- Avoid giving your business e-mail address when registering to use Web sites (to avoid spam), and be cautious in general about

to whom you give your e-mail address, to avoid spammers who send malicious viruses

The Internet Crime Complaint Center is an alliance between the Federal Bureau of Investigation and the National White Collar Crime Center. They have additional tips on how to avoid being the victim of Internet-related crimes at *www.ic3.gov/preventiontips.aspx*.

With a bit of knowledge, common sense, and caution, you can operate a safe and secure Web site and keep your business out of the hands of fraudsters.

KEEPING YOUR WEB SITE FRESH, FANTASTIC, AND FREQUENTED

It is important for you to maintain accurate and current information at all times on your Web site. You can generate retail excitement for your Web site by these methods:

- Update your site as frequently as time permits to keep people interested and coming back
- When you sell notable items, add a photo and the sale price to your Hall of Fame page
- Have your Web site's address printed on packing slips, business cards, letterhead, and any other printed documents
- If you have a retail drop-off store, include your Internet address on your store's signage
- If you have a Yellow Pages listing, be sure to include your Web site's address

If you are listed in your local telephone directory, most of the Internet telephone directories will pick up your business listing from it, but it's important to check if you can add additional information, such as your Web site's address. Here is a list of some of the more popular free online telephone directories that people use every day to find businesses such as yours:

- *www.google.com/local/add*

- *www.superpages.com*
- *www.switchboard.com*
- *www.yellowbook.com*
- *http://yp.yahoo.com*

Of course, you should take advantage of any free listing options in other business guides, and another way to promote your site is to submit its address to the top search engines. Millions use search engines each day to find all kinds of information on the Internet. You can register your Web site with virtually all of these search engines free of charge, or you can use the "paid search" feature, where you purchase targeted advertising on the search engines for your company's site. Usually you pay for each click—each time a user links from the search engine's site to your own site after they type in keywords—such as *Trading Assistant*—to find what they seek. The link to your Web site (and others) will be prominently and separately displayed on the search engine's first page of Trading Assistant listings. If you choose paid search, be certain it is highly targeted. Because your client base will be limited primarily to businesses and individuals within no more than about 25 miles from your business, you don't want to pay to attract customers beyond this trading area. Google.com, at present the most popular of the search portals, does offer this kind of pay-per-click, performance-based advertising that can be targeted to display your ad only to users within a specified number of miles from your business—very handy!

A cost-effective way to submit your site to thousands of search engines and other sites is a program called SubmitWolf, which is software that will automate the submission process for you. It's a one-time cost, because you are paying for the software, not permission to submit to the many Web sites. You can accomplish the same thing by hand, submitting to one site at a time, but this tool will pay for itself many times over in time saved. You can find this software at *www.trellian.com*.

I also suggest promoting your new site on *craigslist.org*, if one of its many sites is in your area. Craig's List has a section where you can post free classified ads for business services, and it is very popular.

HIRING TALENT

Hiring a Web designer can be an expensive proposition, and once you turn over your virtual storefront to an outside contractor, the critical ongoing maintenance of your site can be a perpetual cash drain.

You may try the following happy medium for a new site:

- Develop all the textual content yourself
- Provide all the edited photos and graphics
- Provide the designer with a clear idea of how you want the site to look and function
- Require in your contract that the designer train you on content maintenance and uploading, and have a basic HTML reference handy. (Most Web site creators loathe the update and maintenance function, anyway, and are happy to be out of the ongoing maintenance loop.)

★ **TIP**

Be creative and come up with other ways to promote your new site. It's helpful to keep a written record of these ideas and add them to your business plan as you formulate them.

---

15 STREAMLINING STRATEGIES

A client dropped off a Masonic apron that was encased in glass, with a few notes on the back that dated it to the Civil War. She told me that she had paid $40 for it at a garage sale and that she wanted me to sell it on eBay. Shortly after the bidding started, I was flooded with offers of up to $500 to sell it offline. When I relayed this to the client, she said "Do it!" Well, I didn't, because my experience has told me when you get offers like this, it will go higher. The apron ended up selling for $1,100, and the client was very pleased. She brought me some additional items that generated over $5,000.

Tom Shanley, Allen, Texas;
eBay user ID "treeline2"; trading on eBay since February 24, 1999

Just as you use a business plan to help define your business and pitch it to investors and banks, you need to have systems in place to keep your business running smoothly. Being organized will pay off in a number of ways, including higher productivity and reduced stress for you. A well-oiled machine will make you profits. Being badly organized will cost you in lost time and frustration.

DE-CLUTTER

Are you a naturally organized person? I'm not. And knowing this, I have to work hard at being organized. When I was the only person working for me, it was actually harder to stay organized than now. As my business grew and I added employees, who are very organized themselves, I was able to see and define the "big picture" of my company, and together we keep things in order and operating to my great satisfaction.

Now it's time to get out your pen and paper and add some work flow strategies to your business plan, to help you define how you will actually operate. Being a smooth-running, organized business will take some time and a ton of discipline. You will find many distractions along the way, but you can never be too focused when running your very own business.

You can start getting organized by shedding as many of the unnecessary and undesirable activities in your life as possible. This is *not* off-topic. Look at your daily routine and see what you presently do that consumes your valuable time without benefiting you. Do you wash your own car? Do your own laundry? Clean your own house? Are you running errands that could be delegated to someone else? Finding ways to delegate tasks will free you up to mastermind your business and help to bring that sharp focus to what you really want and need—tremendous financial success! Before you reject these remarks as some sort of rah-rah motivational speaking mumbo jumbo, realize that highly effective people are highly organized—constantly avoiding unnecessary activity, instead planning each minute of their day. Think about the additional time you will free when you delegate chores to other people.

DIVINE PLANNING

Please don't be in a rush. Rushing your new venture will lead to mistakes and create havoc. You are playing a very important game of chess that requires strategy and intelligence. If you are used to punching a time clock, keep in mind that you are now your own boss and are no longer paid by the hour. Though you may be proud of how hard you work, focus instead on efficiency—how much you can accomplish with the least amount of effort. Ideally, owning your own business will give you the luxury of being able to do what you want, when you want. Creating a well-thought-out plan for managing your business will allow you tremendous freedom to enjoy more time with family and friends—

taking a vacation when you feel like it and not having to wait for the boss to say you've earned it!

You can help make your days go smoothly by thinking of all of the tasks you have to accomplish each day and compartmentalizing them. You don't need to make listings or pack orders every single day. You should write down all the tasks you need to accomplish and place them into "buckets" of time when you will complete them. It's very tempting to try to get everything done all at once, and many new business owners make this common mistake.

Here is a sample weekly list of tasks for a store that operates Monday through Saturday.

Monday	Tuesday	Wednesday	Thursday	Friday	Saturday
Answer buyer questions	Answer buyer questions	Answer buyer questions	Answer buyer questions	Answer buyer questions	Answer buyer questions
Pack and ship orders	Photograph items	Process payments and deposit checks and money orders	Pack and ship orders	Photograph items	Process payments and deposit checks and money orders
Inventory and order supplies	Make eBay listings	Pull and check paid orders	File documents	Make eBay listings	Pull and check paid orders
Compress and reorganize shelves	Store items	Clean and vacuum store	Compress and reorganize shelves	Store items	Pay clients
Clean and vacuum store	Clean and vacuum store		Clean and vacuum store	Clean and vacuum store	Clean and vacuum store

I am assuming that most clients will come to your business at unscheduled times—so these largely random visits aren't on this daily schedule.

Sunday is a day of rest on this sample schedule. However, because Sunday is actually a good day to end auction-style listings (because more bidders are at home and on their computers), you may choose to list auctions ending on Sunday and, therefore, will need to answer bidders' last-minute questions from home. This also means that you will be scheduling the seven-day listings to start on a Sunday, even though your listing days shown here are Tuesday and Friday. With software or using eBay's scheduling feature, you can easily start listings on any day you want, whenever they were created. If you use listing software, you will be making the listings and then launching them at your leisure. Nonetheless, you will need to answer buyer/bidder questions on a daily basis, so I have placed this at the top of each day.

★**NOTE**

Depending on the volume of merchandise you receive each week, you can be flexible about scheduling the photography and listing tasks, but you want to have at least two days dedicated to creating listings.

Processing payments and pulling items for shipping can be done the day before the actual shipping. This allows time to create a strategy about which packing materials you will need and which shipping carriers you will use for which items, as well as estimating the amount of time required to pack the paid orders.

Personally, I find packing and shipping a relaxing task, and so I prefer to do it on specified days, for variation in the work week. And I suggest doing packing no less than twice a week to keep your buyers as happy as possible. But I have done shipping as infrequently as once a week when I used Priority Mail (for lighter items) only—when I didn't send out any heavy shipments, for which I usually use UPS. After each shipping day, it's helpful to reorganize and compress your merchandise storage shelves to utilize the additional space left by the shipped items.

You can inventory and order shipping and office supplies just once a week. Filing can be done twice a week. Stay on top of your filing so that you can quickly put your hands on a contract or paid bill. If the filing gets behind, it will snowball, and you can get burned when you really need to find a specific document fast. The time spent foraging for unfiled or misfiled documents will quickly amount to more hours than you would have spent just doing it right the first time.

Keeping a clean and orderly store will attract repeat customers and also helps you stay efficient and organized—so I put this task down for each day.

The weekly tasks can be rearranged any way you feel is appropriate. If you have full-time employees handling specific tasks such as photography, listing, and/or shipping, you would obviously add this task to *every* day.

You'll be paying your rent or mortgage, bills, and possibly taxes monthly. And if you see your Trading Assistant business growing steadily, you'll want to plan your spatial needs, staffing requirements, and equipment purchases on a fairly long time line. As I type these words, my warehouse is full to the ceiling with merchandise. I had to give up my personal office to store client items. We could move to a bigger location, but because the flow of client merchandise does not always fill our store, we are conservative about long-term expansion planning. We can control the volume of our work by being even more particular about the value and nature of the items we accept for listing. You may decide that you don't want to be huge but you do want to make great money. Selling higher-value goods is a work flow strategy to help you reduce volume and maintain revenue.

HANDLING THE STUFF

Always keep your client contracts handy and maintain a generous work space to receive new items. If you offer to clean client merchandise, you should have an area dedicated to this chore. And I do mean chore: Cleaning is a major time bandit and normally we don't do it—we actually turn down items if they need more than just a quick dusting. It's difficult to turn away people, but we aren't in the cleaning and restoration business. If someone brings you a rare piece of art or a spectacular sterling tea service, you may offer to do the cleaning, but I suggest you refuse bins of filthy common items.

You might remind the client that cleaning antiques and collectibles can significantly reduce their value to collectors. This is especially true for silver and other metals, wood, fabrics and fiber, Lucite, and similar "degradable" items. When in doubt, don't clean. Wipe off dust with a soft cloth. (And clearly state in the auction that you have not cleaned the item because it could decrease its value and that the buyer should seek professional help if they wish to restore these items after purchase.)

★ **NOTE**

Some items such as coins should *never* be cleaned and should only be conserved by an experienced professional. Most coins will lose value if cleaned (sometimes this can mean thousands of dollars lost).

You should have small labels for numbering client items (inventory control numbers). I use a Dymo label printer to create *sequentially* numbered inventory stickers (one-inch by one-inch self-adhesive labels). You can always buy small labels at the stationery store or online and simply write your item numbers on them by hand. You have to do a pretty hefty volume to justify a printer dedicated to this task.

The labels will help you track your consignments, and you should also keep a log of your incoming client merchandise. You can do this with software, but when you are starting out, it's just as easy with a spiral-bound notebook or steno pad. The information you want to capture includes:

- Client name
- Date of receipt of the item(s)

- Brief description of the item(s)
- Status columns to show date of photography and then listing (to help track what is still unlisted)

You need a good supply of bubble wrap bags (or simply bubble wrap) for storing fragile items. You should have various sizes of these bags, and you can find them on eBay by searching the term *bubble bags*. You don't want the self-seal type, and don't confuse bubble bags with the padded or bubble mailing envelopes (these are great for shipping but not good for merchandise storage). Plastic bins will also come in handy. They can be used for storage of client items before, during, and after making listings. I buy the large, heavy-duty, stackable type with the hinged dual flaps that form the lid. I number each bin to identify it and also tape an index card with the client's name on the bin. But until you start making money selling on eBay, you can always use free boxes from your local supermarket or department store.

A high-quality, plastic, resin-top folding table works well for sorting and even photographing items. I don't suggest the bigger six- or eight-foot tables, as they are heavy and hard to handle. We find that four-foot tables are inexpensive and easy to move around, and we can easily make an eight-foot table out of two four-foot tables. At my store, we have six of the four-foot resin-top tables, and we use them for temporary work tables, desks, staging areas, shipping tables, and photography. We even use them at small events and trade shows because, covered with a tablecloth, they look great!

OFFICE SUPPLIES—THE BASICS

You'll need some basic office supplies:

- *Stapler and staples*
- *Manila file folders.* For filing paid bills, client contracts, and other documents
- *Manila envelopes (9 inches by 12 inches).* For storing flat items such as photos, postcards, magazines, and small books

- *Pens.* And lots of them. They're super cheap, and you will have clients "borrowing" them all the time and forgetting to give them back—you can never have too many
- Sharpie brand permanent markers
- *Scissors.* For making custom box sizes along with all the usual tasks. Get a couple of pairs as they are cheap and will be used a lot
- *Calculator.* Get the solar type so you'll be battery-free, and look for one with large buttons. You'll have a lot of math "problems": calculating commissions, adding up shipping and handling charges, etc.
- *Lighter fluid.* A miracle product for removing residue and old labels from plastic, glass, and other surfaces. Have it on hand always
- *Glass cleaner.* For quickly touching up glass items and a lot more (and cleaning your store windows, of course—and try a squeegee for that)
- *A huge supply of index cards.* For writing yourself quick notes, identifying large or sticker-resistant items, and to accompany items with notes for writing the listing
- *Re-sealable sandwich and larger freezer bags (various sizes).* For storing items such as flatware, jewelry, small porcelain or crystal items on your shelves—anything delicate that will fit. These are also handy because you can number the item by placing an index card in the bag instead of using a sticker on the delicate item itself.
- *Large clear plastic trash bags.* You can put your outgoing mail in them to allow for quick transportation to the post office or to make your postal carrier or UPS driver's job easier. Get the clear type so no one mistakes them for trash and accidentally throws them out
- *A good selection of basic tools.* This includes screwdrivers, pliers, hammer, and rubber mallet (*the* tool for assembling and taking down those locking metal shelving units) as well as a standard, compartmentalized plastic toolbox
- *A good vacuum cleaner with a full array of attachments.* For quick cleaning of dusty merchandise, not just your floor

- *Super Glue and two-part epoxy adhesive.* For quickly resetting loose stones in costume jewelry or reattaching parts that may have fallen off of an item with age
- *Clear tape and masking tape.* Use the latter for labels that come off easily and cleanly
- *Air compressor.* We have found our small air compressor (100 pounds per square inch [psi]) invaluable for dusting items quickly, and we keep it by the photography table. These are available at any big hardware store and are not expensive, but it will probably be a down-the-road purchase, depending on the volume and nature of your listings

Your business may be completely different from mine, and you may find that you need other tools for your own specialties. If you sell a lot of computer equipment, you may want to set up a test bench with an open-case computer for testing hard drives, expansion cards, and peripherals. Your particular tools and supplies will reflect your own unique needs.

UNDER YOUR THUMB

Staying on top of a growing inventory of merchandise is challenging, and I suggest that you start using inventory control numbers. At my store, each item is issued a unique control number. We call this the item ID number and track it in our inventory system. Using such a number system with eBay's Selling Manager Pro or Blackthorne Pro, you will easily be able to keep tabs on the merchandise. If you don't use listing software and are listing items on eBay manually, you can enter the unique item ID number at the end of your eBay description as a way of tracking the item through its sale and shipment. Keep your inventory in numeric order and neatly arranged on your storage shelves so that you can put your hands on any item in a matter of seconds. Your store will be the height of organization and efficiency, very handy when a prospective buyer calls with a question minutes before the auction ends (it happens!).

Think of your items as having different "statuses" and keep them segregated in different staging areas. New items should have a dedicated table or shelf for examination, cleaning, and listing. Items waiting for photography should have their own committed area. Items being stored after listing will have a dedicated "listed item" shelf. Have an "awaiting shipment" area for after items sell.

Be disciplined, and you will find that everything flows well and stays very organized. Your biggest time bandit can be to trying to locate misplaced things, whether a client item, a contract, or that darned screwdriver, and staying neat, tidy, and organized will prevent this from burning up your day!

There are so many ways to set up a system and work flow procedures, and you will settle into your own personal methods as you gain more experience. You can also change your system at will if it does not work for you—creating new systems to replace the old is part of running an entrepreneurial enterprise.

16 STAYING FIT AND TRIM

I sold a Greek amphora dating back to around 250 B.C. Amphoras are ceramic jars that were used to transport wine and olive oil in ancient Greece. The owner of this relic was a deep sea diver in the 1950s, and he had exhibited this in his house all these years. He was forced to sell it because he was downsizing, and he had been given an approximate value by Sotheby's of $800. I listed and sold it for $1,575 to an Italian buyer who paid an additional fee to crate and ship it back to his country. We collected a commission of $525, and the buyer paid all of the transportation and crating charges.

Wayne Lehman, Portsmouth, New Hampshire;

eBay user ID "cogebi"; trading on eBay since July 20, 1997

Even the most successful athletes use personal trainers to get them into shape for competition and to keep them that way. Unfortunately, many of us in business don't get enough exercise (I'm one of them); but as a business professional, you need to embrace fiscal discipline. I would like to be your financial personal trainer for a chapter, so that you can keep as much of the money you earn in your new Trading Assistant endeavor as possible.

As you look at different ways to purchase the supplies necessary for the successful operation of your business, you will often find massive differences in prices from one vendor to another. Being financially competent can be challenging.

BE A MISER

It's okay to be stingy—not stingy to a fault, though, such as tripping over dollars to save pennies. When you walk into a post office, you'll pay $1.50 for a shipping box at the retail supplies counter, while you can go online and obtain free shipping boxes from the U.S. Postal Service—including free shipping to your location.

When you work for another company, worrying about the cost of everything the company purchases is probably someone else's problem. But when you own your own business, you will have to analyze every purchase to ensure you are getting the best possible price.

Do you enjoy saving a penny just to see if you can? Being frugal can be lots of fun!

Companies spend a great deal of money figuring out ways to part us from our money—from extravagant advertising campaigns to colorful packaging, designed to compel us to buy their products. In this society based on consumption, even our government encourages us to spend, with tricks like lower interest rates to help spur spending when the economy is struggling. In your new position as the CEO of your own company, you may feel a sense of greater spending power, but for practical purposes it's an illusion. We all need to stay focused on our real financial goals. Just say, "No!"

In our society, temptations to dive into more debt are everywhere. Here are some tips for you to stay fit and trim financially:

- Before making any purchase, ask the question, "How much will this investment return for me in actual dollars?" or, "Is this purchase absolutely necessary for the successful operation of my company?"
- Never finance anything that will not predictably provide you with additional profits—otherwise, pay in cash or wait until you can afford to do so.
- Compare three different vendors' prices for every item you purchase. When contacting vendors for prices, be sure to let them know that you are price shopping and that your company's policy

is to buy from the cheapest vendor (given of course that the product is the same from vendor to vendor).

- Shop on the Internet and pay reasonable shipping costs to save time, as a result allowing more focus on what makes you money—selling, not shopping.
- Pay all credit cards off *in full* at the end of each month. Keep a record of all charges so that you know exactly how much you have spent and whether or not you can pay for those items when the bill comes due. Interest charges on an ongoing credit card balance can eat up any savings you may have realized from careful shopping.
- Pay in cash if you can receive a substantial discount for it.
- Buy any items you use frequently in volume to get the best discount possible.
- Maintain impeccable credit so that you can obtain the absolute best interest rates for any purchases that you can reasonably argue must be made on credit.

Being frugal does not necessarily mean settling for generic brand or inferior products. It means finding the best possible wholesale or discounted price for the brands and products you need.

At my company, one of our most frequent purchases is shipping boxes. One major office supply superstore (who will remain nameless) sells 12 x 12 x 12-inch cardboard boxes in packs of 25 for $34.68, which comes out to $1.39 per box. Another vendor sells the same box for $0.51 each. I can get free delivery from the first vendor with no minimum purchase, but the second company with the lower price requires a minimum order of $300 for free delivery. Because of my volume, I can always get free delivery, and I am saving more than 63 percent on this box. We stock up on many low-cost supplies from this discount vendor and order much less frequently, perhaps once a month or less, to get our order up to at least the $300 minimum for free shipping, in order to get the best prices.

NO HARM IN ASKING

Certainly not everything in life is negotiable, but most companies offer some form of discount. And even if they don't, there's no harm in asking. Being a member of AAA (American Automobile Association) allows me a wide array of discounts from many sources. Using my American Express card gets me discounts with Kinko's and FedEx. There are many ways to save a little money here and there, and trust me—it adds up.

At any business establishment or when I shop by telephone, I always ask for a discount. And I receive a discount surprisingly often simply for asking. Employees of various businesses are empowered to grant discounts to customers on a discretionary, per case basis, and from my experience, will do so if they like you. So be sure to pour on the charm everywhere you go, and you will be amazed at the results. You won't get a discount at your local 7-11, but there are many, many ways to save.

Here are some tips for getting discounts:

- Maintain a current AAA membership (a good idea anyway) and ask for this discount at all business establishments
- Ask for free shipping or delivery—it's the same as getting a price reduction
- Offer to pay in cash if the merchant will then agree to pay the sales tax
- Go to Google.com and see if you can find coupon codes for online merchants—on one occasion, I was able to get a rental car for less than $10 per day this way

Developing great relationships with your vendors will help you get those discounts. Never take the attitude that you are entitled to a discount, and always express great appreciation when you get one. Sending thank-you and holiday cards to vendors who allow you discounts and remembering key employees' birthdays are ways to keep the relationships you develop strong and fruitful.

POWER IN NUMBERS

Co-op purchasing is the concept of pooling purchasing power with others to obtain quality products and equipment at significant savings. When you network for your business, seek out like-minded individuals with similar businesses to save big money. If, for example, other companies in your area use shipping supplies as you do, offer to work with them on making bulk purchases to get free delivery and volume discounts.

SHIPPING FOR FEWER DOLLARS

Did you know that most shipping companies have different prices for their customers depending on their volume? If you are a high-volume shipper, you can work with your account manager to get these discounts. Arrange a meeting with your shipping company's business office and ask them to discuss these discounts with you. You may be required to meet minimum shipping volumes to qualify for these discounts, but as your business grows and so does your monthly shipping bill, you can realize huge savings when you maintain the volume needed to qualify. Ask and you shall receive!

You can also ask all your vendors to ship items to you on your own UPS account, as a way to increase your overall shipping volume. Simply provide them with your account number and ask them to bill the shipping charges directly to your account.

You may be surprised to learn that even the U.S. Postal Service will give you discounts on shipping. We use the Delivery Confirmation service with all our parcels to provide online confirmation that parcels have been received by our buyers. The normal fee for this service is $0.50 when shipping by Priority Mail and $0.60 when using First Class or Media Mail. If you use their online mailing service or a software program that prepares mail (including PayPal's built-in shipping feature), you will be able to obtain Delivery Confirmation free on Priority Mail parcels and a discount of $0.14 with all other classes of mail. If you can save $0.50 per package by using software to prepare your mail, you will save $500 for every 1,000 parcels you ship out.

GIVE YOURSELF A BREAK

One of my oldest and most cost-saving tips is to "Remember the breaks!" I have preached this at nearly every seminar I have taught for eBay University since I started evangelizing the site years ago. You will recall that eBay charges one fee for listing (Insertion Fee) and another when an item sells. eBay does not presently offer any discounts on their fees (except for special events and promotions), but you can save big money when you start a listing at the proper minimum bid, Buy it Now, or Reserve price to take advantage of the breaks in the price structure for the eBay Insertion Fees.

Starting or Reserve Price	Insertion Fee
$0.01–$0.99	$0.20
$1.00–$9.99	$0.35
$10.00–$24.99	$0.60
$25.00–$49.99	$1.20
$50.00–$199.99	$2.40
$200.00–$499.99	$3.60
$500.00 or more	$4.80

Fees for using eBay may change from time to time. To get the latest fee information, go to *www.ebay.com*, click "Help" and enter the keyword *fees* in the search box at eBay's system help. When randomly browsing listings on eBay, I notice that for the most part, people do not consider these price breaks when setting their starting prices. If you drop a penny and list your item for $49.99 instead of $50, you will pay $1.20 to list it instead of $2.40—a savings of 50 percent off the eBay Insertion Fees.

If you list 1,000 items at $49.99 instead of $50, you would save $1,200 in insertion fees. I want you to be the most financially successful person you can be, and by using this little secret, you can save huge money—perhaps even enough to help you pay your entire rent. Not paying close attention to these fee breaks cost me thousands of dollars in my early eBay days, but no more.

GET IT ON EBAY

As you already know, I love using eBay. There are many things I can't buy for my business on eBay simply because we need them fast, but when there's a little time, there are many ways to save big money on eBay. With patience and planning, you can stock up on many of your operation's necessities at very low prices.

Here are just a few of the bargains I found for my company on eBay:

- *Nikon digital camera.* Paid: $135. Retail: $250.
- *Credit card terminal (for phone orders).* Paid: $135 . Retail: $650.
- *Foam peanut dispenser.* Paid: $76.50. Retail: $183.00.
- *Novatron lighting kit model V240.* Paid: $333.00. Retail: $996.80.

These are just four examples from the hundreds of items I have purchased for my company over the years. I refuse to pay retail for anything I can buy on eBay at a big discount. Some quick eBay buying tips:

- Research completed listings on eBay to make sure you are not overpaying

- Always review the seller's feedback and avoid bidding if there are complaints for nondelivery
- Always consider shipping charges as part of the total price, and if they aren't specified, always e-mail the seller *before* bidding to ascertain the total shipping charges—some sellers do charge rather high handling fees
- Ask the seller if you can use your own UPS account for sending the parcel (ask before bidding) and, if so, whether they will charge you a "boxing" fee
- If possible, purchase heavy and bulky items from a seller nearby so that you can pick them up or get lower shipping costs
- Bid on items you don't need fast to get lower prices, or use Buy It Now if you need it immediately
- Use software to bid at the last minute (called "sniping") and avoid a bidding war (I use *www.auctionstealer.com*)
- Look for items ending at odd times (like 2:00 AM) and then place your bid with the sniping software to assure a restful sleep while the auction ends—there is usually less competition for items ending at off times
- Avoid getting emotionally involved with the item—you will always find another one on eBay if you don't win the bid
- Use PayPal or a credit card for payment so that you receive the maximum protection possible for your purchase (never mail a check, money order, cash, or send a wire transfer)
- Use the "Add to Favorite Searches" link on any search page to bookmark searches for items you buy frequently, and eBay will e-mail you daily when these items are listed
- Try using "Want It Now," which allows you to post a want ad on eBay when you can't find the item you need—sellers can review these and post appropriate listings to fulfill requests
- Try eBay's wholesale lots site at *www.ebay.com/wholesale*, to find even better bargains on larger lots of products you need

17 ACQUIRING NEW CLIENTS

I am a former commodities broker and decided to try something different and less stressful. When I used to live in New York, I always loved secondhand stores and decided to try selling for others on eBay. I loved the idea of going out for dinner and coming home to find I'd earned money while I was out! A client brought me a Chrome Hearts Biker jacket that is no longer in production. It was in immaculate condition, and she wanted to start it off at $1,800, knowing my commission was 50 percent. She thought I had gone mad when I told her I would want to start her listing at $4,999.99 because of the jacket's rarity. She was extremely pleased when it sold at my asking price.

Debra Kent, Miami, Florida;

eBay user ID "mightykismet"; trading on eBay since June 16, 2000

You will need business cards. Not the kind you print on your own printer but high-quality cards that reflect your high-quality business services. I usually have 5,000 printed at a time. That may seem like a lot, but if you are actively marketing and promoting your business, you use your business cards on a daily basis. The coffee shop where I get my daily brew has agreed to carry a large stack of my business cards. The lady who cuts my hair keeps a bunch at her reception desk. The man who services my three cars regularly hands out my cards.

Many of your fellow chamber of commerce members and local businesses will gladly display your business card if you reciprocate. Business cards are a highly effective and inexpensive way of marketing your company. I get 5,000 full color, two-sided, glossy business cards printed for only $129 at *www.nextdayflyers.com*. I use this company for printing my postcard-size flyers as well. They do the job in one day, they'll ship anywhere in the United States, and their prices and quality are unbelievable. You can design your own cards or have someone else do it. The printing is only as good as the design, and some effort needs to be put into the creation of a business card if you want to make a great impression. Once you have your design file, all you have to do is send it to the printer via the Internet.

You must realize that simply being good at what you do is not enough. The best product in the world will be a complete dud if nobody knows about it, and you must be a great promoter to run a successful business. Don't let this intimidate you. Self-promotion, or marketing yourself, is usually a learned skill, not something that comes naturally to everyone—certainly not to me! Anyone can master the basics of marketing a Trading Assistant business without poring over marketing textbooks or taking expensive courses.

Your total marketing package is not one element but a recipe made up of many ingredients. You've already started—your market research was a critical part of writing your business plan, and you have developed valuable contacts with other Trading Assistants.

Big companies can hardly determine the tangible benefits of each ad they place, but they understand the value of consistent marketing as a core part of their financial success. With a small business such as yours, you will have a far greater handle on the results of your marketing efforts to acquire new clients, and with a little testing, you will find the ideal ways to promote your new Trading Assistant business.

Marketing and promoting your business will require focusing on these general areas:

- Market research
- Pricing your service
- Advertising
- Promotions and tracking
- Public relations

WHO'S IN YOUR CROSSHAIRS?

Who can use your service? You must identify your target audience before you begin the marketing process. Some of the possibilities are:

- Individuals who are retiring or downsizing their lives for some other reason
- Estates of deceased individuals (a situation that often leaves a family with lots of unwanted items)
- Wealthy individuals who enjoy buying new things and want to shed used items
- Bankruptcy attorneys
- Divorce attorneys
- Probate attorneys
- Dissolved businesses or partnerships
- Charities who need donated items sold for cash
- Local government agencies with surplus property
- Auctioneers with unsold items
- Businesses that need to liquidate excess inventory
- Banks and finance companies with repossessed merchandise
- Leasing companies with off-lease inventory
- Rental companies that need to retire their assets
- Insurance companies with damaged (but salable) goods for which they have already paid out claims
- Manufacturers with overruns, canceled orders, and factory seconds
- Custom imprinting companies with misprinted items
- Installers and movers who routinely come across unwanted client items
- Public storage unit operators
- Hotels and motels that are renovating

There are a zillion more categories of folks who need your service. But don't forget that you will do better targeting individuals or businesses from whom you will receive a steady flow of merchandise. One of my clients is a busy probate attorney and a very consistent source of good material. Another client helps elderly individuals with downsizing and moving and has brought us hundreds of high-quality items. Another is an antiques dealer who uses us for ongoing high-end art and antiques liquidations.

You can't reasonably market to everyone at the same time—it will be best to focus on a few market segments at a time and work your way down the list. Joining the local chamber of commerce will give your company immediate networking capability. If your chamber is an active one, they can be a source of constant referrals.

You can usually get free marketing information from your chamber or local newspaper, both of which normally have a ton of financial and demographic data, such as buying habits and preferences, which can help you understand your trading area. The economics of your community will play a significant role in the nature and quantity of unwanted merchandise available to you.

HAPPY CLIENTS SPREAD THE WORD

I've already talked quite a bit about setting your rates and using them effectively. Your rates are also an important part of marketing your business. You want to steer clear of people who are much too sensitive about the starting prices of their items or the commission you charge. I have interviewed Trading Assistants who are getting up to a 40 percent commission on each sale, but their clients are happy with the fees because they are moving *unwanted* items. Your marketing should focus on this concept—you move items to which your upscale clients have no emotional or financial attachment. How do you reach them? Many Trading Assistants tell me that they find this type of client by word of mouth.

You can always adjust your rates if you find you are not getting enough high-quality merchandise or if you receive too many complaints about your rates. You need to be flexible with your rates if you are not reaching your target audience.

MARKETING YOURSELF

Budgeting advertising is very, very tricky. You can blow a lot of money fast by advertising in the wrong places. First, avoid any form of advertising that requires a long-term commitment, unless you can get out of the contract easily by paying some form of nominal cancellation fee. If you agree to 52 weeks of advertising in your local paper to get the lowest possible rates from them, be sure that you can easily stop the ad if it's not bringing you customers.

There are so many forms of advertising, they might make your head spin. Be disciplined with your ad budget—frugally try different kinds of advertising until you find what works, then keep the successful ad campaigns running.

Whatever kind of advertising you use, strong ad copy is critical. I see big corporations throwing advertising budgets away on messages that seem just plain bizarre, and I wonder how such copy could possibly generate interest in their product. The message should grab our attention right away and hold it, without extraneous fluff. Your ad copy should be direct and engaging—you want people to call you and stop by your store.

I suggest advertising your business with these proven tools that have worked very well for me:

- Telemarketing
- Personal sales calls by appointment
- Small, strategically placed classified ads or inexpensive display ads
- Fliers
- Sales letters to organizations (corporations, nonprofits, and others)

BLOW YOUR HORN

Before you spend a dollar from the advertising line item in your budget, I strongly urge you to take your business cards and start hitting the pavement. Joining the local chamber of commerce will provide a complete list of all of the chamber members, and you can start networking with them at the chamber's various mixers and meetings. It will take time for people to get to know you, but as you distribute your business cards at these functions, your name will start to circulate and people will become familiar with what you do (especially if your company has a catchy name).

You will want to follow up with chamber members you meet and ask them for an appointment to discuss what you do. Visit each business you can, offer your printed brochure, and ascertain any possible need for your service. Just remember that literally *anyone* is a potential client.

Take the chamber's membership directory and start telemarketing. Forget any negative image you may have about telemarketing. You're simply making phone calls. Call the members of the chamber, inform them that you are a new business and a chamber member, and ask them for an appointment to discuss your services. If you are turned down for the appointment, offer to mail a brochure and business card. Your goal is to become as well known in your local community as possible. This process requires a great deal of patience, because people are not always friendly to solicitations. Members of the chamber will be a bit more friendly than most, because they joined the chamber to develop their own businesses and understand that you are simply networking in the same way they do. You will also find a warmer reception if you take the time to learn a little about your fellow chamber members' businesses and offer to network for them with others when you see the opportunity.

Be pleasant and natural on the phone—don't talk fast. Try to avoid a "sales pitch" tone, and you'll get a lot more appointments.

Here's a good way to approach an initial telephone call:

Hi, this is Jane, and I'm a fellow chamber member. I am calling you because I have recently joined the chamber and am networking with other members. My business sells unwanted items for other people on eBay. I would like to stop by your office and discuss what I do with you. Would you have time to see me tomorrow?

A WARM RECEPTION

Asking for a specific day and time will make you sound professional. Gauge the tone of the other person. If you do not get a warm reception, thank them and go on to the next call. You only want to talk to people who want to talk to you, so focus on the calls where you receive a friendly and warm reception. When calling larger firms, you may need to speak with the purchasing agent, or whoever handles the acquisition and liquidation of the company's assets. At manufacturing businesses, this title may be production manager. Usually, whoever handles the purchasing for a company is also responsible for the liquidation of excess items.

You will notice that I am focusing on commercial clients in this discussion of telemarketing and sales calls. The reason for this is simple—cold calling homes is not very productive. You will get a chilly reception from most people when you call them at home, and your efforts will result in few items. But when you score a new commercial client, you will receive a steady stream of merchandise from them as well as plenty of high-quality referrals to other businesses that may need your services.

After hitting up your local chamber members, you will want to start expanding your cold calling efforts to the list of different types of businesses mentioned earlier in this chapter. You will find that ads in the local newspaper will be a helpful tool in locating auctioneers, attorneys, and the other types of appropriate businesses. Try to set up appointments as before, to explain your services. When visiting a law office that handles divorce, bankruptcy, or probate matters, take a large stack of your business cards. Ideally, the attorneys will give them to clients when they feel it's appropriate. Be aware that giving a referral fee to an attorney may be considered unethical or even be illegal in some states, and you would do better to position yourself as a valuable service for these attorneys, to help their clients rid themselves of unwanted assets.

You can apply these networking concepts to many different kinds of situations. Focus on where there is money!

GETTING PUBLISHED

Go easy here, tiger! Print advertising is relatively expensive but not very targeted. You can burn up a lot of cash placing print ads in quality newspapers or magazines with large circulations—but your target audience may be only a minute fraction of those numbers.

I suggest placing small classified ads to attract new retail clients. With print advertising, most of the new clients you attract will be individuals with personal or family items to sell.

If placing print ads, you want them in the most popular, widely read newspapers and magazines, but I rarely advertise in magazines unless they are the local weeklies. Magazines have very long publishing lead times and tend to have a broader distribution than local papers. You want to pay for advertising that will reach people in a radius of no more than about 25 miles from you. At least 90 percent of all of my clients are located within ten miles of my store—this is very telling! Consider using papers that are distributed exclusively in your town. The larger the circulation beyond your area, the more money you will be paying for advertising that is of no real use to you. You certainly don't want to have someone call up with great stuff to sell only to find out they are located 100 miles away.

Before placing a single ad, you should request an advertising kit and rate information from the publication. This information will provide insights into the demographics and financial profiles of the publication's readers. Study this information carefully. If you are seeking wealthy individuals with unwanted goods, you would want to advertise in a paper they read.

DAILY MIRACLES

Virtually all classified ads are billed by the word. To keep costs down, you want simple ads that grab attention and create a call to action. Here is a sample of such an ad:

We perform miracles every day on eBay! Sell through us without the hassle—we do everything! Call today for more info: 818-555-1234, Trade-It-Away, Inc.

In this particular ad, you assume that the reader knows a little about eBay and maybe even has considered selling their items themselves. The clients you seek will be relieved when they see your ad, because they always wanted to find that spare time to sell their unwanted stuff but just never got around to it—but you are the hero who can do it for them—relieving them of a chore they were avoiding—and they'll call you. This type of marketing takes advantage of eBay awareness, while the short, succinct ad copy keeps the cost way down.

FAMILIARITY BREEDS BRANDING

When buying ads, you will benefit greatly from frequency. It's a proven advertising axiom that people usually respond after seeing an ad over and over again. If you can run your ad for several months, you should see improved results over time as people read it repeatedly. As in the above example, include your company name in all advertising—you are building a brand, so be sure to reinforce that brand in people's minds at every opportunity.

You can also purchase display advertising. It's more expensive, because typically display ads are larger and the publication will charge by the size of the ad. For a small Trading Assistant, these ads can really eat up your profits fast. But if you are going to buy display advertising, I suggest that you create the basic message yourself, perhaps expanded from one of your classified ads. Then someone has to design the ad. Many newspapers will design your ad free of charge as a part of their service to you as an advertiser. And although I prefer to design my ads personally in Photoshop, I have found that quite a few publications have in-house design personnel who do a fantastic job. As before, frequency is important. And as always, you need strong ad copy to grab the reader's attention.

Ad placement can be just as important as the ad copy itself. If I am trying to bring in clients with musical instruments, for example, I will place my classified ad in the section of the paper where such items are sold. If I want to attract commercial clients, I will write a targeted ad touting my abilities to help liquidate excess inventory and run it in the business section of the paper. Your copy should focus on your target demographic.

When you become an eBay PowerSeller (and you will if you are making enough to pay your rent), eBay's Co-op Advertising Program will reimburse 25 percent of your qualified advertising expenses, as of this writing. Qualified publications must have a circulation of at least 10,000, among other guidelines (including preapproval of ads by eBay), but under the program you can be reimbursed up to $8,000 per quarter. To learn more about this program, visit *www.ebaycoopads.com*.

FREQUENT FLIERS

I feel that a well designed business card is an advertising flier in itself, but it would be effective to have a larger, printed advertising flier for your business as well. I use four-by-six-inch, full-color (both sides) glossy postcards. The postcard-size ads are easy to handle and distribute. As with any printed advertising, your message should be simple, catchy and compelling, and, as always, strong copy is critical. On my fliers, I use a large headline to grab attention and concise copy to explain what I do. Because most people are familiar with eBay, your message can be brief. You don't need to explain eBay; rather, focus on the fact that you sell items on behalf of others. In addition, your flier should include:

- Some sample sale prices of items you have sold for others (with photos if possible—you're paying for full color printing, after all)

- Testimonials from clients
- Your complete contact information
- A call to action, such as a discount for your services if the customer presents the flier

You can design simple fliers in Microsoft Word, but to produce a fancy flier yourself, you will need a graphics program such as Adobe Photoshop. Or you can look for a reasonably priced graphic designer, and here again, a post on craigslist (if available in your area) may do the trick. Through craigslist, I have hired people all over the country to do various clerical jobs as well as more specialized tasks, such as graphic design. If you use a graphic designer, be sure you get your design's native source files so you can update or change the flier in the future. The basic template can be repurposed as often as you want, saving you money.

You can also use eBay's Trading Assistant resources. At *www.ebay.com/ta*, you will find numerous templates for fliers and posters available for download. You simply fill in your information and print them, in black-and-white and full color. Short-run color printing is rather expensive, so I invested in a high-quality color printer to print my short-run fliers in-house. The cost is much lower in the long run, especially if the printer is designed for high-volume printing. But investing in a high-speed color printer is something you can grow into when you've made some money—black-and-white will be fine in the meantime. The highly glossy paper I use costs about three times as much as normal paper at my local office supply store, but I think its impact makes it worth it.

I distribute the fliers by having them dropped off at homes and offices and in our busy Burbank downtown shopping district. I also have them in various local shops. I find that most small business owners will display my flier if I agree to reciprocate in my own store. A flier is a good place to mention the charity-related aspect of your service: People can donate to a good cause by giving you items to list on eBay and designating the proceeds, less your commissions, to go to a charity.

I also enclose a few fliers when I mail customer payments, using 9 x 12-inch manila envelopes. It costs a tad more in postage, but the benefits are worth it.

★ TIP

Mail out ten fliers to each person who calls in response to your advertising, along with a friendly introductory letter. Even if this person doesn't ultimately use your services, they will often refer others to you.

A co-op advertising company can create and mail another type of highly targeted flier for you. There are many of these companies, and we all know the packets of coupons they mail. I use Money Mailer (*www.moneymailer.com*). For just over $300, they design, print, and mail 10,000 full-color, one-sided fliers to residents in my local area. This is called cooperative advertising, because a number of businesses with coupons in the packet share the costs, thus keeping them low for each merchant. These programs are highly effective, because the mailings target specific zip codes, and Money Mailer also makes your coupon available for download on its Web site. For me, direct mail other than co-op or a very targeted list (such as your own clients) is much too costly. An advantage that Money Mailer offers is its sheer size—my sales representative could quickly access their numerous other Trading Assistants's ads, which we used for ideas for my ad. It was also reassuring to know that other Trading Assistants were having success with Money Mailer's program.

TRACKING YOUR SUCCESS

It's important to track and test any marketing program before making a significant long-term financial commitment. Testing involves tracking the success of your ads. If you use printed ads, fliers, and other printed media, be sure to include a coupon—for instance, for a discount on your services or for one free eBay listing—to see which ads are generating the most responses. The coupon should have a code that indicates the source of the ad. For example, your ad in the *Main Street Trading Times* would include a coupon coded "MSTT0606," indicating the paper's name as well as the month and year you placed the ad. A coupon can generate a positive sense of urgency—very productive with busy people who procrastinate in disposing of their surplus items.

I suggest pulling all the coupons and offers in the Sunday paper that really impress you and putting them in an ideas folder to help you create your own promotions. I love to look at other people's ads to get ideas for my own, and I'm constantly reading newspapers and magazines to get ideas for my business.

YOU'RE A PUBLICIST, TOO

A great Trading Assistant is a minipublicist too. Publicity is routine in most major and midsize companies. Issuing a press release about your business when you open your doors will almost certainly result in free publicity in your local newspaper, and possibly even radio and TV coverage. Our firm has been has been featured on the local NBC news and in the *Los Angeles Times*, *Entrepreneur Magazine*, and *Time Magazine*, among others. We've had lots of articles in major antiques periodicals, and on the Internet, about amazing prices we've realized for collectibles on eBay. The free publicity from these many articles and interviews resulted in a higher awareness of our business. After an article about us appeared in the *Los Angeles Times*, new clients were still mentioning it more than six months later. The benefits of this form of free advertising are priceless.

Fear usually stops people from writing a press release. Professional publicists will tell you that writing a press release is like open heart surgery—a very complex and specialized job that you couldn't possibly do yourself. This might be true for a *Fortune* 500 company's publicity, but for a small business like yours, there's no reason you can't do your own publicity. It soon will become just another part of your routine.

EBAY CAN HELP

The eBay Trading Assistant program has sample press release templates that you can use to announce your new business to the local media and for future press releases. You can find them at the eBay Trading Assistant Education and Training Hub under the link entitled "Toolkit," or you can download them immediately by going to *http://download.ebay.com/tas/5125.zip*. With these sample templates, you simply fill in the blanks, being certain to add any additional important or interesting details about your business. The media tend to be attracted to human interest stories, so if there is something interesting about your personal situation, you should include those details to help sell your press release to the media. Sally B. Donnelly wrote about me for *Time* after hearing about my business from one of my customers who knew her personally. You can never underestimate the value of networking for publicity—ask your chamber of commerce contacts if they know any writers or reporters.

Before sending out a press release, it helps to call ahead and probe a bit to try to find out which reporters might be interested in your story. Directing a press release to a specific reporter will yield better results. Get their e-mail address if you can and send the press release electronically along with some high-quality photos of yourself and your business, in the format that they prefer (just ask).

If interested, many busy newspapers and magazines may simply print an article without asking for an interview. But if you are asked for an interview, it helps to have some talking points written ahead of time, addressing the benefits of your Trading Assistant services. Media training and tips on handling interviews are beyond the scope of this book, but for the most part, if you are an outgoing and well-spoken person, you should find that doing such interviews will go smoothly. If you are having your photograph taken or will be on camera, it is very important that you are well groomed and look professional. If pictures or video will be taken at your business location or home, it's very important to organize and clean up to create the most positive visual image possible—put your best foot forward!

If you sense that a reporter is writing a negative story about eBay or the Trading Assistant business, decline the interview. You will be better off not participating in such interviews. I have never run into this situation, but it's good to be cautious. You have probably heard the adage originally spoken by P.T. Barnum, "There's no such thing as bad publicity," but personally I prefer not to get involved in anything that may be negative—I think it creates bad energy and karma for me.

If you are uncomfortable in front of cameras, then stick to print media. I would suggest doing some supplemental reading about media training and writing press releases if you intend to expand your publicity beyond the templates eBay provides for Trading Assistants.

★ TIP

If you write well, you can literally write an entire article about yourself for the print media. More often than not, my published press releases are printed nearly verbatim, because I make a point of both writing the story as I think it can be printed and sending the text electronically to help the reporter get the story turned in without having to retype anything.

DON'T BE SHY

Spread the word! I encourage you—no, I *demand* that you become a loudmouth! The greatest business (like yours) will fall flat if no one knows about it. Don't be shy in asking others to spread the word about your business. Hand everyone you know a bunch of business cards and fliers.

If they were pleased, even amazed, by your valuable services, your existing clients will provide the bulk of your referrals. But don't just assume that these individuals will automatically think to talk up your services—ask them to do so! After you pay your clients, talk to them about their experience with you, and if it was a happy one, ask them if they know anyone else who might be interested and give them some of your business cards.

Paying a referral fee is a compelling incentive. I pay 5 percent of my commission on a new client's first item listed on eBay to whomever sent that new client. You can pay a flat fee or you can pay a percentage, but be sure to *pay*. I write down the name of the referring individual on the client's item submission form so I will remember to pay the fee, which of course I only pay when I have successfully sold at least one item for the new client. Smart and experienced businesspeople pay for referrals, just as they pay for any other form of advertising. If you want a consistent flow of new clients, referral fees will help.

★ TIP

When networking with your business cards, use a felt-tip permanent marker to code the cards with a tracking number or initials matched to each person you give cards to. This allows you to track the card back to the person who originally gave it out and pay them their referral fee.

18
HANDLING NEW CLIENTS: THEIR ITEMS, PERSONALITIES, AND CONCERNS

A resident in my town noticed that many wonderful and adoptable pets were being euthanized. This outraged her greatly so she decided to establish a rescue shelter to help prevent these wonderful animals from being put down. After hearing about her efforts, I made the decision to use my earnings as a Trading Assistant to help her in this worthwhile cause. Today, my Trading Assistant dollars provide the organization, Compassion in Action, with the much needed funds that help save the lives of hundreds of beautiful, loving pets.

Elizabeth Ziegelbein, Elmendorf Airforce Base;

eBay user ID "eczblack"; trading on eBay since May 29, 2003

Learning the art of handling your customers can be a daunting task for a new Trading Assistant. You are so eager to get clients for your new enterprise that you will invariably make mistakes. I will help you avoid this, but the unexpected will happen, and you must be prepared to make errors and learn from them. Be patient—dealing with people is probably the hardest part of being a businessperson. You have to juggle the different facets of your client interactions and determine what to do and when. Take a deep breath and put on your thinking cap. And don't worry—you will be great with each of your valuable new customers.

On any given day, my staff and I wonder who will walk in the door or call with myriad questions, concerns, ideas, and items for submission. Some days are so quiet you can hear a pin drop; other days, the telephone rings off the hook, and a small army of clients lines up in our lobby. All these individuals have special concerns and needs, and we have to be on our toes to assist them properly and quickly in any one of a hundred scenarios.

THE INTERVIEW

The new client either stops by or calls. Each situation requires different strategies and tactics for closing them on your services. If you do not operate a convenient walk-in location as I do, you will be handling these new clients mostly by telephone, and sometimes by visiting their home or workplace.

The first thing you should do with a prospective new client is ask them for their contact information. Explain to them that you keep your client list confidential and that you will not share this information with anyone else. Individuals who are serious about using your services will give this information freely, and your asking sets a tone that you are serious about what you do and that you value them as a potential new client.

You should get the following details:

- Name
- Address
- City, state, and zip
- Telephone number
- How they heard about you (As discussed in the previous chapter, this information is critical, because you will want to measure the success of your advertising, to track referrals, and to get a general idea of what kinds of marketing work well.)
- A detailed description of the items they would like to sell

An easy way to capture this data is on a 3 x 5-inch index card, or if you type fast, you can enter it directly into a spreadsheet on your computer.

Some of your visitors will be competitors, tire kickers, and, in the case of a physical store, people killing time while their spouse is busy shopping nearby. Quickly identify the situation and determine who warrants your valuable time and who should simply get a brochure and be on their way. Of course, you should always be enthusiastic, affable, and polite regardless of the situation.

Be professional and courteous, as you never want to alienate a potential new client. Not all prospects will immediately understand the value of your services, and you want to make sure that they fully comprehend exactly what you can do for them: All the great services you provide and the convenience of having an expert handle their items, thus maximizing their return.

For anyone who is new to eBay, explain how auction-style and Fixed Price listings work and the reasons for and benefits of each. Explain eBay's fees and have a printed copy of them to show to your clients. If you charge the client for eBay and payment processing fees (such as PayPal's), make sure these fees are all in writing. You can easily put this list together from the details available on the eBay and PayPal sites. If you offer eBay buyers direct credit card payments and pass the charges on to your seller clients, you should explain that, too.

We have found it very useful to have a breakdown on our rate sheet of what clients can expect to *net* on a sale of $50, $100, or $1,000, and you may want to include high-ticket sales figures, too, if you are dealing with more expensive items.

Explain that buyers can bid up the auction-style listings, and that the seller, your client, can expect to get a fair market value. Tell your prospective client that the amount their item will ultimately bring on eBay will almost always be higher, even after your fee, than what that item would have brought at a yard sale or flea market. Make it very clear that you are by far the best method for maximizing the money in their pocket, better than any other method of liquidation.

> ## ★ CLOSING THE SALE
>
> There is no right or wrong way to close a sale. The old stereotype of the fast-talking, slick salesperson is definitely not you. Remember that to build your business, you must sell yourself, and that means that you should always *be yourself* when closing with clients on your services. Make them comfortable, and they will feel good about dealing with you. The key is to create a relationship built on trust, respect, and appreciation. Relax, don't try too hard, and you will develop a routine and rhythm for dealing with prospective clients.

QUESTIONS, QUESTIONS, AND MORE QUESTIONS

One benefit of referrals from existing clients will become evident immediately, as you will have fewer questions about your services from referrals. Without a doubt, your superior work with your existing customers will reach others by word of mouth, and these new clients will be eager to work with you, with few or no questions about what you do.

Initially, most of your clients will come from their searching the eBay Trading Assistant Directory or from your advertising and marketing efforts. These clients usually have a few questions. Here are some frequently asked questions and what you can say in each situation.

Q: Your fees seem awfully expensive. Are they negotiable?

A: We provide outstanding service and an extremely good value. Our fees are comparable to other eBay drop-off stores in (your city). We don't consider ourselves a cut-rate operation and we don't give discounts on our service, because we don't provide lower-quality listings. I think you will find our fees very fair considering all your options, such as a garage sales, local auctions, and pawn shops. With eBay, you receive the benefit of a global marketplace with millions of buyers. More often than not, you will get more money even after our fees than any other options you would have for selling your item.

Q: I already know how to use eBay, why should I use you?

A: If you prefer to sell your item personally, then you should. We provide excellent service, high-quality photography, and added value to you in terms of time savings. We often get more money for items because of our experience and excellent eBay feedback rating. A great many of our clients know how to use eBay but prefer the convenience of allowing us to do it for them.

Q: How much can I expect to get for my item?

A: In all but the rarest cases our clients don't set a minimum starting price or Reserve price for their items. Our experience selling on eBay has shown over and over that the highest final prices are actually realized from auctions with low starting prices, such as $0.99 or $9.99. Bidders enjoy bidding items up and competing with other bidders, and starting at a very low price point attracts bidders and adds to the excitement. We let the marketplace determine the value, and therefore, the final selling price is unknown. If we do start an item at a minimum or Reserve price, we charge a nonrefundable $9.99 fee to defray the higher fees eBay charges us for such listings. And if you do have a minimum price, it's important that it be realistic, because we would like your sale to be successful. The reality is that we cannot guarantee any particular item will sell at a particular price, but we will do the best job we can for you and hope that we get a buyer to purchase it on eBay.

Naturally, this response can vary, according to your own policies—you may choose to be more liberal in accepting items with minimum starting or Reserve prices. The above reflects my own company's policies.

Q: I have a [such and such] at home and would like to know what to expect on eBay. What would it sell for?

A: Well, we will gladly provide you with an evaluation of your item if you bring it in or allow us to come to your home [or office] and look at it.

The critical thing to remember here is to get the client to commit to bringing their items to you or allowing you to look at it in person. Many supposed new clients will eat up large chunks of your time asking you to look up final sales figures in "completed auctions" on eBay, ostensibly for insights into what their own items would bring. Then they never bring the items in—they were just using you as a free research service. We never give an evaluation of more than one hypothetical item, because the research takes time and our time is valuable. Give your time to someone who has actually let you look at the item in person. But be careful if you sense that the client has unrealistic price expectations—another case where you want to keep the research time to a minimum.

Q: How do I know you are going to be honest about what my item sells for?

A: That's one of the great things about eBay—it's completely transparent. We provide you with the eBay listing number, and you can see for yourself what the item sold for.

Q: How soon after it sells will I receive my payment?

A: We pay (weekly, biweekly, monthly) and we can mail your check, you can pick up your check, or we can PayPal your money to you. Please keep in mind that even after an item successfully sells on eBay, we sometimes have to wait for payment from the buyer, after which we can pay you.

Q: What happens if a buyer returns the item to you? Do I have to give the money back?

A: Ultimately, you are the actual seller of the item. We do our absolute best to list it accurately, based upon the information you give us and our research. We guarantee that the item will arrive as represented. If the buyer demands that we accept a return, we usually work with them to try to avoid this. But if the item is in fact returned, we will inform you, and it is your responsibility to make sure that we can give them an appropriate refund and hopefully relist your item for sale on eBay. Returns are extremely rare, but they do happen.

Q: Can I keep possession of my item during this process?

A: We prefer to keep all items under our control to assure the fastest possible shipment to the buyer.

★A BIRD IN THE HAND IS WORTH TWO IN THE BUSH

I urge you always to keep possession of items you are selling for clients on your eBay seller's account. Regardless of how good your relationship with a client, things can happen. "Seller's remorse," sentimental attachment, a change in their financial condition, damage, and many other factors can cause problems for you. When their own eBay feedback isn't at stake, clients aren't always reluctant to change their mind about parting with their items. Of course, if you list on the client's own eBay account, this is not really an issue for you.

Q: What am I required to do as part of this deal?

A: Absolutely nothing! We handle the research, photography, listing, collection of money, and shipping. After your listing sells successfully, we mail you a check!

No doubt other questions will pop up from time to time, and it would be a great idea to keep track of the questions and of effective ways to address them. On index cards in my store, I jot down little notes about customer interactions for later reference and brainstorming. I take the time to discuss the details of these interactions with my employees, to help them better handle clients and any new topics that might come up.

COMFY CLIENTS

If your new-found client chooses to start working with you immediately, this would be a great time to review final prices actually realized on eBay for one or two of their items (exact matches if possible, or closely comparable items if not) to give them an idea of what they might expect. You accomplish this with a search of completed items on eBay. But make sure they understand that, of course, the figures of completed auctions *guarantee* nothing.

You will need to gauge the level of research needed on a client-by-client basis. Some people really don't care what things sell for—they just want to get rid of them. Others will be hesitant to part with their cherished heirloom and might be very angry if it doesn't sell for top dollar. Be careful of the latter. Make sure you always have an item submission form or contract for each item that clearly states the authorized starting price, which the client and you both sign. Be absolutely certain that the client understands that the starting bid amount or Reserve amount should be the minimum (don't forget—less your commission!) at which they will be *completely comfortable* in letting the item go. Even if it's just $0.99, it's always possible, and does happen all the time, that an item will sell for the starting price.

★ DIG DEEPER

If you want more in-depth research tools, you can use Terapeak.com, a subscription-based eBay research Web site. This site provides average price data, charts, time of day, and day of week sales trends, and much more.

STUNNED BY A RUG

I once listed a common, machine-made (and ugly) area rug for a client, and he authorized me to list it for a $1 minimum bid with no reserve. The shipping was so expensive that no buyer would bid more than $1, and the rug sold for that amount. The client was devastated. Now he told me that the rug was the "joy" of his life and a cherished family heirloom. I was stunned. I had failed to realize that my client was emotionally attached to this rug, and I shouldn't have agreed to list it at all, because he had totally unrealistic expectations of the auction outcome. It's critical that you make sure your client truly understands your procedures and the possible outcome of an auction. If you set minimum bids requested by clients, I suggest that you insist that they make those minimums realistic and low enough to leave room for the possibility of a sale. Remember that bad word of mouth is ten times worse in the long run than simply turning down an item that you don't feel is appropriate for your services.

COMPLETED ONLY

As for your research, if you have a small number of things to look up on the eBay site, you can conduct the research while your client waits. When looking at the eBay listings, be sure to sort your search results by price, starting with the highest prices realized. And make absolutely certain that you only review the completed listings. If you are not readily familiar with the completed items search function on the eBay site, you should take the time to use eBay's help system to get a full tutorial on how to search for an item.

Remember that in Completed Auctions, you can search only the Subject words, the title of the listing, not the more detailed description, so in many cases you will need to try different search words. Be very specific whenever possible and use make, model number, and any other specific words to narrow the search.

THOUSANDS OF RESULTS

A search for "diamond ring" will pull up thousands of results. You might try "1ct diamond ring" to narrow the search. For certain kinds of items, such as the diamond ring categories, eBay adds a Product Finder, a series of pull-down menus that allow you to specify the carat size, ring size, and other item specifics to aid in the search process. Be sure to look for these tools, as they vary from category to category and can really help in the research process.

Add date, color, brand, etc. to narrow a search. If you are looking up a hubcap from a 1970 Volkswagen, you would want to use a search similar to "1970 Volkswagen hubcap;" or if you wanted simply to look for any Volkswagen hub cap from the 1970s, you could search "197* Volkswagen hubcap," in which the asterisk provides a wildcard. This would return any listing for the hubcap from that decade.

When searching, try plural and singular variations, for example, "Gorham Etruscan fork" and "Gorham Etruscan forks." You can learn about other advanced search methods by going to the help system on eBay.

JUDGMENT CALL

At this point, you should have a general idea of the value of the items you are dealing with. If you are unable to find similar items on eBay and have doubts about the value of what you are being asked to sell, you may be wasting time on something that won't be worth the effort.

But you also make a big mistake by rejecting an item simply because you don't know, or can't find out, anything about it.

You have to use some judgment. After all, your time is extremely valuable, and the last thing you want to do is fill your day listing junk. And frankly, junk is what about 80 percent of clients bring us. We literally turn down over three-fourths of what comes in the door. Often, individuals with junk have already tried to pawn it or sell it at a flea market or yard sale and have had no luck getting anywhere near the value they want. Believe it or not, until people really get to know you, you might be a target for folks who take you for a sucker, and they will try to waste your precious time listing their worthless stuff on eBay. Many people who come to us have already tried other eBay Trading Assistants who have turned them down.

GOLD MINING

One eBay phenomenon is that many people unfamiliar with eBay have the perception that it's a gold mine. Another, related phenomenon is that eBay has brought massive quantities of certain kinds of items out of the woodwork. Thus, the 1960s *Life* magazine issue on the moon landing might have brought $20 in a used book store or antique mall ten years ago (before eBay) but now might bring $1 on eBay, because so many copies of this issue have come out of the woodwork and onto eBay. Supply and demand has driven the price into the basement. A woman once walked into my store and *proclaimed*: "I have 50 Beanie Babies, and I want to sell them on eBay." I sensed from her tone that she had extremely unrealistic expectations for the amount these would realize on eBay, thinking that they were now rare collectibles and that eBay was a gold mine for such things. I searched "Beanie Baby" in the Completed Listings on eBay, and turned our front desk computer monitor for her to see. The search results showed nearly 30,000 completed Beanie Baby auctions—almost all had started at $0.99, and most of the relatively few that had actually sold had fetched that price—$0.99. The woman was in shock. When she recovered, she said, "You know, I think I'll give them to the children's hospital." I told her I thought that was a wonderful idea.

DODGING THE DELUGE

Focus only on those things for which you can obtain good value. Try using different methods of valuation. It's always good to get help from others. You can tap into your network of knowledgeable friends for advice. I routinely confer with experts in their fields to help me properly grade and identify merchandise that falls outside the scope of my expertise. I pay them 5 percent of the final selling price for their help. This is a great arrangement that works beautifully for everyone. We keep a roster of experts all over the country (and even some in other countries) who can quickly identify and value items from a brief description and photograph.

Another defense against the legions of junky merchandise is a simple one—tell your clients you want "good" stuff. I keep a list of specific things that do well, and I hand it to my clients. Part of this process is education. Just because someone paid $22.50 for a collector plate in 1975 does not mean it is worth $300 today. Most of the "collector" series editions people buy are so mass-produced that they don't hold their value.

But there are pitfalls to listing only items that can be easily researched. Sometimes you will have a "sleeper" item. Sleepers are things you would never imagine to be worth anything that turn out to sell for an amazing windfall. One such item was the 1930s Lenci figurine, described in the Introduction, which the client had almost thrown out because she thought it worthless (and ugly). This ultrarare porcelain sold for $17,000 on eBay.

★SOME AMAZING AND UNEXPECTED SALES AT OUR STORE

- An antique photo of Abraham Lincoln that sold for $5,000
- A four-inch Tiffany lamp shade that sold for $1,525
- An old Indy 500 felt pennant that sold for $1,414.87
- A set of Towle stainless flatware that sold for $1,136.11
- A two-and-a-half inch tall Wedgwood covered box that sold for $1,025
- A 1950s Nikon camera that sold for $1,000.03
- A rare Hummel figurine that sold for $917
- A nonfunctional vintage Fender tube amplifier that sold for $871
- An old (and beat up) cornet wind instrument that sold for $835
- An old Toby drinking mug that sold for $810
- A used storage tin from the 1800s that sold for $771.99

ON THE COLLECTIBLES LIMB

The challenge for you will be to have some vision and be willing to go out on a limb with items like this. Sometimes (not always, of course), a little intuition, going with a gut feeling, or playing a hunch will pay handsomely. You just want to avoid finding yourself bogged down with tons of unsold items that you should never have agreed to list for your clients.

We sell in just about every category on eBay for our clients. The collectibles category is one area where prices are not easily researched and determined. Collectors are an interesting bunch who will often pay any price to get what they want. It's important with collectibles to have knowledgeable friends, dealers, and experts who can identify potential treasure. A terrific way to get this help quickly is by posting a photo of the item on one of eBay's great Community Boards and asking other eBay community members to give you their opinion.

When you are dealing with large lots or estates, you won't have the time to research each and every item while your client waits. It's important to explain this and assure them that their items will be handled efficiently and thoroughly at a later time.

GRANDMA'S BROKEN PORCELAIN

Sometimes a client will have an inventory list of the items they have brought to you, and at other times, the items will arrive simply piled in a box. Regardless of how these new listing items arrive, it's important that you go through them physically one at a time to note the condition and take a physical piece count. Write a short description of the item on your submission form or contract that is sufficient to identify it. If your client has their own list, you can simply check the pieces off this list. You must be very careful to note any problems with item condition. The last thing you want is to be accused later of breaking Grandma's porcelain figurine and ending up in a dispute. If an item has issues such as a scratch, a ding, or some other damage, be sure to make a note of it and make the client aware of it when you receive it.

You should try to accept only clean merchandise. Think back to what I said about cleaning in Chapter 15. We see so many boxes of dirty, dusty, and even filthy things that we simply have to draw the line somewhere. We ask our clients to bring items that are clean and ready for listing. Cleaning merchandise is no easy task, and eventually it leads to a dingy, dirty office or home. Sometimes it's hard to say no to a good lot of dirty merchandise, but unless you get a huge group of fabulous, dirty Steuben glass or a filthy three-carat diamond ring, you really need to ask your clients to come back when the cleaning has been done. Be careful also not to turn down items that should *not* be cleaned, such as many antiques, collectibles, coins, etc.

Once everything has been inventoried on the submission form or contract, have the client sign it as evidence that you both agree on the item count and the condition of each item that is less than perfect. If you collect an up-front listing fee, now is a great time to total up what is owed and collect the money.

THEY STEAL MORE THAN TIME

If this is the first time you have done business with an individual, you should request and photocopy their identification as due diligence to protect your business in the event that you mistakenly accept and list stolen property.

I once received a call from the Glendale, California, police department. They had found one of my company's check stubs in the apartment of a robbery suspect. Apparently, he had brought us some camera equipment to list on eBay. Because we had provided serial numbers on all of the equipment in our listings, the police were quickly able to identify it as part of the stolen property they were seeking. The great news is that this was the first such call we'd had in our seven years in business. The transparency of the eBay marketplace, its easy search functions, and our good records helped to solve a crime!

Watch out for red flags. If you are offered a submission of ten brand-new, in-the-box, high-end portable DVD players from a client you don't know well or at all, you should probably ask some questions. Where did they get them? Do they have a receipt? You also must get government-issued identification from 100 percent of your clients 100 percent of the time. Use common sense. You will find that 99.9999 percent of the time, the submissions you receive make sense and seem logical, but if something bothers you about a client's items or the circumstances, don't be afraid to inform them tactfully that you don't feel their items would be appropriate for your service.

Hopefully you will never have to face a situation where you have accepted stolen merchandise for listing on eBay. If you become aware that an item may be in question, it is your immediate responsibility to contact the police and discuss the item with them. If you follow some basic processes, such as always requiring government-issued identification and mailing payments by check (never paying in cash), you'll probably never have to face a stolen merchandise issue.

And you don't want to buy anything outright until you have checked the laws of your state and city regarding the buying of merchandise from the general public. As an eBay Trading Assistant, you are acting as a listing service and a bailee—an individual or entity (as a business organization) having temporary possession of another's personal property. You are not the owner of the items you sell; rather, you are simply listing and selling them on eBay for others, for a fee, while providing interim storage until the items sell. You are not taking clear title to the merchandise, nor are you buying it from the client. The rules change drastically when you start buying outright from the public.

YOUR LIFEBLOOD

Referrals are a Trading Assistant's lifeblood. We discussed giving each of your clients ten of your business cards to distribute, ideally with their name or some code on each card to enable you to track referrals back to their source. I routinely give cash incentives for referrals, but to my wealthy clients, I prefer sending cookies or other tokens of appreciation rather than cash. Many of these high net worth individuals came to you primarily to declutter their lives, not to make money. And don't underestimate the value of a simple thank-you card. The important thing is that you do *something* to show appreciation.

Your best marketing tool is success. Success for clients with good merchandise will bring more clients. You have to be patient as you build your business, but when you get a great price for someone's item, the word spreads, and the referrals come in.

THE CLIENT RAINBOW

Caution, or even skepticism, about you and your work is natural and common with new clients. This is their first time dealing with you, and they may try to give you a few small, low-end items to test the waters. Be prepared for this situation, and be prepared to be firm in your position.

One of our former clients was an avid eBay seller himself who had put himself though chiropractic school with his eBay earnings. He was an eBay veteran with impressive feedback. But now he was busy with his new practice, and was seeking the services of a qualified Trading Assistant to sell for him. He said that he had storage units filled with excellent, high-end merchandise, but because he didn't know us, he would give us a chance to prove ourselves by listing an initial group of low-ticket items. He gave us some fishing lures, surplus medical supplies, and a few other odds and ends to list on eBay.

I warned my store manager about the potential downside of accepting these "test" listings. Not only did we end up spending a lot of time researching, photographing, and listing these inexpensive things, but once they were listed, we were being second-guessed by the client on every listing title, description, and decision we had made on his listings. He was high maintenance on this low-end stuff, and I immediately got to the bottom line with him, telling him that this type of merchandise didn't warrant the time needed to give him the quality work he was seeking.

When most of these items sold and the client contacted us about "test marketing" some more things to see "how we would do," I politely declined and asked for his best, high-ticket items. I realized that he was dumping the stuff he didn't want to bother listing on eBay himself, and that we would probably never get his best merchandise, no matter how good our work for him. I cut my losses and moved on, and this was the right decision.

CHATTING YOU UP

Use caution with the extremely chatty people, too. Getting into long and unproductive conversations with clients is what I call the chit-chat rathole. An apparently lucrative one-item submission can quickly turn into a client you just can't get rid of. A $50 doll may have a history and pedigree that the proud owner must share in such detail you might start thinking, ". . . then the earth cooled." Be professional and to the point, focusing the client and your conversation on the basics needed to put their item on eBay. Don't be afraid to explain politely that your work involves many other tasks and that you need to attend to them. This may be hard for you if you are not a natural-born closer, and you may have to practice this skill. But if you are going to grow and quickly, you need to be able to manage your clients professionally and politely while adhering to good time management. Your time is money, and you must consider how much time you can give each client based on the potential returns.

Some clients to avoid:

- Clients who keep trying to cut your fees.
- *Dealers who just want to unload their low-end, dead merchandise on you.* You will become their free storage facility, while they hope to move a few items that would not sell anywhere else.
- *Profit maximizers who hope to buy something and resell it immediately for a quick profit.* This plan only works if they have an exceptionally great eye for a bargain and/or extraordinary luck. Usually, such people demand high starting prices that will result in few sales.
- *Clingy people who really don't want to sell their items.* They often make daily phone calls, asking if their item has been listed yet or if it has sold. Typically their sale price expectations are too high and/or they have extreme remorse for selling something they really didn't want to part with in the first place.
- *Desperate individuals who need money today.* Avoid these folks—they're trouble. Often a telltale sign, their first request will be that you buy their merchandise outright. You should have a nice

long list of pawnshops and other cash buyers who can help them. But if you do have a listing agreement with them, they will behave much like the clingy people—calling daily to see if their item has sold.

- *People who can't produce photo identification and insist on picking up checks rather than having you mail them.* Don't take their stuff!

Clients you should welcome with open arms:

- *Wealthy individuals with too many things.* They simply want to get rid of unwanted items and declutter their lives.
- *Corporations and businesses.* They may want you to dispose of excess inventory, customer returns, and open-box merchandise.
- *Charities that receive quantities of good donations.* This group can be a challenge because they often want you to handle everything— the good and the bad. You need to make them aware that some of the merchandise won't be suitable for eBay, and you should have an agreement with them that any such items will be returned to them or donated to a thrift store by mutual agreement.
- Any clients with quality unwanted items and realistic expectations.

A QUICK CHEAT SHEET

Here is a review of what to remember when handling clients and their merchandise:

- Be helpful and friendly—your customer service skills must be exceptional
- Explain your service in detail for the first-timer
- Give prospective new clients your services brochure and fee schedule
- Get the new client's basic information and note how they found out about you
- Ask that you see all items before you research more than one

- Try to accept only clean merchandise
- Research completed listings on smaller lots; do research for larger ones later
- Carefully and thoroughly review the piece count and condition with the client
- Fill out your item submission form or contract
- Give your client ten business cards to give to others and ask them to write their name on them, and specifically ask for referrals
- Watch out for the tire kickers, time burners, and competitors seeking to pick your brain with no intention of listing anything
- Avoid the picky and difficult clients
- Avoid the chit-chat rathole
- Stay very organized—you are dealing with other people's valuable things

19 PAYING CLIENTS

We had a walk-in customer bring us an 1870-CC Seated Liberty dollar coin to sell for them. We submitted it to a nationally recognized coin-grading company because we felt it had a rare date and was in outstanding condition. It came back as one of the finest possible grades. We listed and sold it on eBay for $98,900. The client admitted that he was prepared to accept an offer of a few dollars or less. I think he was pleasantly surprised.

Louis Palafoutas,

Superior Galleries, Inc. of Beverly Hills, California; eBay user ID "superior"; trading on eBay since March 29, 1999

On the surface, paying clients might seem a simple matter—you sell something, collect the money, deduct your commission, and pay your client. But there are some subtleties to this process, such as the frequency with which you pay clients and how to handle buyer returns. Keeping good, accurate records will help immensely.

TIMING IS EVERYTHING

When your business is small, you can pay clients very frequently, and this will create high levels of satisfaction and thus result in more referrals. As you grow your business, you will increasingly need to work smart to make your workload as manageable as possible and compartmentalize your various tasks, including paying your clients. As your volume of clients and their sold items grows, you will want to pay on a periodic basis that makes sense for your schedule and your ability to process the payments.

At my company, we pay our clients on a monthly basis for a very specific reason—we want to attract upscale clientele. By paying this way we accomplish three things:

1. We weed out the desperate clients who usually do not have high-quality merchandise anyway.
2. We allow time for the buyers to receive the sold items and leave us positive feedback or let us know if anything was not 100 percent satisfactory to them.
3. We reduce our administrative costs for handling these payments.

If you plan to pay more frequently than we do, weigh the pros and cons of doing so. Paying quickly will thrill your clients and hopefully encourage more item submissions. The downside is that you will spend more time dealing with payments. More important is the possibility that a buyer may wish to return an item for which you have already paid your client (see below for more on this).

If you do decide to pay weekly or every other week, you will have to micromanage each payment by monitoring the status of the shipment to the buyer. You can set up some check boxes on your item submission form that allow you to track some additional attributes of the sale, such as:

- Whether ten days have elapsed since you deposited a payment check, which helps to ensure that the check hasn't been returned (bounced)
- Whether the buyer has left you positive feedback for the transaction
- Whether the time allowed for returns has expired, if you have a returns policy

MOVE THOSE FUNDS

You can pay your clients by check or through PayPal. If your client has a free personal PayPal account, they can receive payments from you electronically without the service charge associated with PayPal's Premiere or Business accounts.

You should open a separate bank account where you will hold your clients' money until it's time to pay them. It may be tempting to spend money sitting in your regular operating account that actually belongs to your clients. Calculate what you expect to owe your clients after taking your commissions, and then move these funds to the client account for safekeeping. Many banks allow you to make quick and free transfers between accounts online.

If you are operating a Trading Assistant business from within your existing retail business, you can also offer your clients a store credit to make purchases in your establishment. You may want to offer reduced commissions for clients who opt for a store credit as a further incentive to receive payment this way, because you will make a profit on the items they take in credit.

★TIP

If your client has unsold items that must be picked up, you can hold their check and unsold items together and ask them to pick up both at the same time, as an incentive for them to remove the unsuccessful merchandise quickly. I have found that items waiting for client pick-up may sit at my store indefinitely if I mail their payments.

THINGS BOUNCE BACK

When you ship orders, it's very important that you have the capability to track the status of their delivery. If you do not receive positive feedback immediately after delivery, send the buyer a quick e-mail asking them if they were completely satisfied with their order so that you can pay your client. There is a very good possibility that your clients will be looking at your eBay account to see if their items have sold, and in the rare instance that a customer service problem does arise, you should let the client know so that they realize their payment may be delayed until the problem can be resolved.

If you do receive a return on a shipment, hopefully you haven't already made a payout for that item and you can simply relist it. If you have already paid out on the sale, you will have the somewhat uncomfortable task of informing your client and asking for the return of the money. In the entire time I have been in business, I have only had to do this with clients who bring me large quantities of items. With such clients, there is an ongoing flow of payments against which I can make an adjustment. You may, however, run into a client who feels that the sale is a sale regardless of the return and refuse to repay you. Thus, you may wish to add some specific language to your contract that requires clients' cooperation in these situations. But if you are careful, this will rarely, if ever, happen, and you won't be stuck holding the bag.

At my company, fewer than 1 in 500 shipments results in any form of customer service issue or return. If you take care to be accurate and honest in your eBay listings and pack items well, you will rarely face return issues.

KEEPING EXISTING CLIENTS COMING BACK FOR MORE

As the ambassador for your own company, you must keep in touch with your clients' needs and work on ways to keep them bringing in more merchandise. I am on one of my many business trips as I write this, sitting in my room at the Wynn Hotel in Las Vegas. Although the room costs an astronomical $269 a night, I am quite impressed with the hotel's service—from the wonderful sundries to the little chocolates I find each evening after I receive turndown service—everything is brilliant and impeccable. Such exceptional service goes a long way in offsetting any sticker shock I would otherwise feel from such an expensive hotel stay. And though sticker shock won't normally be an issue with your clients, this is the very same type of service they should expect from you.

THE CLIENT IS KING

Keeping clients happy means using exceptional customer service skills. It all starts with an authentically great attitude, something that's deep within you as a person. It's important for you to maintain positive energy at all times—it will definitely spill over into your professional behavior. Treat every client exactly as you would like to be treated, and you will find that real excellence surrounds you. Giving great customer service takes some practice, but eventually it will be second nature.

Forging positive relationships with people will make your business thrive and turn first-time customers into long-term clients. It's also critical that the quality of everything you do as a Trading Assistant is *consistent*—do what you say you will every time, without making difficult-to-keep or empty promises, and people will judge you by your actions. Keep your word at all times.

In your eagerness to acquire a new client, you should never puff up the anticipated value of a client's items or promise something you may not be able to deliver just to score a deal. Train your staff to be helpful and knowledgeable. Every person who works for you should have the power and ability to make the decisions necessary to service your clients properly while still bringing profit to you.

Use Kid Gloves

From the moment you touch an item belonging to another person, you must handle it with the utmost care. Regardless of your own perception of the value of someone else's personal belongings, show that you value their cherished possessions to the same extent they do from your initial contact with the item all the way through its packing and shipping.

Their Call

Most of us are turned off by pushy salespeople. Even though you are selling yourself and your services, I urge you not to pressure clients to make any decision. You must nurture your relationships with your clients and treat them like gold. Despite my normal policy of not listing items on eBay with minimum starting prices or Reserves, at a client's request, I once put a very fine set of sterling silver flatware on eBay with a $1,700 minimum starting price. I received no bids at that price, but several offers to purchase the item for prices several hundred dollars less. I presented all the offers to my client, but he declined them. I didn't try to pressure him, even influence him, or complain about his decision in any way. In fact, I told him it would be fine to keep the set in my eBay Store, because I really liked it and wanted to give it a fair chance to get more offers. And a few weeks later, it sold for the full price on eBay. I could have encouraged the client to accept one of the lower offers, but I didn't. I simply informed him of the offers without comment and deferred to his wishes. It was the right decision—when a buyer finally did surface, we both made money, everyone was happy, and my client brought me more high-quality items—he felt totally comfortable with me.

Giving Good Phone

A friendly voice on the phone welcoming prospective new clients is a must. Don't underestimate the importance of giving good "phone." Train everyone in your organization to answer promptly and courteously. I don't screen my calls, and I tell my staff not to do so, either. Personally, I find it irritating when I call a business and hear ". . . and this is? What is this regarding?" and I do not allow my employees to answer the phone this way.

Always return phone calls regardless of their nature—even if doing so seems to be without benefit to you. Years ago, when I worked in the entertainment industry as a personal manager of actors, I once asked one of the most successful talent agents for her secrets of success. A key part of her formula, she told me, was that she returned every single telephone call every single day before leaving her office—without fail, without exception. Have a member of your staff do so when you are away or can't do it personally. The result will be professionalism on the highest level.

Make yourself available whenever possible. Have an answering machine to answer calls when you are not at work. This may seem obvious, but some companies don't have one. Your message should include your hours of operation to help clients in scheduling their visits.

Become an Oracle

Be an authority and let people know it. Providing advice to people about what you do will get you more referrals. Numerous times, someone has declined my services, but because of my gregarious nature and willingness to be of assistance, they later referred others to me who then became clients themselves. Being charismatic and commanding attention with your great expertise and knowledge will attract people to you automatically.

You can speak at local organizations as a way of educating others about your business. I have spoken to many different groups, creating more business for me. Most people who fear sharing information will fail. Being generous with your time will attract other generous people to you.

Integrity Sells

You can't possibly know everything. As a seller of unwanted items, you will have to be able to assess complex situations related to the sale of a wide variety of merchandise. When you don't know something, it's important to be honest about it. You can't fake your way through—you must make every effort to find the answer. Take responsibility and never pass the buck.

Open Your Ears

Everyone is a unique individual. We all speak and think in different ways, and it's very important that you listen carefully to your clients. While talking with them, never interrupt, and be thoughtful and open-minded. Maintain eye contact and ask questions about any points you do not fully understand. This is particularly important during initial client consultations to ensure that you understand your client's expectations of your services. If a prospect has never used a Trading Assistant before, you need to be very clear about their perceptions of your work and to identify and clear up any misconceptions.

Learning to listen effectively will bring you closer to the needs of your clients. Never ague verbally (or even mentally) with them; rather, try to understand how they think and feel—and try to relate to them. Because yours is a service business, customers are your number-one priority. This applies both to the clients who bring items and to the buyers who purchase them. Get to know the needs of each person with whom you do business. We speak to a lot of our buyers on the phone, but we also "listen" to them by keeping tabs on what they buy from us, and we keep lists of our buyers and their interests, so that we can notify them of specific upcoming sales.

Cross Your Ts

People appreciate efficiency, especially when it comes to getting paid, and your clients will feel more confident in working with you if your payouts and records are accurate. We can generate a list of both sold and unsold items for any client in a matter of minutes. Each time you pay your clients for sold items, provide them with a list of their unsold inventory and let them know if they are required to retrieve it from your place of business or if the items will be relisted. Keep copies of all your payout sheets so that you can refer to them in the event of an error. Generally, it's a good idea to keep a copy of everything you do for a client. Keep client-specific documents in their alphabetical file. Keeping everything chronological in the client's folder will help in finding documents quickly. There's a lot to be said for keeping a manual filing system. Although computer records are great, having hard copies is very handy in the event of computer data loss.

THE "WOW" REPORT

Consider each successful sale an opportunity to promote your fine work. Try compiling a list of your most notable and amazing sales each month and include a copy of it (along with a photo, if possible) with your check when you pay your clients. Many people have items similar to those you have sold but may not have realized their true value or considered bringing them to you. Providing this "wow" report to your clients will help keep you and these items in the front of their minds.

When someone calls you and asks for more information about your service, you might want to capture their mailing (or e-mail) address so that you can send these prospective clients a monthly update of your successes as well. Being a good self-promoter is a necessary part of being a businessperson.

★TIP

I encourage you to keep your item photos indefinitely. You never know when you may want to use them at some future date for publicity or marketing purposes. If you start running out of space on your computer's hard drive, you can always burn them to a CD or DVD and save them in a secure and safe place. Save the auction information so that you can match it up to the photos if needed.

COUPON CULTURE

Coupons and discounts are a part of American life. The word *sale* strikes a chord that gets us spending. I certainly love to save money, and

I've caught myself putting off washing my car until the Sunday newspaper arrived with the car wash discount coupons in it. Whether your business is going through a slow period or growing robustly, consider mailing out coupons to your clients. Make them fun and create a call to action. A coupon should provide enough value to get someone to act quickly. You can offer a discount on your commissions, for example 5 to 10 percent off your normal fee for a specific month, or if a client brings in ten or more items, etc.

Another coupon idea could be a charity contribution program. You can work with your local charities and get their permission to mention that a portion of the proceeds of every sale (taken from your commission, of course) would be donated to a specific charity. People tend to respect and admire those who do good for their community.

MAKE IT PERSONAL

People appreciate personal service more than ever in this increasingly impersonal world. It's always a good idea to give clients a call, and not just to let them know the status of their items. If one of their items sold for an amazing amount of money, you should call the client the same day and give them the good news. Generally, it's a great idea to touch base with your clients on a monthly basis, even when they don't have items in your care, to see how they are doing, check to see if they have more items that need listing, and find out if they have friends who may need you. Staying fresh in their minds is great marketing, and they will appreciate your personal service. It is important to ask your clients if they welcome such calls and to also give them the option to opt out of them.

20 CONFLICT RESOLUTION: HANDLING CLIENT (AND BUYER) DISPUTES EFFECTIVELY

I sold a collection of 35 match safes on behalf of a local minister whose grandfather had collected them. I sold one alone for $485 on eBay. Most of them sold to a California doctor who collected match safes and was willing to pay whatever he had to pay in order to get them.

Len Smoke, Orlando, Florida;

eBay user ID "superdealsusa"; trading on eBay since February 27, 1998

WHEN THE GOING GETS TOUGH, THE DIPLOMAT GETS GOING

Don't ever duck a complaint. It can be scary dealing with an irate person, but you have to do it. Be strong and wise in your solution to every problem that presents itself. On occasion, as we have discussed, someone may be unhappy with the price their item realized, or they may regret having sold it at all. Simply reminding them that they are bound by a legal contract will probably only further fuel the fire. Stand your ground and explain your obligations to your buyers, but express sincere empathy and understanding for your client. Diplomacy and a spoonful of sugar will go a long way to calm nerves and get the situation under control. Bring the same kindness to all your business interactions and complaints will be rare.

And *always* follow through with your commitments. Once the bonds of trust are broken, it will take a tremendous amount of work to try to heal a soured relationship. An unhappy client can share one bad experience with ten other clients, impacting your reputation exponentially. So be very proactive with misunderstandings—clear them up as fast as possible.

As much as we might like to think otherwise, an attraction to conflict is part of human nature—conflict makes movies and television programs interesting. In real life, some people like to argue as a part of the fabric of their daily lives, while others prefer to acquiesce and avoid conflict. You will encounter many different personalities and cultures as a Trading Assistant, and the possibility of conflict looms whenever doing business with other people—both buyers and clients. The art of diplomacy must be learned, and you must work towards mastering the skills necessary to resolve conflicts as they arise to the satisfaction of all parties.

I believe that in general conflicts can be resolved using unemotional logic seasoned with a bit of understanding and compassion for your customers—whether a client or eBay item purchaser. Most conflicts arise either as a result of a misunderstanding or out of ulterior motives.

- *Misunderstanding.* In my experience, communication problems are the biggest cause of conflicts. Maybe your client didn't fully understand their contract, or perhaps some of the terms in your eBay listing terms were unclear. Usually such conflicts can be managed and resolved fairly easily. If you are careful, clear, and honest in your dealings with people, a conflict of this type that cannot be resolved is a rare event, because most people are fair and honest and have reasonable expectations.
- *Ulterior motives.* Some conflicts result from factors beyond your understanding or control, such as a person with ulterior motives who actively seeks conflict. Either a client or buyer may try to leverage a better deal from you after the fact by cooking up a conflict—commonly, for example, by claiming dissatisfaction with your service. These conflicts are much more difficult to

resolve, because the other person will be playing games with you to obtain the results they seek.

TEMPER TANTRUMS

First of all, remain *calm*. There is absolutely nothing to be gained from flaring tempers, and there's plenty to lose. I am a stubborn and, quite frankly, often rather difficult person by nature. It's very hard for me to remain calm during a conflict incident because of my personal programming. I have blown a number of business deals over the years because of shortsighted stubbornness and a lack of vision. Remember that you are a businessperson now, and being "right" doesn't necessarily always work in business situations. You have to approach every situation with confidence that you can resolve any conflicts that might arise. Keep in mind that one vocal individual can do tremendous damage to you and your business's reputation, even if you are completely innocent. Your goal is to have satisfied clients and buyers, and although you can't make everyone happy, you can achieve a high success rate with bad situations if you follow some basic ground rules.

Have you ever seen a small disagreement escalate into a big fight? Have you ever suddenly found yourself caught in the middle of a verbal battle? How did the situation get out of control? What were you feeling and thinking? Did you feel badly afterwards? What could you have done to avoid the conflict in the first place?

CONFLICT MANAGEMENT TIPS

- Don't let the conflict escalate by allowing yourself to get angry; stop and take a mental "time out" to allow yourself to think the situation through
- Determine the cause of the other person's problem and mentally inventory their objections and concerns so that you can address them individually

- Put yourself in the other person's shoes and try your best to see their point of view while coming up with ways to come to an understanding and resolution
- Be a great listener and remain open-minded about the possibility of a compromise
- Try to think of any and all options that might allow both parties to get what they want and walk away happy
- Be extremely truthful—do not simply tell the other person what they want to hear, but instead be honest in your handling of the conflict
- If the conflict is face-to-face or on the phone, do not interrupt the other person—take turns talking
- Don't engage in finger pointing—blaming the other person will only escalate the conflict further
- Be a lightning rod for the other person's anger—take some of their pain away by saying things such as, "I understand your feelings and want to help resolve this situation . . ."

Lighten up. It's not appropriate to make light of another person's feelings or problem, but being congenial and friendly goes light-years farther towards conflict resolution than being stern and hardheaded. People are by nature intuitive about others' moods and feelings, and projecting an affable and genuine attitude will help to bring a conflict to a swifter conclusion.

INFLATED EXPECTATIONS

Because you will have many clients with different personalities and levels of business experience, at some time or another you will no doubt run into a conflict with one of them. The most common issue that will arise is that of a client's inflated expectations for the amount of money their item will bring on eBay. If you list clients' items with the minimum bid price they specify based on their expectation for the item (taking into account your commission), then you shouldn't have a problem. If you charge for this minimum bid service with an up-front listing fee, some clients with inflated expectations of the value of their items may opt to save on these fees. But their "treasures" may not be as valuable as expected. This can cause, to put it mildly, disappointment.

As with my client described previously, whose family heirloom rug sold for $0.99, some clients may experience "seller's remorse" after the sale. It turns out that they had a strong emotional attachment to the item and, deep down, never really wanted to sell it (and probably never should have). Now that their item has another owner, they're miserable and may, in rare cases, try to block the sale. As always, you must be understanding and empathetic but firm—you have a contract!

Some folks are so excited about being able to sell on eBay that they lose sight of the fact that things can sell for low prices. Inflated expectations are not uncommon, especially when based on the original purchase price of the item. Always let clients know at the outset that there is a very real possibility, without a high minimum bid or reserve price, of an item selling low. I make a point of trying to head off later client disappointment by reinforcing to them that eBay should be their venue for selling unwanted items—items for which they have no emotional or financial expectations or attachment—at a low starting price that encourages bidding interest. And if an item sells for more than they expected, there will be nothing but smiles.

TAMING THE UNRULY

What happens if you present your client with their accounting statement and check and they become irate over a low selling price? It's critical that you (and they) understand your role as the liquidator of unwanted merchandise. Never overcommit yourself or puff up your abilities beyond what you can actually deliver. You are at the mercy of the eBay buyers and what they are willing to pay for an item.

Protect yourself through the process by saving critical e-mails between you and your clients and documenting everything. The contract is only the first step in this—any important decisions that you and your clients make together should be on paper and initialed by both parties, or in saved e-mails, to ensure that you have proof if a dispute arises later.

Be patient, understanding, and clear about your role throughout any disagreement. Don't let an unruly client make you an unruly Trading Assistant—keep a positive attitude and things will sort themselves out.

Make certain that your staff also understands the risks involved in performing services for a difficult client so they can conduct themselves in ways that minimize conflict. Often difficult people are more difficult with the staff than they are with the owner. If a client accuses an employee of poor service or improper conduct, present this information to your employee for their response. If it is a onetime complaint, then you should be prepared to support your employee, as you can easily lose a valued staff member over a client's ranting and unreasonable behavior. Never let the difficult client treat your employees in an abusive manner.

A difficult client is also likely to be unhappy about your fees and may ask you to take a lower commission on a poor outcome. Stick to your guns and your contract in these situations.

Know when to fold—it's not always possible to service everyone's needs, and your sanity is at least as important as servicing the client. If you find that the client is angry, hostile, overly involved, obsessive, dependent, or otherwise high maintenance, you should complete whatever work you have outstanding for them and then sever the relationship. The client who feels that they know more about eBay than you do is to be avoided, too, because they will constantly be telling you your job and second-guessing your decisions.

If you surround yourself with great clients, they will refer more great clients, and eventually your business will be based on people who are positive and appreciative of the fantastic results your eBay Trading Assistant business provides.

UNHAPPY HAPPENS

You have carefully crafted your eBay listing; taken wonderful, clear photos; sold the item and collected the payment; and packed and shipped the item with great pride. The world looks bright, and you are elated with your eBay transaction. But the buyer, on the other hand, receives the item and sends you an e-mail tersely stating that they are not pleased. The vase is smaller than expected, the shoes are a bit too loose, or the painting doesn't really look like it did in your listing. What do you do? Take a deep breath—it happens. Even with the most incredibly accurate description and pictures, buyers aren't always pleased. So what do you do now? Here are the steps to take in making the buyer happy:

- Acknowledge their dissatisfaction by saying something like, "I'm very sorry to hear that you were not completely satisfied with your eBay purchase."
- Ask the buyer what would be required to resolve their complaint and decide whether you feel their requests are reasonable and if you are willing to comply.
- Depending on the nature of their request for resolution, ask if a partial refund would be acceptable, even if it means losing your profit or possibly a few dollars more; or assess the cost of taking a return of the item (your time and return shipping costs) and determine if it would be better to accept the return and simply relist the item.
- If a return is the final result, be sure to pay return shipping as a good faith gesture—assuming the unhappy buyer is without ulterior motives, you want to retain their good will for possible future transactions.

STRIPPING MIDGE

There are some dishonest buyers out there, and you have to deal with each situation on a case-by-case basis. Rarely, buyers will try to swindle you. I once sold a 1960s Midge doll (Barbie's best friend) on eBay, and the buyer claimed it was not as described and asked me to re-fund $30 of the $34 he paid for it. I politely explained I felt it was unfair to practically give the doll away, and I asked him to return it for a full refund. The buyer declined my return/refund offer and then disputed his payment with PayPal. In my response, I informed PayPal that I would accept the doll back as a return (giving the buyer a full refund) and they mediated the issue in my favor. But when I finally did receive the doll back, it was completely nude! The buyer had conveniently kept the clothes, which obviously had some value. Although I was completely shocked by this conduct, I had to weigh the crime against the cost of recovering the property—it was obviously not worth pursuing, and I had to let it go. Realizing that situations like this will arise now and then, you must be prepared to walk away and move on—putting your energy into more profitable pursuits. If I were to dwell on such problems, it would cost me both emotionally and financially—not a good investment of energy.

Most people are good, and you can count on many happy and successful transactions. When a wrinkle does pop up, it's important that you provide incredibly good customer service to your buyer and resolve their issue to the best of your ability. Even if you cannot honor an unreasonable request, be cordial, professional, polite, and customer oriented.

STAYING POSITIVE

Negative feedback is normally the result of a buyer not receiving the service they expected. New members of eBay are more likely to jump the gun and leave a negative feedback comment for you before first attempting to resolve an issue directly with you. Your feedback score is the backbone of your eBay business, and maintaining the highest possible overall positive score will encourage buyers on eBay to purchase items from you. It's extremely important to protect your feedback by taking measures to ensure total buyer satisfaction.

Here are my pointers for keeping your feedback free of negative comments from buyers:

- Carefully review your eBay listing descriptions for complete accuracy—from the wow to the warts.
- Research items and elaborate on their provenance and any other pertinent details you can provide.
- Be comprehensive and conservative in your description of the item's condition, carefully pointing out any physical flaws or

damage. In our photos, we often show such flaws with labels—
we draw a red arrow on a small white label and point it towards
the flaw in a close-up photo.

- Place a ruler next to the item in one photo to provide a scale reference (we use a penny, dime, or quarter for scale with small items such as jewelry).
- Ship promptly upon receipt of payment.
- Include a thank-you card or note in the shipment that also encourages the buyer to contact you immediately if they are not completely satisfied with their order.
- Send a quick follow-up e-mail after the shipment has been delivered (you will be able to determine this from the postal service's Delivery Confirmation service, which you should always use with mail, or UPS's tracking number system) to ask the buyer if they were completely satisfied with their merchandise.

To avoid retaliatory negative feedback, think very carefully before leaving a buyer a negative feedback yourself, and do all that you can to resolve disputes before you leave a buyer a negative.

When a dispute does arise, it may be helpful to review the buyer's feedback and also the feedback the buyer has left for others. You can see the feedback a buyer has left for other eBay members by going to the eBay member's feedback profile and clicking on the "Left for Others" tab. This will give you a good idea of the member's own reputation and how they treat other eBay members. If they tend to leave other sellers negative feedback, you should review their negative comments— maybe you have a habitual complainer. Sometimes, as unfair as it may feel, bending over backwards for these complainers will benefit you in the long run, because a negative feedback can result in lost sales when other buyers see the comment, even if it is unwarranted.

> **★TIP**
>
> If you feel it's appropriate after a heated dispute with a buyer or an encounter with a dishonest buyer, you may want to block them from being able to bid on any of your future auctions through the "Block Bidder/Buyer List" link on the eBay site map, in the "Sell" section. This will prevent future purchases (and the possibility of more disputes) from this eBay member.

21

HIRING, PAYING, MOTIVATING, AND MANAGING EMPLOYEES

I own a jewelry business and decided to start selling through eBay as a Trading Assistant. My clientèle is mostly attorneys and estate trustees. I have four full-time and two part-time employees running my eBay business. In our last four months of business, our eBay fees were only 4.88 percent of our total sales. I look for employees with good computer skills, and then I teach them everything else they need to know. I presently use a software program called Liberty for Trading Assistants from a company called Resale World. We sell exactly 71 percent of the items brought into our store.

Stan Shelley, Hendersonville, North Carolina;

eBay user ID "shelleys_yes"; trading on eBay since October 5, 2004

I've heard other businesspeople say that it's amazingly difficult to find good help these days. I've been very fortunate in my hiring, consistently finding people who are superb at what they do. Hiring is an art that requires some vision on your part. You want a certain balance— happy employees who work hard and know how to follow your directives, anticipate your wishes, and follow your business style. Being someone's boss is an acquired talent that will require patience and time. Not everyone will think the way you do, but they can still provide significant value to your company.

One great attraction for many of my employees, past and present, is the flexibility of working in an online business. My employees can work just about any day of the week to handle such tasks as photography, packing and shipping, and clerical work. Most of the tasks I delegate can be saved up if necessary and completed a few days later.

Some things to look for when hiring for your Trading Assistant business:

- Employee honesty—do they have past employer references?
- Strong computer skills (even shippers use a computer!)
- Prior eBay selling experience
- A friendly, outgoing personality—a must for great customer service skills
- Willingness to be flexible about days of work and hours
- Someone who is enthusiastic about your business

Employee honesty tops my list, because we are handling other people's items, many of high value, and I really and truly need to have total confidence in the people working for me. It's important to find out as much as you can about whom you are considering hiring before bringing them into a position of trust and responsibility.

Here are some additional tips for hiring employees:

- Write clear, thorough, and realistic job descriptions for your employment ads, and make sure your ads provide sufficient information about the job. Or, with the high cost of advertising, you may want to shorten your employment ads and provide your Web site address for a job description and further information.
- Advertise, but also put out the word to existing employees, friends, and family—referrals from people you know and trust can bring you great employees.
- Find out what other comparable employers are paying, to be sure you are competitive.
- Interview carefully, looking at the prospective employee's qualifications and attitude during the interview and listening closely while you let them do a lot of the talking.

- Ask current employees to sit in on the interview—the opinions of those who intimately know your business and your ways can be very valuable.
- Check all job and personal references carefully—call them.
- With the applicant's permission, conduct a background check (*www.sentrylink.com* does them for $19.95).
- If your applicant will be running errands, review their driving record, even if they would be using their own car.
- When making offers of employment, specify all of the terms (hours, pay rate and frequency, benefits, etc.) in writing.

THE BEST MONEY YOU WILL SPEND

Timing is everything, and the time to start hiring is well before you become overwhelmed with work. If you are doing a great job as a Trading Assistant, you will be getting client referrals in droves, and when you find yourself working more than about 40 hours a week, it's time to hire employees, whether full- or part-time. If you've never had employees, hiring can be a difficult decision. You'll find yourself giving up some of your profits to have help, and it can be hard to part with those dollars, but it's something you'll have to do to expand your business. Yes, I've cautioned you to be frugal, but great employees are an exception—their paychecks will be the best money you will spend.

When you are feeling extra tired at the end of the day, diffuse or unproductive, having other people helping and supporting you can make a humongous difference in your own productivity and success. And if your budget has been kept in order, you should be able to accurately project how much extra money you will have at the end of each month that can be allocated to pay staff.

WHEN YOU'RE THE BOSS

When you hire others, you will have some legal responsibilities as their employer, and the Internal Revenue Service as well as your state government will impose some rules on you as well.

Different kinds of business relationships can exist between you and others providing services to you, usually either that of hired employees or of independent contractors. The latter status can be tricky, and I strongly discourage you from treating your help as independent contractors without first consulting a tax professional.

With employees, you must withhold and pay income taxes, withhold and pay Social Security and Medicare taxes, and pay unemployment tax. You are not normally required to withhold or pay any taxes on payments to independent contractors, but be careful: Incorrectly classifying an employee as an independent contractor can result in your being liable for the payment of taxes and penalties.

Your liability insurance will cover nonemployee injuries at your place of business. But before hiring anyone, speak to your insurance broker about the required workers' compensation insurance, which covers your employees in the event of an on-the-job injury. A handy resource for information about workers' compensation laws for your state is located at *www.workerscompensation.com*.

To withhold and report taxes, you will need to fill out an SS-4 form for the IRS, which will provide you with a Federal Employer Identification Number (FEIN) to be used with all payroll services. You can apply for this online at *http://sa.www4.irs.gov/sa_vign/newFormSS4.do*, or you can simply enter "apply for FEIN online" at *www.google.com* to get the link to the form.

Some states do not levy a personal income tax (mine is not one of them—boo-hoo). However, in case yours does, you will need to contact your state to determine if they require withholding and payment of state taxes.

PAYDAY

As a Trading Assistant, you have to keep your costs under control. This means budgeting your payroll—and personalities are a factor. Some people love the comfort of a steady paycheck, while others prefer to work on commission. A few rare individuals who were naturally obsessive about getting things done have worked in my store. A person who likes to keep the ball rolling is ideal for jobs like photography and shipping, where the task is repetitive and you need to be very productive to keep things profitable.

Finding fast, diligent, self-starter workers may be harder than you think—but certainly not impossible. I suggest bringing on *all* employees initially as temporary, part-time workers so that you can see the quality and speed of their work. If they impress you, then you can hire them full-time.

There are different ways to compensate employees with different talents and speeds. You can:

- pay a salary;
- pay an hourly wage;
- pay on a per piece basis, such as for photographing items or packing and shipping; or
- pay a commission or flat rate for listing each item.

If you hire creative people, such as photographers, you may find that they are perfectionists. You need high-quality work of course, but only up to a point. If the photography, for instance, is great but simply taking too long, the law of diminishing returns may be gobbling up your profits; and paying on a per piece basis for this task may help to give your talented photographer much needed perspective.

Recently, I came upon a large estate of very expensive and rare antique pocket watches, and I know nothing about pocket watches. Looking for pocket watch experts on the Internet, I found a new friend, too, in Lance Thomas, who worked in my office for several days creating eBay listings for these valuable rarities. I didn't pay Lance a flat per-listing fee, but instead a 10 percent commission on each final sale. If he could make a compelling listing that sold successfully, I would be happy to share a nice piece of the pie with him. Because he was only paid when an item sold and I received payment, the situation was truly win-win. I believe that this knowledgeable expert generated substantially more profit for my company than if I had tried to muddle through making the listings myself.

Work on your communication skills with prospective and existing employees, because how you compensate people is really a matter of negotiation. You will want insights into their compensation wants and needs, and involving them in the process will help to make them feel appreciated.

★ TIP

Pay is not a subject for public consumption and should be discussed privately. Employees often compare notes, however, so don't play favorites, or it may come back to bite you.

PAYROLL JOY

Payroll is a pain in the . . . well, it can be a chore. I have tried many different payroll services over the years—I've even tried processing payroll myself without a payroll software program. But I've discovered that an online payroll service is a joy. You can't be a "Jack or Jill of all trades." Focus on your Trading Assistant business and use a payroll service or software to help with the accounting tasks.

Now I use Paycycle.com as my payroll processing company. I have found them to be by far the simplest, most reliable, and most cost-effective service available. Paycycle.com charges a monthly service fee, which includes processing all paychecks, withholding and paying all taxes, making contractor payments, producing annual W-2 forms and 1099-MISC forms, and basically any other payroll tasks. Their set-up process guides you through every step required, including providing forms or links to obtain your federal and state employer identification numbers. All taxes are filed electronically whenever possible, and you get phone support from real people. I was paying nearly as much per week with my prior processing service, so I'm saving about 75 percent by using Paycycle.com.

With Paycycle.com, you can handle your entire payroll online from anywhere in the world, and if your employees take the free direct deposit option, you don't even need to go near your checkbook or Quick-Books program to pay them. Paycycle.com even allows you to run a sample payroll from their Web site so you can test drive the service. In any case, be sure to compare the costs and ease of use before choosing a payroll solution.

WHY THEY LOVE YOU

Let's be realistic: Most people won't come to work simply to experience your charming wit and enjoy your wonderful company—they're usually working for the money. If you hire a retiree or student, their financial requirements may be lower, but employee incentives are a viable way to help create employee satisfaction for all.

Offering a flexible schedule to accommodate your employees can be an incentive. You must find ways to motivate and retain the great employees who do so much for you each and every day, and incentive programs are designed to award achievers. Having happy employees will result in amazing customer service, and it is very important that they feel a sense of belonging at your company—this invariably translates into a positive and upbeat attitude.

In today's highly competitive business environment, incentives show appreciation that a salary, no matter how large, can't convey. Most companies, even smaller firms such as yours, offer incentive packages to their staff.

Here are some basic tips for any incentive program:

- Separate incentives from normal pay so that they stand out as something special
- Consider monetary and nonmonetary incentives combined to keep things interesting for your employees
- Reward individual performance and avoid giving group incentives—people love to receive personal acknowledgement for their hard work

- Solicit frequent feedback from your employees to determine how they feel about your treatment of them—listen to them carefully and effect changes when needed

And here are some incentives to consider:

- Scheduling flexibility
- A bonus for bringing in a large new account
- Bonuses for referrals
- A substantial discount on your fees when employees list their own items for sale
- Gift certificates from local merchants
- Full or partial health insurance reimbursement or a group plan to which you contribute 50 percent or more of the premiums
- Baby- or even pet-sitting for employees when they need it
- Offering to drive employees home if they have no car and live close to work
- Offering to match IRA contributions up to a certain limit
- Writing heartfelt thank-you cards
- Remembering employees' birthdays and/or anniversaries
- Taking the staff out for a monthly dinner
- Holding holiday parties
- Providing constant verbal appreciation and acknowledgment

There is really no right or wrong way to give incentives. You should do what your heart tells you. Treat your employees the same way you would want to be treated if you were in their shoes. If you take good care of them, they will return the favor by doing a wonderful job for you.

WHO WILL CLEAN THE BATHROOM?

The ability to delegate is a truly critical management skill. Effective delegation will save you time, reduce personal stress, and help you motivate employees, too. To get tasks accomplished in your Trading Assistant business by delegating, you must first gain the respect of your staff. You won't get instant respect merely because of your position as the employer—you must earn it. Be consistent and ethical in all your dealings. Lead by example: If you expect honest, hard-working employees, you must also be honest and hard working. Simply handing off all of the work to your staff while you drink coffee and talk to friends on the phone all day will result in resentment and, ultimately, employee dissatisfaction. Lead by example.

You must also make a real effort to treat all employees equally and with great respect. Employees are the backbone of your company, and you will want to show them how important they are to you. You must be willing to do any task that you delegate. If you ask someone to take out the trash, you should temper this by doing it yourself as well. Nobody likes to clean the office bathroom, but unless you can afford a maid service, you will have to schedule the employees to take turns doing it, including *yourself*.

Here are some tips for delegating projects to others:

- Choose the right person for the job—don't give a computer project to someone who types "hunt and peck"
- Be very concise in your instructions—think them over carefully and write them down before giving out a job
- Train well if the project is new to the employee
- Provide all needed resources to complete the job
- Give advice and support at all times
- Give deadlines and ask your staff to keep them, but make certain you allow enough time to do so
- Keep it real—never ask for the impossible
- Ask for measurable progress, with reports both verbal and in writing (e-mail is okay)
- Ask each employee to keep a measurable record of their productivity
- Give honest and fair feedback on all work
- Always praise someone for doing a great job

> **★ TIP**
>
> Create a wall chart showing your company's weekly and monthly progress. Put up total sales figures, number of items listed, and other fun facts to keep everyone focused on the business's success.

Effective delegation may require some finesse as well. Sometimes, an employee may express resistance when asked to do something that they don't agree with. Never ask an employee to lie on your behalf or do something uncomfortable. You should explain and justify your reasons for delegating to them.

I would also suggest giving employees varied tasks to help keep the job interesting. If your shipping clerk is an amateur photographer, then perhaps you can give them a day here and there to photograph items. If you already have a full-time photographer, you will want to tell them why you are doing this and assure them that you are not trying to replace them. After all, who will shoot the items if your regular photographer is sick or on vacation? (If you want to have creative workers, give them enough time to play!)

RUNNING LIKE CLOCKWORK

Like the routine tasks discussed previously, delegating requires scheduling. And if your staff is to achieve the highest productivity levels possible, you will want to write up a schedule. It is critical that you carefully outline what is expected and when. If you know, for example, that you are expecting a large drop-off of items at your store, you might want to schedule the entire staff to help receive, review, and store them.

Although employees often like to take breaks together, this may cause you to be without the personnel you need to handle multiple phone lines and various situations that come up. Schedule staggered breaks and lunches so that you will have the help you need when you need it. Be sure to communicate your reasons for doing this.

If you run a physical drop-off location and are open more than five days a week, you will want to overlap your staff so that you have help every day. If you are open Monday through Saturday and have two employees, for example, you can schedule the photographer to work Monday through Friday and the eBay lister/shipping clerk to work Tuesday through Saturday. If your employees want to work less than full-time, it's important that you do whatever you can to accommodate them, while still ensuring sufficient coverage for the work that needs to be done.

22

BOOKKEEPING, ACCOUNTING, AND TAXES

Working from home can benefit you greatly—you can stop at any point and take a break—but working at an office really allows you to concentrate and focus on building a customer base. When you have an office, it is a place of business, and that is what you are coming in for. eBay is the best thing that ever happened to a lot of people—I recently sold a rare book published by Salvador Dali, number 27 of 39, which brought $12,600 for one of my clients. We only estimated its value at $7,000 to $8,000. We were extremely pleased. I made $1,260 commission on the sale. With the right clientele, you will do really well. I quit my job two years ago to become my own boss and sell on eBay full-time.

Michael Rybak, Los Angeles, California;

eBay user ID "ezbaywest"; trading on eBay since April 2, 2001

Frankly, I feel that this book demands a lot of the reader and that if you have made it this far, you have the "right stuff." That's good—because most people like bookkeeping about as much as a cold shower, but for a small business owner, keeping up with the books is a necessary evil. You'll thank me later. In the past, cleaning up the bookkeeping messes caused by my lax attitude has cost me dearly in outside, professional bookkeeping and accounting help. Don't make this same mistake.

You'll need to learn the bookkeeping ropes yourself, even if you eventually decide to delegate this task to someone else. Small business accounting is different from that of a big corporation, and you should focus on keeping your accounting as simple as possible. With a basic understanding of bookkeeping and some help from software, you will be able to create a balance sheet, a profit and loss statement, and a cash flow statement for your company. The balance sheet shows your company's total assets and liabilities (its value), the profit and loss statement shows if your business is profitable, and the cash flow statement gives you a good idea of your future cash flow patterns. With these documents, you will feel the pulse of your company's financial well-being.

COUNTING YOUR BEANS

If you decide to use a payroll service such as Paycycle.com, you have already taken a big step towards keeping excellent records and staying on top of one of your most daunting tasks—payroll.

As previously discussed, you should set up a separate bank account for your business, even when you operate as a sole proprietor. Keeping business records completely separate from your personal finances will really help when it comes time to do your tax returns. You can use accounting software to pay bills and keep track of general ledger (G/L) codes—used to group expenses into manageable categories that will later translate into line items on your tax returns.

Tax Liability Issues

There will be a number of tax liability matters that you and your accountant will need to deal with.

Income taxes. If you start as a sole proprietor, you will be reporting your business activity on a schedule that is attached to your IRS form 1040, called Schedule C. Not only will a sole proprietor pay income tax but also Social Security and Medicare taxes, reported together as a separate item on the income tax return. The Social Security and Medicare taxes can be quite a surprise for the new small businessperson, who usually doesn't expect to pay roughly 15 percent of net income on top of the income tax. Operating as a partnership or LLC doesn't relieve a partner of the obligation to pay self-employment tax. Your accountant can help set up estimated tax payments that will lessen the burden of your final tax bills and help you avoid the penalties for underwithholding.

Payroll taxes. If you have employees, you'll need a Federal Employer Identification Number, or FEIN, to file payroll tax returns. Also, depending on your location, various state and other local taxes will be required. In California, for instance, you need a state identification number as well as your FEIN, enabling you to pay the state tax and disability insurance monies withheld from your employees and a state unemployment tax.

This is a great time to tap your SCORE counselor once again for help, this time on setting up your new business's bookkeeping and accounting procedures.

WHEN IN DOUBT, AUTOMATE

I use the de facto industry-standard accounting program for my business: QuickBooks (*www.QuickBooks.com*). Many business accounting software packages are on the market, but you will find that most people "speak" QuickBooks, and my accountant recommends it. The program's wizard walks you step by step through the process of setting up your company's accounts, including allowing you to quickly and easily set up those general ledger codes I mentioned.

★TIP

You can now purchase a special edition of QuickBooks for eBay.

Instead of ordering preprinted checks for my business, I purchased a software program called CheckSoft Home and Business (*www.avan questusa.com*). This handy software was $39.95 and allows me to create checks on my laser printer, using the company's special check paper. Some banks may require that you use a special magnetic ink or laser toner (called magnetic ink character recognition, or MICR) for your checks, and you can obtain these supplies through CheckSoft's Web site, on eBay, or from any major office supply retailer.

eBay's Accounting Assistant program provides a simple way to import your eBay and PayPal sales data, as well as an accounting of your eBay fees, into QuickBooks and works with these QuickBooks programs:

- QuickBooks Pro, Premier, or Enterprise editions, 2002–2006
- Simple Start 2005 and 2006
- QuickBooks Online

Accounting Assistant is free for subscribers to eBay Stores, Selling Manager, Selling Manager Pro, and Blackthorne products. Using Accounting Assistant will also reduce the possibility of data entry errors when tracking your eBay and PayPal numbers. If you are using a listing management tool, such as Blackthorne Pro, you will be able to print sales reports and financial statements from most of these programs as well. To avoid information overload, it's a good idea to map out your accounting plan ahead of time and use the simplest tools you can to manage your business.

★TIP

If you use PayPal to receive money from individuals and businesses outside of your eBay sales, you can download the handy (and free) PayPal Payment Request Wizard for QuickBooks. This cool tool allows you to invoice your customers quickly from your QuickBooks program and receive payment in your PayPal account.

Many savvy small business owners use TurboTax (*www.turbo tax.com*) to prepare their own income taxes, which can be a help or a burden depending upon the complexity of your business. If you have a very simple business, no real estate assets, and nothing too fancy going on, you may want to consider using TurboTax or other tax preparation software. TurboTax integrates smoothly with QuickBooks, and there's a Premier edition that helps you prepare self-employment tax returns. Because I run a more complex business these days, I use the services of a CPA, but if yours is a small, start-up sole proprietorship, you can use software to prepare your own tax returns. TurboTax and TaxCut both have software you can install on your computer and both now offer online tax preparation solutions, too, so that you can prepare everything right on their Web sites.

If your business is a corporation or partnership/LLC and earns no more than $250,000 a year, these software solutions work great. If you're doing more business than that, you really will want to consult a tax professional. The downside of using any software is the lack of intuitive guidance that a human accountant with years of experience can provide.

PINCH THOSE PENNIES

Many people feel that debt is the American way—spend on credit and hope for a better tomorrow! I think that you should focus on becoming debt-free—that's not unpatriotic! And for this, the Trading Assistant business is ideal, because you will be able to sell other people's items on a percentage basis with no direct up-front costs except for relatively minor eBay fees. You can't simply incur bills in the hope of being able to pay them later without a clear understanding of your budget and cash flow.

Just as your business plan contained some specific financial projections, it's critical that you keep yourself on a strict monthly budget. You will know what your recurring expenses, such as rent and utilities, will be; to create a monthly budget, you will have to make estimates beyond these fixed costs. Most accounting software, including the popular

QuickBooks, offers a budgeting feature that you can use to create a projected budget for your business and to compare your actual expenditures against this budget.

★TIP

Save your money for a rainy day! When you get an avalanche of merchandise to sell and you make a bunch of cash, save your money. It's very tempting to spend it, but remember that you work on a percentage of what will probably be an unknown amount from month to month, so you need to save as much as possible.

You will be receiving substantial sums of money that belong to other people in the course of your business, and it's important that you keep this money separate from your fees. You can physically move these funds to another bank account, which would be your "client trust" account. You can also setup a G/L code in your accounting software that will designate this money as a liability, that is, something you owe to someone else (your clients). Keeping the clients' funds physically separate will help you stay disciplined, until you become more experienced with accounting.

ACCOUNTING PARTNERS

A great accountant usually comes by referral. Ask someone with a business about the same size as yours for a referral to a good CPA. You can also seek an accountant through the local chamber of commerce or through the American Institute of Certified Public Accountants (AICPA). The AICPA has been serving the accounting profession since 1887, and you can locate a CPA in your area on their Web site: *http:// pfp.aicpa.org*. The commercial tax preparation companies can do the work for you, too, but when using such firms, it's very important that you provide them with well organized, clean financial statements.

Having highly organized financial information can save you money, too. Most accountants charge by the hour, and their rates can be pricey (compared to those of a bookkeeper), so it really benefits you to give your accountant the most concise information possible to keep their hours, and thus your accounting costs, in line. The accounting for a Trading Assistant business, provided it's not connected to any other businesses, should be fairly straightforward. A good accountant will also help you plan legal ways to lower taxes or even avoid them altogether.

Just as with anyone you hire, your accountant must mesh well with your personality. You should sit down and talk with (in other words, interview) a prospective accountant, discussing your business and their fees and just getting to know them a bit before hiring them. It's helpful to get an estimate, based on your initial meeting, of your projected accounting costs so that you can factor them into your budget.

DEADLINE SANITY

Because my business is fairly simple in terms of accounting, I find that I can write checks, assign general ledger codes to them, and reconcile my own bank statements at the end of each month. Because I type very fast and have a pretty good working knowledge of accounting, I have chosen to do my own bookkeeping—I find it fun and a welcome distraction from my other daily routines. I also like to keep my business running smoothly with tight, personal control.

If you are not comfortable with software programs such as Quick-Books, you will find that hiring a full-service bookkeeper can help you greatly. Many bookkeepers work from home. You can fax or mail them copies of your checks, and they will do all the computer work on your behalf. If you need copies of your checks for the bookkeeper, you can order a checkbook with a carbon duplicate option. The bookkeeper can manage your finances for you, reconciling the end-of-month bank statements and sending your quarterly data to your accountant, who estimates your quarterly tax payments (when applicable).

KEEPING UP WITH THE JONESES

One of the major benefits that a bookkeeper and/or accountant can offer is to keep you on top of your accounting deadlines. And when you use a third-party payroll service, it will automatically handle your tax deadlines, lifting a great burden from your shoulders. This alone is worth the price of the service—hands down! Because the deadlines for filing payroll taxes are rather complex and I fully expect you to outsource it, I won't go into detail about them here (it would make your head spin—use a payroll service!).

Here are some of the common accounting deadlines you will need to meet if you operate on a calendar accounting year (one that ends December 31, as opposed to a fiscal year).

Federal Form 1040

Due April 15. A valid extension automatically extends the filing deadline by four months, to August 15, and a second extension is available that extends the filing deadline by an additional two months, to October 15, the maximum deadline for filing. If you are filing a return for a corporation, S corporation, partnership, or LLC, your tax return may be due based on your company's fiscal year, which may be different from a calendar tax year if your accountant feels that's helpful with your tax planning.

Quarterly Estimated Payment

Due dates (primarily for the self-employed):

- January 15
- April 15
- June 15
- September 15

Early in my business career, I fell behind on my taxes, and cleaning up my accounting mess ended up costing me a boatload in both time and money. I realized that I had been making my accounting much too complicated. With solid preplanning, a simple approach to accounting will keep your business running smoothly and paying the least in legally required taxes.

★TIP

Make an effort to pay for all business-related expenses with a credit or debit card with online access to your account. From the card, you will be able to upload the transaction data directly into QuickBooks. This will save you a tremendous amount of time in assigning appropriate G/L codes to those expenses and will maintain a good accounting trail. And this procedure will reinforce your frugality, too, as you'll see what you're spending in real time, rather than in a statement at the end of the month. Avoid paying cash, as this requires tedious manual data entry of expenses into your accounting software. Also receipts are often lost or forgotten—losing your precious tax deduction. Finally, remember that most expenditures for your business are tax deductible.

23

DISASTER PLANNING, PREVENTION, AND RECOVERY

I became a Trading Assistant three years ago, and in my prior job, I worked at several museums in collections management, having previously owned an antiques store. My husband suggested that I try selling some of my antiques on eBay. I thought that I was doing well with eBay, and eventually I ran out of things to sell, so I wanted to start helping other people sell their items. I recently helped a client sell two very distinctive and valuable Pablo Picasso Madoura ceramics. He had paid $100 for both of them, and after researching them, I realized their great value. Both ended up selling for a total of $5,376 on eBay.

Carol R. McGeehan, Miami Shores, Florida;
eBay user ID "luvantiqs"; trading on eBay since December 14, 1998

When I ventured into writing this book, I made a commitment to myself and to you, my reader, to be very frank and factual about the realities of running a Trading Assistant business. As with any business, things can go awry. The world is your oyster, and with a great attitude you will be a very successful businessperson, but you must also be a careful one—to avoid or mitigate losses due to disasters, accidents, or emergencies that may arise.

You can't possibly avoid every unknown event that could throw a wrench in your day, but being prepared, both mentally and procedurally, can soften, or even dodge, the blow.

IT HAPPENS

Some possibilities that may ruin your day include:

- Loss of your Internet connection (yikes!)
- Power surges that damage equipment and data
- Theft of property
- Identity theft
- Acts of God (force majeure)
- Accidental damage to merchandise

These are just a few of the possibilities. Of course, I hope that you never have to confront any such situations, but although the odds are against it, it's best to be ready.

Here's what you can do to help keep things running smoothly.

Internet

Not all Internet carriers are created equal. Be sure to pick yours wisely. Not only do you want to have fast Internet, but reliability is critical. Be sure to ask around before settling on a provider and learn as much as you can about the various Internet service providers' (ISPs) track records. If you use broadband (and you really should), you should have a backup means of getting on the Internet in case of a total loss of your primary connection. Set up a dial-up account, and make sure it's useable at all times. Virtually all broadband providers will give you free dial-up access to their network if you use their broadband service. Create a dial-up connection on your computer and test it at least once a month. Most ISPs make an array of dial-up numbers available, leaving little chance you will be left in the "virtual dark."

Power Surges

The quality of the power you receive can vary greatly. I've had several power outages over the years, and power surges (and even brownouts and blackouts) are not uncommon. Therefore, having surge protection is important. If your city has very inconsistent power and you are prone to blackouts due to heavy power usage during the summer months (when people really crank up the air-conditioning), or because of bad weather, it might be prudent to get a battery-based, uninterruptible power supply that kicks in when the power fails. These power supplies are readily available at your local computer store (or on eBay), and many brands have a special software program and computer connection that automatically closes your open programs and safely shuts down your computer when the power fails.

Theft of Property

A major reason I moved to Burbank was that I mistakenly believed it was virtually crime-free. Just two days before I wrote this chapter, the bank two doors from my office had a failed robbery attempt. Oddly enough, I was not at all alarmed, surprised, or stressed-out about this situation, because we have a great police department here. More importantly, my office is secure, and I am confident we are not at much risk for a break-in.

★**TIP**

You will do well to be security conscious at all times when you run a business. Don't leave anything valuable lying in plain view. Smaller, high-value items should always be locked away out of sight.

Here are some additional tips:

- When items come into your store, put them in bins out of view until you are ready to list them
- Keep a good physical barrier between your clients' merchandise and the public—avoid creating temptation

- Never leave your store unattended, even for brief periods of time. If you work alone, lock up when you have to use the restroom or step out (keep an "I'll be back at _____" sign handy to display when needed)
- Deposit checks, money orders, and cash daily, and try to bank as close to your office as possible so that this is convenient
- Check an eBay buyer's feedback before considering taking credit card charges by phone (if you offer direct credit card payments). Ask buyers with questionable feedback, and any buyers of items costing more than you would be willing to lose in the event of a credit card scam, to fax proof of identification. This situation demands a judgment call, because without hard copy proof of the transaction, the buyer can deny the charges
- Always insist on picture identification from buyers who pick up merchandise
- When accepting PayPal, ship only to the confirmed address on the PayPal payment to avoid the possibility of a chargeback, and make certain to ship by methods that allow tracking and proof of delivery
- If you have employees, require two members of your staff (you can be one of them) to inspect every item before it is shipped. My company's packing slips require that two staff members physically sign off that the merchandise was verified to be the correct item and packed in the box
- If you have employees, file a police report when items are missing, so that the incident is documented both for your files and for possible insurance claims. Showing that you are serious about such matters will also discourage employee dishonesty
- Conduct a criminal background and credit check of employees. Employees with horrible credit have had trouble handling their own finances and may have trouble handling your business, too.
- Install an alarm system with remote monitoring notifying the police when the alarm is tripped
- Immediately report any suspicious activities to the police, even if they seem trivial

If you are handling merchandise of extremely high value, you may want to consider installing cameras that record on a continuous basis. With the advances in computer technology, recording to a hard drive with lots of storage space is cheap, and you can store massive amounts of camera footage on them. But make sure "the juice is worth the squeeze"—that the cost of security is not higher than the potential loss you might suffer without it.

Identity Theft

You will be privy to other people's important personal data during the course of your business. Operate your company much like a law firm or doctor's office—keep sensitive client information secure. Designate which employees are allowed to handle and view client folders, and be sure to keep these files locked up if they contain sensitive information about your clients. Never throw any documents containing such information into the regular trash. Use a shredder or have a box for document destruction (we use a bonded company for this).

Acts of God (Force Majeure)

If you live in an earthquake or hurricane zone, it will be very important to secure shelving units to the walls so that they won't tip over. Put heavy merchandise towards lower shelves. In a heavy rain, our company's back door tends to allow a small flood, so we keep merchandise off the floor to prevent water damage. Check your building's roof regularly (even if you are a tenant) to make certain it is not leaking. Fix leaks or report them immediately to your landlord regardless of how minor—little ones turn into big ones. Check any trees that might cause damage to your windows, façade, or sign on a windy day, and keep such trees trimmed to control limbs that could spoil your day. Inspect plumbing regularly to check for leaks, and if you live in an area that's cold enough to freeze pipes, keep your items as clear of these pipes as possible (and off the floor).

Accidental Damage to Merchandise

If you are handling very delicate or breakable items such as china, crystal, etc., consider prepacking them after you photograph and list them. Putting these items into bubble wrap and boxing them (ready for shipment) will prevent the accidental breakage that happens in a busy environment. Items with small, breakable appendages, such as porcelain figurines, are very likely to meet their doom if left unprotected. We use Ziploc bags for nonbreakable items to keep them free of dust (and coffee spills). Don't allow employees to eat or drink beverages when handling clients' merchandise. It's not a matter of if, but simply when, a coffee or soda will spill and ruin something expensive or rare.

YOU NEED BACKUP

It is very important to your business that you protect the data on your computer. Computer data can inadvertently be lost for many reasons, including a power surge, equipment failure, file corruption, or even operator error. You need to be able to back up this critical data regularly and keep the backups in a separate place in case of data loss. In small companies, a regular backup can easily be neglected among the myriad of other tasks to be remembered each day. A daily checklist of must-do tasks that includes making a backup of critical, business-related files would help.

The data you may wish to back up regularly can include:

- Digital photographs for your listings
- Software that you have purchased and downloaded from the Internet
- Data files for software that you use in your business
- Your address book for e-mails, business calendar, and Internet browser bookmarks
- All business-related documents and files

You can store this data on removable storage media such as a CD (for smaller amounts of data), a writeable DVD, another hard drive on your network, or a removable drive. I use a very large, removable USB drive. A USB drive is very inexpensive these days and can rapidly store huge amounts of data. Tape drives are slow and no longer very cost-effective.

Many people currently have a computer running Windows XP Home Edition, and oddly enough, the backup program that comes free with this operating system is not installed on your computer by default. The backup software, a basic program that allows you to back up your system files and settings and restore them in the event of a disaster, normally sits quietly on the original installation CD. To install this free software, insert your Windows XP CD in your computer, and when the Welcome screen pops up, click "Perform Additional Tasks," then click "Browse This CD." When a Windows Explorer screen opens, click the "ValueAdd" folder, then "Msft," and then "Ntbackup." Double-click the file called Ntbackup.msi, and the backup utility will then install.

★NOTE

If you use Windows XP Professional, this backup utility will be installed already.

Once the program is installed, you will find it by following these menus on your Windows computer: click on Start > Programs > Accessories > System Tools. The software comes with a wizard to help you create your first backup and another for restoring backed up files.

Mac users can use the subscription-based Mac services to move files to a secure, off-site Internet storage vault for safekeeping.

Many third-party backup software programs and Internet storage services are available to help with your data protection needs. You may wish to look at the various software solutions available by visiting *www.download.com* and following the link for "Utilities." There, you will find hundreds of free and inexpensive software programs.

Norton Ghost is a software program that takes a snapshot of your system, creating an exact copy of your entire hard drive at the moment you make the backup. This "image" of your computer's hard drive will come in handy if your entire system crashes due to hardware failure. You can store the backup copy on your network, another hard drive, or removable media such as the USB hard disk mentioned earlier.

Having a good backup plan will save you money. It only takes one incident of data loss to cost your business hundreds or even thousands of dollars in lost data, time, and frustration.

GETTING BACK ON YOUR FEET

If you planned carefully, recovering from a disaster will be a smooth process. The first thing you want to do is stay calm. Regardless of the nature of your disaster, you are still alive and healthy, and you will recover from it.

If your disaster was the result of theft, accident, or force majeure, then the first thing you should do is contact your insurance company. If you intend to start putting your business life back together, you should videotape or photograph the damage before you start repairing it. Speak to your insurance company about the steps required for you to process a claim successfully.

It's important that you pick up the pieces carefully. If your loss involves computer equipment, don't panic, even if the equipment has been damaged due to fire or natural disaster. Don't assume that the data is a total loss. If the equipment is intact, there's hope that data can be recovered. For data recovery projects, getting professional help is important. Don't try to do it yourself. If your system is damaged, forensic computer service companies can assist with data recovery. Choose this specialist carefully, because your company's entire data will be in their hands.

It is estimated that only 40 percent of companies recover from a total catastrophic loss of their business data. For your company to be among the living, you should run regular drills of your disaster recovery plans. For your computer data, try restoring your data onto another, non-mission-critical computer to see if you can successfully put it back into action during a simulated emergency drill. Do a monthly drill to ensure that you and your employees are ready for anything.

★NOTE

When a viable backup is not available in the event of equipment failure or data corruption, you can seek guidance from your computer's hardware manufacturers for assistance in data recovery.

CONCLUSION

I moved from Los Angeles to Las Vegas in 1995, and I had to start my life over here. Being a single mom was challenging. I knew nothing about the Internet or computers, but in 1997, I bought an old telephone modem and went online for the first time, and I was absolutely astonished by this new frontier. I discovered eBay, but I could not afford a digital camera because at that time they were close to $1,000. I saw an ad for a scanner on sale for $100, and I learned how to scan jewelry and was selling it on eBay. We became Trading Assistants to help increase our sales without having to buy merchandise. We now operate a 12,000-square-foot antiques mall in Las Vegas that includes an eBay drop-off store. We have quickly become PowerSellers, and we sell under several eBay user accounts. I can honestly say eBay has changed my life!

Renee Poole, Las Vegas, Nevada;

eBay user ID "notjustantiquesmart"; trading on eBay since August 22, 2004

INDEPENDENCE DAY

You made it! It's Independence Day—for you. eBay is an idea whose time has come, and so has yours. Because now you have all the tools you need to start an eBay Trading Assistant business—and to be the success you've always wanted to be. Selling for others on eBay can give you the financial independence you've been dreaming of while you help other people, and with creative, varied, exciting work on the very cutting edge of the Internet and new technologies—what could be better? You can do it. I'm so certain of it that I'd like you to e-mail me at *spencer@ebayentrepreneur.net* with your eBay Trading Assistant success story. I want to hear it, and maybe you'll see it in the next edition of this book—by that time, you'll be an old hand at the Trading Assistant biz!

You can do it—you really can. But don't just take my word for it—as Trading Assistant Teresa D. Bankston says at the top of Chapter 12, "If I can be a successful eBay seller with six kids running around the house, then anyone can do this."

APPENDIX

Content in this Appendix has been generously provided by Joseph E. Sullivan, legal counsel for eBay, Inc.

---

1. AUCTIONEER/SECONDHAND DEALER LAWS

More than half of the states in the United States have laws regulating "auctioneers," and most states and many municipalities have laws regulating pawn shops and secondhand dealers. These laws require certain business owners to pay fees, obtain licenses, post bonds, take classes, collect and store certain records, and make filings with government agencies. Right now, questions abound regarding whether these laws should apply to eBay sellers. eBay takes the view that the laws should not, because the regulations generally were written before eBay existed and were created to deal with issues that do not arise in the eBay context. eBay's government relations team is working hard right now to convince local officials to not apply these laws online or, if unsuccessful in doing that, to convince legislatures to change these laws to make exceptions for eBay businesses. However, even during this unsettled time, sellers remain personally responsible for investigating and complying with all local laws to the extent that local authorities believe they apply to eBay sales.

a. Auctioneer Laws

While eBay transactions are commonly referred to as "auctions," there are several fundamental differences between traditional, regulated auctions and the transactions that take place on the eBay platform.

Traditional auctioneers control all aspects of their sales, from the members of the audience invited to the bids that get recognized, while eBay sellers conduct business very differently. A large percentage of sales advertised on eBay are fixed price sales or sales that provide that the "bidding" will end at a fixed time. eBay itself manages much of the interaction between sellers and buyers, eBay provides significant trust and safety services to buyers, and eBay offers buyer protection programs to protect buyers against loss. To recognize these large differences between auctioneering and eBay sales, eBay prohibits Trading Assistants from using the term *auctioneer* to describe their businesses, unless the Trading Assistants are licensed as auctioneers under traditional auctioneer licensing laws.

Important eBay rule. Trading Assistants may not use the term *auction* or *auctioneer* in their name or advertising to describe their sales on eBay, unless they are licensed under their state laws as an auctioneer or auction business or are conducting a traditional auctioneer business in a state that does not license traditional auctioneers. Trading Assistants may use the term *auction-style* instead.

The current state of the law. As of this writing, the only state agency to hold affirmatively that consignment sellers on eBay need to be licensed as auctioneers has been the Louisiana Auction Board. eBay is currently working to try to change that interpretation or change the law. Regulators from North Carolina, North Dakota, Tennessee, and Wisconsin have issued statements concluding that their auctioneer laws do not apply to eBay sellers. Auction boards in Arkansas and other states are also reviewing the issue and may issue decisions in the near future. Because the interpretations of law in this area are changing so quickly, do not rely on what you read here—independently verify the standards required in your location.

b. Pawnbroker/Secondhand Dealer Laws

Storefront drop-off stores have grown in popularity around the United States as alternatives to pawn shops as places where people can bring their goods to be sold on consignment. In response, pawnbrokers have argued that these stores should face the same regulations that apply to them—fingerprinting of all customers, reporting of all goods to local police databases, and, in some cases, application of holding periods before sale of the goods. However, on a closer look, drop-off stores offer a business model very different from pawn shops. Unlike when a person brings goods to a pawn shop and walks out the door with cash, a person who brings goods to a drop-off store only receives funds after the item sells on eBay, frequently over a month later. Moreover, pawn sales are not open to the world, whereas eBay is a transparent marketplace searched by millions of users every day. There has been little evidence of sales of stolen property via these drop-off stores on eBay; and eBay believes that application of the strict pawn laws would be overkill that would serve no valid purpose and instead would have the unintended consequence of stifling small, local entrepreneurs.

In an effort to prevent stolen property from being listed on eBay, to provide a substitute for pawn laws that meets law enforcement concerns without overburdening eBay users with inappropriate regulatory requirements, and to provide efficient support for law enforcement, eBay now makes listings from Internet drop-off stores that list $25,000 or more worth of items on eBay per month available to law enforcement in the l.e.a.d.s.online searchable database. l.e.a.d.s.online is the nation's largest online investigative system in use by law enforcement for the investigation of crimes involving property. More than 2,200 pawn and secondhand stores in 41 states electronically upload their transaction to l.e.a.d.s.online for use by local law enforcement, and l.e.a.d.s.online's service is in use by nearly 500 law enforcement agencies in 21 states. l.e.a.d.s.online will provide the service to subscribing law enforcement at no additional cost, will ensure that this data is available only to law enforcement conducting legitimate ongoing investigations where the evidence relates to the ongoing investigation, and will also confirm that the records are provided in compliance with eBay's privacy policy.

Important eBay rule. Trading Assistants that operate as storefront businesses must include accurate city and state item locations in their listings; must include item serial numbers if available in their listings; must record identification, billing, and listing information of all consignors; must retain those records for at least 60 days; and must make those records available to local law enforcement officials upon request during regular business hours.

The current state of the law. This issue continues to be debated around the country, and you must check with local and state officials on what is expected of you. In California, Michigan, and Florida, police have taken action against drop-off stores for failing to comply with local pawn and secondhand dealer laws. A Florida court rejected the police action there, but the issue is not settled. California's attorney general recently released an opinion stating that drop-off stores likely fall under the California definition of secondhand dealers and directing the legislature to clarify the situation.

2. REAL ESTATE LAWS

Real estate advertising services on eBay are offered by eBay Real Estate, Inc., a wholly owned subsidiary of eBay, Inc. ("eBay Real Estate"). eBay Real Estate offers two formats for the advertisement of real estate: Auction-style format items and ad format items. Auction-style advertisements of real property do not involve legally binding offers to buy and sell. Instead, auction-style postings are simply a way for sellers to advertise their real estate and identify the most interested potential buyers. Following the close of the auction-style bidding, sellers and buyers are expected to contact each other to prepare and deliver the appropriate paperwork to transfer the property and to take such other actions as may be required by local laws and regulations. eBay Real Estate also offers sellers the option of advertising their property in an "ad" format that also does not involve legally binding offers to buy and sell. Sellers can specify their asking price, and no bidding takes place. Interested buyers fill out a contact form, and their information is sent to the seller.

Important eBay rule. Trading Assistants may not post real estate advertisements on eBay on behalf of third parties, unless the Trading Assistants are licensed real estate agents.

The current state of the law. Some local authorities have laws and regulations that may cover the types of services that Trading Assistants provide to clients. Please take particular care in connection with the advertisement, sale, or marketing of real estate, because some government agencies may require that you first become licensed as a real estate broker or otherwise impose local regulation on your activities. Just as you are responsible on eBay to ensure that the items you sell are legal to sell, you are responsible for ensuring that the services you provide to clients are legal. A consultation with an attorney may help you clarify questions you may have.

3. MOTOR VEHICLE SALES LAWS

Please be aware that motor vehicle sales, especially across state lines, may carry higher legal liability than selling other merchandise on eBay. eBay highly recommends that you check with your state's department of transportation to understand licensing and liability issues before engaging in motor vehicle-related sales activities. The eBay Motors Trading Assistant program is modeled after the eBay Trading Assistant program, but it differs in a few ways because of the legal complexity of this area.

Important eBay rules. Trading Assistants who are not licensed motor vehicle dealers cannot do the following:

- List vehicles under their own user ID
- Charge a fee for services based upon a percentage of the sales price
- Interact with bidders, filter, or otherwise control the flow of information between bidders and the owner of the vehicle

Trading Assistants who are licensed motor vehicle dealers may do the following:

- List cars under their own user ID
- Charge service fees based on the final sales price
- Communicate directly with bidders
- Accept payment directly for the sale
- Arrange for registration and title transfer

The current state of the law. Most states require anyone who sells cars or motorcycles for another to have a motor vehicle dealer's license. Laws and requirements vary from state to state (check with your state's department of transportation). Whenever required by law, eBay Motors Trading Assistants must become licensed as dealers, brokers, or salespersons.

The following services usually require a dealer's license:

- Selling vehicles on consignment
- Auction management (responding to e-mails, calls)
- Negotiating final terms of the sale
- Collecting payment from the buyer
- Processing title transfer between seller and buyer
- Accepting a fee from the seller based on percentage of the sale

4. CHARITY SALES

Charitable fundraising is a highly regulated area subject to numerous state and federal laws. eBay allows sellers to list items and collect proceeds on behalf of charity either with eBay Giving Works, the dedicated program for charity listings on eBay, or without eBay Giving Works, as long as the listings meet specific guidelines for charitable solicitations.

eBay selected MissionFish, a licensed nonprofit service of the Points of Light Foundation, to serve as the dedicated solution provider for eBay Giving Works. MissionFish's valuable service and support includes: Powering the nonprofit directory for eBay Giving Works, verifying that nonprofits are eligible for this program, collecting and disbursing sellers' donations, providing sellers with tax receipts, and tracking donations online. eBay features Giving Works listings on the Web site by differentiating these listings with a distinctive ribbon icon and including them within a specialized charity search functionality.

Important eBay rules. Sellers may only list with eBay Giving Works if they:

- use the Sell Your Item form on eBay and enable JavaScript in their browsers;
- register with MissionFish and maintain an account in good standing;
- agree to donate at least 10 percent of the final sale price or $10—whichever is greater—to a member nonprofit organization if the item sells (but the $10 minimum donation requirement does not apply to nonprofits selling items on their own behalf, called "Direct Selling");
- select PayPal or credit card as one of the buyer payment options (not required for listings in the Motors or Real Estate categories or for "Direct Selling"); and
- do not list the item in the Real Estate ad format or Mature Audiences category.

Sellers may only list items for charity without eBay Giving Works if they:

- are soliciting on behalf of recognized, tax-deductible, charitable organizations having 501(c)(3) status or equivalent with the IRS; and
- receive advance written consent for the solicitation from the benefiting nonprofit. To verify you received permission, you must include a scanned copy of the consent in your listing. It must appear with the nonprofit's letterhead, be signed by an officer, and include the nonprofit's tax-deductibility status as well as

your name or eBay user ID, dates of event/listings, and donation amount (percentage of the final sale price).

The current state of the law. Most states have laws that require anyone who, for compensation, solicits funds for a charity to be licensed as a professional fundraiser. If you sell items on eBay and a portion of the proceeds goes to a charity but you receive a fee for the sale, these laws probably apply to you. You are independently responsible for complying with these laws.

PHOTO GALLERY

Welcome to my personal Hall of Fame photo gallery. The eBay marketplace is an amazing way to connect to buyers across the globe who buy the most remarkable and interesting merchandise. This amazing photo gallery represents over seven years of my most notable sales using the eBay Web site.

Some of the items were forgotten memories, many were collecting dust in garages or storage lockers. All said this gallery shows the stratospheric prices that can be obtained for used and collectible merchandise on eBay. I know these cool items in my Hall of Fame will inspire you to get your eBay Trading Assistant business started today! You never know what treasure is lying buried in the attic clutter, hidden away in a dark closet, or perhaps sitting idly in a warehouse. You can turn these unproductive items into cash assets for anxious and appreciative clients.

$17,100
Circa 1930 Lenci Porcelain Figurine
by Artist Beltrami Nillo

$5,000
Circa 1860 Abraham Lincoln
Photograph by Alexander Hesler

$736
Wedgewood Small Tri-Color
Pottery Pitcher

$769
Vintage American Airlines Poster
by Artist Walter Bomar

$810
Rare Royal Doulton "Old Charley"
Music Box Toby Mug

$1,250
Antique Carved Ivory Tusk
with Wooden Stand

$1,276
12" Antique Loetz Sterling Overlay Vase
by Artist La Pierre

$2,225
"Court of Appeals" Bronze Sculpture
by Charles Bragg

$735
Circa 1881 Tiffany Sterling Silver Gilded Compote

$1,235.05
Circa 1985 Honda Elite
Model 250 Motor Scooter

$3,150
Circa 1966 Gibson ES335
Sunburst Electric Guitar

$687.53
Circa 1962 Canadian Chatty Cathy Doll

$1,825
Circa 1730 Verge Fusse
French Silver Pocketwatch

$1,000.03
Circa 1950's Nikon SP Model Rangefinder
35mm Camera

$1,414
Circa 1914 Indy 500
Framed Pennant

$1,698
Set of 71 Wallace Grande Baroque
Sterling Flatware

$1,525
Antique Tiffany Favrile Lily Pattern 4" Lamp Shade

$1,900
Circa 1945 Pink Gold Self-Winding
Rolex Watch

$512.56
Vintage Bolex Paillard 16mm Three-Lens
Movie Camera

$4,359.09
Sterling Silver Sangria Pitcher
by William Spratling

INDEX